W9-BJH-370

WEBSTER'S

COMPACT

DICTIONARY OF

SYNONYMS

Webster's

COMPACT
DICTIONARY OF
SYNONYMS

A Merriam-Webster®

MERRIAM-WEBSTER INC.

Springfield, Massachusetts

A GENUINE MERRIAM-WEBSTER

The name *Webster* alone is no guarantee of excellence. It is used by a number of publishers and may serve mainly to mislead an unwary buyer.

A Merriam-Webster® is the registered trademark you should look for when you consider the purchase of dictionaries or other fine reference books. It carries the reputation of a company that has been publishing since 1831 and is your assurance of quality and authority.

Copyright © 1987 by Merriam-Webster Inc.

Philippines Copyright 1987 by Merrian-Webster Inc.

Library of Congress Cataloging in Publication

Webster's compact dictionary of synonyms.

   1. English language—Synonyms and antonyms—Dictionaries.
PE1591.W39   1987   423′.1   86-33138
ISBN 0-87779-186-4

All rights reserved. No part of this work covered by the copyrights hereon may be reproduced or copied in any form or by any means—graphic, electronic, or mechanical, including photocopying, recording, taping, or information storage and retrieval systems—without written permission of the publisher.

MADE IN THE UNITED STATES OF AMERICA

6789WAK92919089

CONTENTS

PREFACE

Webster's Compact Dictionary of Synonyms is designed to be a concise guide to the understanding and use of synonyms. It is intended for people who wish to appreciate the shades of difference that exist among English words that have the same or nearly the same essential meaning and who wish to be able to choose from among synonyms the precisely suitable word for a particular purpose.

The bulk of this book is made up of a collection of main entries consisting of articles in which distinctions are drawn among a group of synonyms. The distinctions usually fall into one of three peripheral areas of meaning: implication, connotation, or application. Implications are the usually minor ideas involved in the meaning of a word. Connotations are the ideas which color the meaning of a word and are the product of various factors, such as etymology and historical and literary associations. Applications are the restrictions on a word's use established by current idiom.

Each main entry begins with a list of the words that are discussed in that article. The words in the list are set in boldface type for easy recognition, and the entries are alphabetized by the first word in the list. Following the list is a concise statement of the element of meaning that the synonyms have in common:

> **abandon, desert, forsake** mean to leave without intending to return.

After this initial sentence, there is a series of statements describing the differences that distinguish the synonyms from one another. The statements are supplemented and clarified by examples, set in angle brackets, that illustrate typical ways in which the words may be used:

> **Abandon** suggests that the thing or person left may be helpless without protection ⟨they *abandoned* their cat at summer's end⟩. **Desert** implies that the object left may be weakened but not destroyed by one's absence ⟨a town *deserted* once the gold ran out⟩. **Forsake** suggests an action more likely to bring impoverishment or bereavement to that which is forsaken than its exposure to physical dangers ⟨*forsook* his wife and family for a younger woman⟩.

In addition to main entries, the book also contains thousands of cross-reference entries. By means of these entries, every word discussed in the article at a main entry is entered at its own alphabetical place, followed by a cross-reference in small capital letters to the main entry at which it is discussed:

> **desert** see ABANDON

When a word is discussed at more than one entry and is treated as the same part of speech at each entry, cross-references list in alphabetical order all of the entries at which that word is treated:

> **casual** see ACCIDENTAL, RANDOM

When a word that is a main entry word is also discussed as the same part of speech at another main entry, a cross-reference note appears at the end of the main-entry paragraph:

> **abandon, desert, forsake** mean to leave without intend-
> ing to return. . . . See in addition RELINQUISH.

This note indicates that the word *abandon,* which is treated
as a verb in this entry, is also discussed as a verb at the main
entry for *relinquish.*

When a word that is entered as a cross-reference is discussed at more than one entry and is treated as a different
part of speech at each entry, separate cross-reference entries
appear:

> **humor** *vb* see INDULGE
> **humor** *n* see WIT

Likewise, if a word that is a main entry is also discussed at
another entry but as a different part of speech, a separate
cross-reference entry appears:

> **malign** *vb* **Malign, traduce, asperse, vilify, calum-
> niate, defame, slander** mean to injure by speaking
> ill of. . . .
> **malign** *adj* see SINISTER

It will be noticed that in the examples for *humor* and
malign the entry word is followed by an italic part-of-speech
label to help the reader identify the appropriate entry and
reference. Such a part-of-speech label appears whenever the
same entry word is listed more than once (whether for a main
entry or a cross-reference entry). The meanings of the abbreviations used in the part-of-speech labels as well as the meanings of the other abbreviations used in this book are given in
a list following this preface.

The manuscript of this book was prepared by Michael G. Belanger, Assistant Editor. Copyediting was the responsibility of James G. Lowe, Senior Editor. Proofreading was done by Eileen M. Haraty and Peter D. Haraty, Assistant Editors. Manuscript typing and data-entry work were accomplished by Georgette B. Boucher and Barbara A. Winkler, under the direction of Gloria J. Afflitto, Head of the Typing Room. Additional clerical help was provided by Ruth W. Gaines, Senior General Clerk, and by Valerie L. Jackson.

Abbreviations Used in This Work

adj	adjective	occas.	occasionally
adv	adverb	specif.	specifically
esp.	especially	usu.	usually
n	noun	vb	verb

A

abandon, desert, forsake mean to leave without intending
to return. **Abandon** suggests that the thing or person left
may be helpless without protection ⟨they *abandoned* their
cat at summer's end⟩. **Desert** implies that the object left
may be weakened but not destroyed by one's absence ⟨a
town *deserted* once the gold ran out⟩. **Forsake** suggests an
action more likely to bring impoverishment or bereavement to that which is forsaken than its exposure to physical dangers ⟨*forsook* his wife and family for a younger
woman⟩. See in addition RELINQUISH.

abase, demean, debase, degrade, humiliate mean to lower in
one's own estimation or in that of others. **Abase** suggests
losing or voluntarily yielding up dignity or prestige ⟨a fine
stage actor who *abased* himself by turning to television⟩.
Demean implies losing or injuring social standing by an
unsuitable act or association ⟨commercial endorsements
demean the Olympics⟩. **Debase** implies a deterioration of
moral standards or character ⟨drunkenness has *debased*
the Mardi Gras⟩. **Degrade** suggests the taking of a step
downward sometimes in rank but more often on the road
to moral degeneration ⟨the public altercation *degraded*
both candidates⟩. **Humiliate** implies the severe wounding
of one's pride and the causing of deep shame ⟨*humiliated*
by his suggestive remarks⟩.

abash see EMBARRASS

abate, subside, wane, ebb mean to die down in force or intensity. **Abate** stresses the idea of progressive diminishing
⟨waited until the storm *abated*⟩. **Subside** implies the ceasing of turbulence or agitation ⟨the protests *subsided* after

a few days⟩. **Wane** suggests the fading or weakening of something good or impressive ⟨the public's *waning* interest in space flight⟩. **Ebb** suggests the receding of something (as the tide) that commonly comes and goes ⟨her love *ebbs* as regularly and predictably as the tides⟩. See in addition DECREASE.

abbreviate see SHORTEN

abdicate, renounce, resign mean to give up a position with no possibility of resuming it. **Abdicate** implies a giving up of sovereign power or sometimes an evading of responsibility such as that of a parent ⟨by walking out he *abdicated* his rights as a father⟩. **Renounce** may replace it but often implies additionally a sacrifice for a greater end ⟨by this marriage she *renounces* any hope of an inheritance⟩. **Resign** applies to the giving up of an unexpired office or trust ⟨forced to *resign* from office⟩.

aberrant see ABNORMAL

abet see INCITE

abeyant see LATENT

abhor see HATE

abhorrent see HATEFUL, REPUGNANT

abide see BEAR, CONTINUE

abject see MEAN

abjure, renounce, forswear, recant, retract mean to withdraw one's word or professed belief. **Abjure** implies a firm and final rejecting or abandoning often made under oath ⟨candidates for citizenship must *abjure* allegiance to any foreign power⟩. **Renounce** often equals *abjure* but may carry the meaning of disclaim or disown ⟨willing to *renounce* his lifelong friends⟩. **Forswear** may add to *abjure* an implication of perjury or betrayal ⟨I cannot *forswear* my principles to win votes⟩. **Recant** stresses the withdrawing or denying of something professed or taught ⟨the suspect *recanted* his

confession and professed his innocence). **Retract** applies
to the withdrawing of a promise, an offer, or an accusation
⟨under threat of lawsuit the paper *retracted* the statement⟩.

able, capable, competent, qualified mean having power or
fitness for work. **Able** suggests ability above the average as
revealed in actual performance ⟨proved that she is an *able*
Shakespearean actress⟩. **Capable** stresses the having of
qualities fitting one for work but does not imply outstanding ability ⟨*capable* of doing simple tasks under supervi-
sion⟩. **Competent** and **qualified** imply having the experience or training for adequate performance ⟨a leap that any
competent ballet dancer can execute⟩ ⟨seek help from a
qualified medical professional⟩.

abnormal, atypical, aberrant mean deviating markedly
from the rule or standard of its kind. **Abnormal** frequently
suggests strangeness and sometimes deformity or mon-
strosity ⟨a classic study of *abnormal* personalities⟩. **Atypical** stresses divergence upward or downward from some
established norm ⟨a markedly *atypical* reaction to a drug⟩.
Aberrant implies a departure from the usual or natural
type ⟨that joyriding incident must be regarded as an *aberrant* episode in his life⟩.

abominable see HATEFUL

abominate see HATE

abomination, anathema, bugbear, bête noire mean a person
or thing that arouses intense dislike. **Abomination** suggests
the arousal of loathing, disgust, and extreme displeasure
⟨in her opinion all of modern art is an *abomination*⟩.
Anathema suggests that something is so odious that it is
dismissed or rejected out of hand ⟨anything that was Yan-
kee was *anathema* to my Southern aunt⟩. **Bugbear** suggests
something so dreaded that one seeks continually to avoid
it ⟨the deficit issue became an annual congressional *bug-

bear⟩. **Bête noire** suggests a pet aversion that one habitually or especially avoids ⟨his mooching brother-in-law was the *bête noire* of his life⟩.

aboriginal see NATIVE

abridge see SHORTEN

abridgment, abstract, synopsis, conspectus, epitome mean a condensed treatment. **Abridgment** suggests reduction in compass with retention of relative completeness ⟨a desk-size dictionary that is an *abridgment* of a larger work⟩. **Abstract** applies to a summary of points of a treatise, document, or proposed treatment and usu. has no independent worth ⟨a published *abstract* of a medical paper⟩. **Synopsis** implies a skeletal presentation of an argument or a narrative suitable for rapid examination ⟨read a *synopsis* of the screenplay⟩. **Conspectus** implies a quick overall view of a large detailed subject ⟨the book is a *conspectus* of modern European history⟩. **Epitome** suggests the briefest possible presentation of a complex whole that still has independent value ⟨"know thyself" was the *epitome* of Greek philosophy⟩.

abrogate see NULLIFY

abrupt see PRECIPITATE, STEEP

absolute, autocratic, arbitrary, despotic, tyrannical mean exercising power or authority without restraint. **Absolute** implies that one is not bound by legal constraints or the control of another ⟨King Louis XIV was an *absolute* monarch⟩. **Autocratic** suggests the egotistical, self-conscious use of power or the haughty imposition of one's own will ⟨the flamboyant, *autocratic* director of the ballet company⟩. **Arbitrary** implies the exercise and usu. the abuse of power according to one's momentary inclination ⟨his high-handed, *arbitrary* way of running his department⟩. **Despotic** implies the arbitrary and imperious exercise of absolute power or control ⟨the most decadent and *despotic* of the Roman emperors⟩. **Tyrannical** implies the abuse of absolute power and harsh or oppressive rule ⟨a new regime as *tyrannical* as the one it had deposed⟩.

absolve see EXCULPATE

absorb, imbibe, assimilate mean to take something in so as to become imbued with it. **Absorb** may connote a loss of identity in what is taken in or an enrichment of what takes in ⟨can quickly *absorb* highly technical reports⟩. **Imbibe** implies a drinking in which may be unconscious but whose effect may be significant or profound ⟨children *imbibe* the values of their parents⟩. **Assimilate** stresses an incorporation into the substance of the body or mind ⟨asked to *assimilate* a mass of material in a brief time⟩.

abstract see ABRIDGMENT

abundant see PLENTIFUL

abuse, vituperation, invective, obloquy, scurrility, billingsgate mean vehemently expressed condemnation or disapproval. **Abuse,** the most general term, implies the anger of the speaker and stresses the harshness of the language ⟨charged her husband with verbal *abuse*⟩. **Vituperation** implies fluent and sustained abuse ⟨subjected his aide to a torrent of *vituperation*⟩. **Invective** implies a comparable vehemence but suggests greater verbal and rhetorical skill and may apply to a public denunciation ⟨a politician known for his blistering *invective*⟩. **Obloquy** suggests defamation and consequent shame and disgrace ⟨silently endured the *obloquy* of his former friend⟩. **Scurrility** implies viciousness of attack and coarseness or foulness of language ⟨a debate that was not an exchange of ideas but an exercise in *scurrility*⟩. **Billingsgate** implies practiced fluency and variety of profane or obscene abuse ⟨a *billingsgate* that would make a drunken sailor blush⟩.

accede see ASSENT

acceptation see MEANING

accidental, fortuitous, casual, contingent mean not amenable to planning or prediction. **Accidental** stresses chance ⟨any resemblance to actual persons is entirely *accidental*⟩. **Fortuitous** so strongly suggests chance that it often connotes entire absence of cause ⟨believes that life is more than a series of *fortuitous* events⟩. **Casual** stresses lack of real or apparent premeditation or intent ⟨a *casual* encounter between two acquaintances⟩. **Contingent** suggests possibility of happening but stresses uncertainty and dependence on other future events for existence or occurrence ⟨the *contingent* effects of a proposed amendment to the constitution⟩.

accommodate see ADAPT, CONTAIN

accompany, attend, escort mean to go along with. When referring to persons, **accompany** usu. implies equality of status ⟨*accompanied* his wife to the theater⟩. **Attend** implies a waiting upon in order to serve usu. as a subordinate ⟨will *attend* the President at the summit meeting⟩. **Escort** adds to *accompany* implications of protection, ceremony, or courtesy ⟨a motorcade *escorted* the visiting queen⟩.

accomplish see PERFORM

accomplishment see ACQUIREMENT

accord *vb* see GRANT

accord *n* see HARMONY

accountable see RESPONSIBLE

accoutre see FURNISH

accredit see APPROVE

accumulative see CUMULATIVE

accurate see CORRECT

accuse, charge, indict, impeach mean to declare a person guilty of a fault or offense. **Accuse** implies a direct, personal declaration ⟨*accused* him of trying to steal his wallet⟩. **Charge** usu. implies a formal declaration of a serious offense ⟨an athlete *charged* with taking illegal drugs before the race⟩. **Indict** is usu. used in a legal context and implies a formal consideration of evidence prior to a trial ⟨*indicted* by a grand jury for first-degree murder⟩. **Impeach** technically refers to a formal charge of malfeasance in office on the part of a public official ⟨the House of Representatives *impeached* President Andrew Johnson of high crimes and misdemeanors⟩.

accustomed see USUAL

acerbity see ACRIMONY

achieve see PERFORM

achievement see FEAT

acknowledge, admit, own, avow, confess mean to disclose against one's will or inclination. **Acknowledge** implies the disclosing of something that has been or might be concealed ⟨*acknowledged* an early short-lived marriage⟩. **Admit** implies reluctance to disclose, grant, or concede and refers usu. to facts rather than their implications ⟨*admitted* that the project was over budget⟩. **Own** implies acknowledging something in close relation to oneself ⟨must *own* that I know little about computers⟩. **Avow** implies boldly declaring, often in the face of hostility, what one might be expected to be silent about ⟨*avowed* that he was homosexual⟩. **Confess** may apply to an admission of a weakness, failure, omission, or guilt ⟨*confessed* that she had a weakness for sweets⟩.

acme see SUMMIT

acquaint see INFORM

acquiesce see ASSENT

acquire see GET

acquirement, acquisition, attainment, accomplishment

mean a power or skill won through deliberate effort. **Acquirement** suggests the result of constant endeavor to cultivate oneself ⟨an appreciation of good music was not one of his *acquirements*⟩. **Acquisition** stresses the effort involved and the inherent value of what is gained ⟨the ability to concentrate is a valuable *acquisition*⟩. **Attainment** suggests a distinguished achievement ⟨honored as woman of the year for her many *attainments*⟩. **Accomplishment** implies a socially useful skill ⟨wittiness in conversation is an *accomplishment* to be cherished⟩.

acquisition see ACQUIREMENT

acquisitive see COVETOUS

acquit see BEHAVE, EXCULPATE

acrid see CAUSTIC

acrimony, acerbity, asperity mean temper or language marked by angry irritation. **Acrimony** implies feelings of bitterness and a stinging verbal attack ⟨a campaign marked by verbal exchanges of intense *acrimony*⟩. **Acerbity** suggests a morose, embittered, or crabbed temperament ⟨an inbred *acerbity* that pervades even his personal letters⟩. **Asperity** suggests harshness or roughness of expression rather than feelings of bitterness ⟨a certain *asperity* of expression was part of her style⟩.

actuate see MOVE

acumen see DISCERNMENT

acute, critical, crucial mean of uncertain outcome. **Acute** stresses intensification of conditions leading to a culmination or breaking point ⟨the housing shortage is becoming *acute*⟩ **Critical** adds to *acute* implications of imminent change, of attendant suspense, and of decisiveness in the outcome ⟨the war has entered a *critical* phase⟩. **Crucial** suggests a dividing of the ways and often a test or trial involving the determination of a future course or direction

⟨for the campaign, the coming weeks will be *crucial*⟩. See in addition SHARP.

adamant see INFLEXIBLE

adapt, adjust, accommodate, conform, reconcile mean to bring one thing into correspondence with another. **Adapt** implies a modification according to changing circumstances ⟨they *adapted* themselves to the warmer climate⟩. **Adjust** suggests bringing into a close and exact correspondence or harmony as exists between the parts of a mechanism ⟨*adjusted* the budget to allow for inflation⟩. **Accommodate** may suggest yielding or compromising in order to effect a correspondence ⟨*accommodated* his political beliefs in order to win⟩. **Conform** applies to bringing into harmony or accordance with a pattern, example, or principle ⟨refused to *conform* to society's idea of woman's proper role⟩. **Reconcile** implies the demonstration of the underlying consistency or congruity of things that seem to be incompatible ⟨tried to *reconcile* what they said with what I knew⟩.

adaptable see PLASTIC

additive see CUMULATIVE

address see TACT

adept see PROFICIENT

adequate see SUFFICIENT

adhere see STICK

adherent see FOLLOWER

adjacent, adjoining, contiguous, juxtaposed mean being in close proximity. **Adjacent** may or may not imply contact but always implies absence of anything of the same kind in between ⟨the price of the house and the *adjacent* garage⟩. **Adjoining** definitely implies meeting and touching at some point or line ⟨assigned *adjoining* rooms at the hotel⟩. **Contiguous** implies having contact on all or most of one side ⟨offices in all 48 *contiguous* states⟩. **Juxtaposed** means placed side by side esp. so as to permit comparison and contrast ⟨an ultramodern office buiding *juxtaposed* to a Gothic church⟩.

adjoining see ADJACENT

adjure see BEG

adjust see ADAPT

administer see EXECUTE

admire see REGARD

admission see ADMITTANCE

admit see ACKNOWLEDGE

admittance, admission mean permitted entrance. **Admittance** is usu. applied to mere physical entrance to a locality or a building ⟨members must show their cards upon *admittance* to the club⟩. **Admission** applies to entrance or formal acceptance (as into a club) that carries with it rights, privileges, standing, or membership ⟨candidates for *admission* must submit recommendations from two club members⟩.

admonish see REPROVE

adopt, embrace, espouse mean to take an opinion, policy, or practice as one's own. **Adopt** implies accepting something created by another or foreign to one's nature ⟨forced to *adopt* the procedures of the new parent company⟩. **Embrace** implies a ready or happy acceptance ⟨eagerly *embraced* the ways and customs of their new homeland⟩. **Espouse** adds an implication of close attachment to a cause and a sharing of its fortunes ⟨spent her lifetime *espousing* equal rights for women⟩.

adore see REVERE

adorn, decorate, ornament, embellish, beautify, deck, garnish mean to enhance the appearance of something by adding something unessential. **Adorn** implies an enhancing by something beautiful in itself ⟨a diamond necklace *adorned* her neck⟩. **Decorate** suggests relieving plainness or monotony by adding beauty of color or design ⟨*decorate* a birthday cake with colored frosting⟩. **Ornament** and **embellish** imply the adding of something extraneous, *ornament* stressing the heightening or setting off of the original ⟨a white house *ornamented* with green shutters⟩, *embellish* often stressing the adding of superfluous or adventitious ornament ⟨*embellish* a page with floral borders⟩. **Beautify** adds to *embellish* a suggestion of counterbalancing plainnesss or ugliness ⟨will *beautify* the park with flower beds⟩. **Deck** implies the addition of something that contributes to gaiety, splendor, or showiness ⟨a house all *decked* out for Christmas⟩. **Garnish** suggests decorating with a small final touch and is used esp. in referring to the serving of food ⟨airline food is invariably *garnished* with parsley⟩.

adroit see CLEVER, DEXTEROUS

adultery, fornication, incest designate forms of illicit sexual intercourse that are clearly distinguished in legal use. **Adultery** can be applied only to sexual intercourse between a married person and a partner other than his or her wife or husband ⟨listed *adultery* as grounds for divorce⟩. **Fornication** designates sexual intercourse on the part of an unmarried person ⟨religious laws strictly forbidding *fornication*⟩. **Incest** refers to sexual intercourse between persons proscribed from marrying on the basis of kinship ties ⟨*incest* involving father and daughter is the most common⟩.

advance, promote, forward, further mean to help (someone or something) to move ahead. **Advance** stresses effective assisting in hastening a process or bringing about a desired end ⟨a gesture intended to *advance* the cause of peace⟩. **Promote** suggests an encouraging or fostering and may denote an increase in status or rank ⟨a company trying to *promote* better health among employees⟩. **Forward** implies an impetus forcing something ahead ⟨a wage increase would *forward* productivity⟩. **Further** suggests a removing of obstacles in the way of a desired advance ⟨used the marriage to *further* his career⟩.

advantageous see BENEFICIAL

advent see ARRIVAL

adventurous, venturesome, daring, daredevil, rash, reckless, foolhardy mean exposing oneself to danger more than required by good sense. **Adventurous** implies a willingness to accept risks but not necessarily imprudence ⟨*adventurous* pioneers opened the West⟩. **Venturesome** implies a jaunty eagerness for perilous undertakings ⟨*venturesome* pilots became popular heroes⟩. **Daring** heightens the implication of fearlessness in courting danger ⟨mountain climbing attracts the *daring* types⟩. **Daredevil** stresses ostentation in daring ⟨*daredevil* motorcyclists performing stunts⟩. **Rash** suggests imprudence and lack of forethought ⟨a *rash* decision that you will regret later⟩. **Reckless** implies heedlessness of probable consequences ⟨a *reckless* driver who was drunk⟩. **Foolhardy** suggests a recklessness that is inconsistent with good sense ⟨only a *foolhardy* sailor would venture into this storm⟩.

adversary see OPPONENT

adverse, antagonistic, counter, counteractive mean so opposed as to cause often harmful interference. **Adverse** applies to what is unfavorable, harmful, or detrimental ⟨very sensitive to *adverse* criticism⟩. **Antagonistic** usu. implies mutual opposition and either hostility or incompatibility ⟨neighboring countries were *antagonistic* to the new nation⟩. **Counter** applies to forces coming from opposite directions with resulting conflict or tension ⟨the *counter* demands of family and career⟩. **Counteractive** implies an opposition between two things that nullifies the effect of one or both ⟨poor eating habits will have a *counteractive* effect on any gains from exercise⟩.

adversity see MISFORTUNE

advice, counsel denote recommendation as to a decision or a course of conduct. **Advice** implies real or pretended knowledge or experience, often professional or technical, on the part of the one who advises ⟨a book of *advice* for would-be entrepreneurs⟩. **Counsel** often stresses the fruit of wisdom or deliberation and may presuppose a weightier occasion, or more authority, or more personal concern on the part of the one giving counsel ⟨Father would often give me the benefit of his *counsel*⟩.

advisable see EXPEDIENT

advise see CONFER

advocate see SUPPORT

affable see GRACIOUS

affect, influence, touch, impress, strike, sway mean to produce or have an effect upon. **Affect** implies the action of a stimulus that can produce a response or reaction ⟨the sight *affected* her to tears⟩. **Influence** implies a force that brings about a change (as in nature or behavior) ⟨our beliefs are *influenced* by our upbringing⟩ ⟨a drug that *influences* growth rates⟩. **Touch** may carry a vivid suggestion of close contact and may connote stirring, arousing, or harming ⟨plants *touched* by frost⟩ ⟨his emotions were *touched* by her distress⟩. **Impress** stresses the depth and persistence of the effect ⟨only one of the plans *impressed* him⟩. **Strike,** similar to but weaker than *impress,* may convey the notion of sudden sharp perception or appreciation ⟨*struck* by the solemnity of the occasion⟩. **Sway** implies the acting of influences that are not resisted or are irresistible, with resulting change in character or course of action ⟨politicians

who are *swayed* by popular opinion⟩. See in addition
ASSUME.

affectation see POSE

affecting see MOVING

affection see FEELING

affinity see ATTRACTION, LIKENESS

affirm see ASSERT

affix see FASTEN

afflict, try, torment, torture, rack, grill mean to inflict on a
person something that is hard to bear. **Afflict** is a general
term and applies to the causing of pain or suffering or of
acute annoyance, embarrassment, or any distress ⟨many
aged persons who are *afflicted* with blindness⟩. **Try** suggests imposing something that strains the powers of endurance or of self-control ⟨young children often *try* their
parents' patience⟩. **Torment** suggests persecution or the repeated inflicting of suffering or annoyance ⟨the horses are
tormented by flies⟩. **Torture** adds the implication of causing unbearable pain or suffering ⟨*tortured* his wife with
charges of infidelity⟩. **Rack** stresses straining or wrenching
⟨a mind *racked* by guilt⟩. **Grill** suggests causing acute discomfort as by long and relentless questioning ⟨they *grilled*
the prisoner for hours on end⟩.

affluent see RICH

afford see GIVE

affront see OFFEND

afraid see FEARFUL

age see PERIOD

aggravate see INTENSIFY

aggressive, militant, assertive, self-assertive, pushing mean
obtrusively energetic esp. in pursuing particular goals. **Aggressive** implies a disposition to dominate often in disregard of others' rights or in determined and energetic pur-

suit of one's ends ⟨books on how to be *aggressive* in the business world⟩. **Militant** also implies a fighting disposition but suggests not self-seeking but devotion to a cause, movement, or principle ⟨*militant* environmentalists staged a protest⟩. **Assertive** suggests bold self-confidence in expression of opinion ⟨*assertive* speakers dominated the open forum⟩. **Self-assertive** connotes forwardness or brash self-confidence ⟨a *self-assertive* young executive climbing the corporate ladder⟩. **Pushing** may apply to ambition or enterprise or to snobbish and crude intrusiveness or officiousness ⟨*pushing* salespeople using high-pressure tactics⟩.

aggrieve see WRONG

agile, nimble, brisk, spry mean acting or moving with easy quickness. **Agile** implies dexterity and ease in physical or mental actions ⟨very *agile* about distancing himself from unpopular issues⟩. **Nimble** stresses lightness and swiftness of action or thought ⟨a *nimble* tennis player⟩. **Brisk** suggests liveliness, animation, or vigor of movement sometimes with a suggestion of hurry ⟨a *brisk* cleaning-up before the relatives arrived⟩. **Spry** stresses an ability for quick action that is unexpected because of age or known infirmity ⟨*spry* older runners sometimes beat out younger competitors⟩.

agitate see DISCOMPOSE, SHAKE

agony see DISTRESS

agree, concur, coincide mean to come into or be in harmony regarding a matter of opinion. **Agree** implies complete accord usually attained by discussion and adjustment of differences ⟨on some points we all can *agree*⟩. **Concur** tends to suggest cooperative thinking or acting toward an end but sometimes implies no more than approval (as of a decision reached by others) ⟨if my wife *concurs,* then it's a deal⟩. **Coincide,** used more often of opinions, judgments, wishes, or interests than of people, implies an agreement amounting to identity ⟨their wishes *coincide* exactly with my desire⟩. See in addition ASSENT.

aid see HELP

aim see INTENTION

air *vb* see EXPRESS

air *n* see POSE

airs see POSE

alacrity see CELERITY

alarm see FEAR

alert see INTELLIGENT, WATCHFUL

alibi see APOLOGY

alien see EXTRINSIC

alienate see ESTRANGE

alive see AWARE, LIVING

all see WHOLE

allay see RELIEVE

allegiance see FIDELITY

alleviate see RELIEVE

alliance, league, coalition, confederation, federation mean an association to further the common interests of its members. **Alliance** applies to an association formed for the mutual benefit of its members ⟨an *alliance* between feminist and religious groups against pornography⟩. **League** applies to a more formal compact often with a definite goal ⟨the *League* of Nations⟩. **Coalition** applies to a temporary association of parties often of opposing interests ⟨formed a *coalition* government with two other parties⟩. **Confederation** applies to a union of independent states under a central government having powers dealing with common external relations ⟨the *confederation* formed by the American colonies following the revolution⟩. **Federation**

specif. applies to a sovereign power formed by a union of states and having a central government and several state and local governments ⟨the United States of America constitutes a *federation*⟩.

allocate see ALLOT

allot, assign, apportion, allocate mean to give as a share, portion, role, or lot. **Allot** may imply haphazard or arbitrary distribution ⟨each student is *alloted* an hour of computer time⟩. **Assign** stresses an authoritative and fixed allotting but carries no clear implication of an even division ⟨each employee is *assigned* a parking space⟩. **Apportion** implies a dividing according to some principle ⟨profits were *apportioned* according to a predetermined ratio⟩. **Allocate** suggests a fixed appropriation usu. of money to a person or group for a particular use ⟨*allocated* $50,000 for park improvements⟩.

allow see LET

allure see ATTRACT

ally see CONFEDERATE

alone, solitary, lonely, lonesome, lone, forlorn, desolate mean isolated from others. **Alone** suggests the objective fact of being by oneself with slighter notion of emotional involvement than most of the remaining terms ⟨everyone needs to be *alone* sometimes⟩. **Solitary** may indicate isolation as a chosen course ⟨glorying in the calm of her *solitary* life⟩ but more often it suggests sadness and a sense of loss ⟨left *solitary* by the death of his wife⟩. **Lonely** adds to *solitary* a suggestion of longing for companionship ⟨felt *lonely* and forsaken⟩. **Lonesome** heightens the suggestion of sadness and poignancy ⟨an only child often leads a *lonesome* life⟩. **Lone** may replace *lonely* or *lonesome* but typically is as objective as *alone* ⟨a *lone* robin pecking at the lawn⟩. **Forlorn** stresses dejection, woe, and listlessness at separation from one held dear ⟨a *forlorn* lost child⟩. **Desolate** implies inconsolable grief at loss or bereavement ⟨her brother's death now left her totally *desolate*⟩.

aloof see INDIFFERENT

alter see CHANGE

altercation see QUARREL

alternative see CHOICE

altitude see HEIGHT

amalgate see MIX

amateur, dilettante, dabbler, tyro mean a person who follows a pursuit without attaining proficiency or professional status. **Amateur** often applies to one practicing an art without mastery of its essentials ⟨a painting obviously done by an *amateur*⟩, and in sports it may also suggest not so much lack of skill but avoidance of direct remuneration ⟨must remain an *amateur* in order to qualify for the Olympics⟩. **Dilettante** may apply to the lover of an art rather than its skilled practitioner but usu. implies elegant trifling in the arts and an absence of serious commitment ⟨a serious art teacher with no patience for *dilettantes*⟩. **Dabbler** suggests desultory habits of work and lack of persistence ⟨a *dabbler* who never finished a single novel⟩. **Tyro** implies inexperience often combined with audacity with resulting crudeness or blundering ⟨a *tyro* who has yet to master the basics of playwriting⟩.

amaze see SURPRISE

ambiguity, equivocation, tergiversation, double entendre mean an expression capable of more than one interpretation. **Ambiguity** usu. refers to the use of a word or phrase in such a way that it may be taken in either of two senses ⟨the *ambiguity* in the directive's wording caused much confusion⟩. **Equivocation** suggests that the ambiguity is intentional and the intent is to mislead ⟨the government's

report on the nuclear accident is filled with *equivocations*).
Tergiversation stresses the shifting of senses during the
course of one's argument and usu. suggests intentional
subterfuge ⟨a thesis that resorts to several *tergiversations*
of the word "society"⟩. **Double entendre** refers to a word
or expression allowing two interpretations, one of them
being risqué ⟨the *double entendres* that are de rigueur in
any bedroom farce⟩.

ambiguous see OBSCURE

ambition, aspiration, pretension mean strong desire for ad-
vancement. **Ambition** applies to the desire for personal ad-
vancement or preferment and may suggest equally a
praiseworthy or an inordinate desire ⟨driven by the *ambition* to be very rich⟩. **Aspiration** implies a striving after
something higher than oneself and usu. implies that the
striver is thereby ennobled ⟨an *aspiration* to become President someday⟩. **Pretension** suggests ardent desire for recognition of accomplishment without actual possession of
the necessary ability and therefore implies presumption
⟨several people with literary *pretensions* frequent her
salon⟩.

ameliorate see IMPROVE

amenable see OBEDIENT, RESPONSIBLE

amend see CORRECT

amiable, good-natured, obliging, complaisant mean having
the desire or disposition to please. **Amiable** implies having
qualities that make one liked and easy to deal with ⟨a
travel club that attracts *amiable* types⟩. **Good-natured** implies cheerfulness or helpfulness and sometimes a willingness to be imposed upon ⟨a *good-natured* boy who was always willing to pitch in⟩. **Obliging** stresses a friendly
readiness to be helpful ⟨our *obliging* innkeeper accommodated our request⟩. **Complaisant** often implies passiv-

ity or a yielding to others because of weakness ⟨*complaisant* people who only say what others want to hear⟩.

amicable, neighborly, friendly mean exhibiting goodwill and an absence of antagonism. **Amicable** implies a state of peace and a desire on the part of the parties not to quarrel ⟨maintained *amicable* relations even after the divorce⟩. **Neighborly** implies a disposition to live on good terms with others and to be helpful on principle ⟨a *neighborly* concern prompted the inquiry about her health⟩. **Friendly** stresses cordiality and often warmth or intimacy of personal relations ⟨sought his *friendly* advice on this important matter⟩.

ample see PLENTIFUL, SPACIOUS

amplify see EXPAND

amuse, divert, entertain mean to pass or cause to pass the time pleasantly. **Amuse** suggests that one's attention is engaged lightly or frivolously ⟨*amuse* yourselves while I prepare dinner⟩. **Divert** implies the distracting of the attention from worry or routine occupation esp. by something funny ⟨tired businessmen looking for a light comedy to *divert* them⟩. **Entertain** suggests supplying amusement or diversion by specially prepared or contrived methods ⟨comedians and pretty girls *entertained* the troops⟩.

analogous see SIMILAR

analogy see LIKENESS

analyze, dissect, break down mean to divide a complex whole into its parts or elements. **Analyze** suggests separating or distinguishing the component parts of something (as a substance, a process, a situation) so as to discover its true nature or inner relationships ⟨*analyzed* the basis for the current problem of trade imbalances⟩. **Dissect** suggests a searching analysis by laying bare parts or pieces for individual scrutiny ⟨commentators *dissected* every word of the

President's statement⟩. **Break down** implies a reducing to simpler parts or divisions ⟨*break down* the budget to see where the money is going⟩.

anathema see ABOMINATION

anathematize see EXECRATE

ancient see OLD

anger, ire, rage, fury, indignation, wrath mean an intense emotional state induced by displeasure. **Anger,** the most general term, names the reaction but in itself conveys nothing about intensity or justification or manifestation of the emotional state ⟨tried to hide his *anger*⟩. **Ire,** more frequent in literary contexts, may suggest greater intensity than *anger,* often with an evident display of feeling ⟨cheeks flushed dark with *ire*⟩. **Rage** suggests loss of self-control from violence of emotion ⟨screaming with *rage*⟩. **Fury** is overmastering destructive rage verging on madness ⟨in her *fury* she started to accuse everyone around her⟩. **Indignation** stresses righteous anger at what one considers unfair, mean, or shameful ⟨behavior that caused general *indignation*⟩. **Wrath** is likely to suggest a desire or intent to revenge or punish ⟨rose in his *wrath* and struck his tormentor to the floor⟩.

angle see PHASE

anguish see SORROW

animal see CARNAL

animate *adj* see LIVING

animate *vb* see QUICKEN

animated see LIVELY, LIVING

animosity see ENMITY

animus see ENMITY

announce see DECLARE

annoy, vex, irk, bother mean to upset a person's composure.
    Annoy implies a wearing on the nerves by persistent petty

unpleasantness ⟨her constant complaining *annoys* us⟩.
Vex implies greater provocation and stronger disturbance
and usu. connotes anger but sometimes perplexity or anxiety ⟨a problem that *vexes* cancer researchers⟩. **Irk** stresses
difficulty in enduring and the resulting weariness or impatience of spirit ⟨his chronic tardiness *irks* his wife⟩.
Bother suggests interference with comfort or peace of mind
⟨that discrepancy *bothers* me⟩. See in addition WORRY.

annul see NULLIFY

anomalous see IRREGULAR

answer, respond, reply, rejoin, retort mean to say, write, or
do something in return. **Answer** implies the satisfying of a
question, demand, call, or need ⟨*answered* all the questions on the form⟩. **Respond** may suggest an immediate or
quick reaction ⟨chose not to *respond* to that comment⟩.
Reply implies making a return commensurate with the
original question or demand ⟨an invitation that requires
you to *reply* at once⟩. **Rejoin** often implies sharpness or
quickness in answering ⟨"who asked you?" she *rejoined*⟩.
Retort suggests responding to an explicit charge or criticism by way of retaliation ⟨he *retorted* to her every charge
with biting sarcasm⟩.

answerable see RESPONSIBLE

antagonism see ENMITY

antagonist see OPPONENT

antagonistic see ADVERSE

antagonize see OPPOSE

antecedent *n* see CAUSE

antecedent *adj* see PRECEDING

anterior see PRECEDING

anticipate see FORESEE, PREVENT

anticipation see PROSPECT

antipathy see ENMITY

antiquated see OLD
antique see OLD
antithetical see OPPOSITE
anxiety see CARE
anxious see EAGER
apathetic see IMPASSIVE
ape see COPY
aperçu see COMPENDIUM
apex see SUMMIT
aplomb see CONFIDENCE
apocryphal see FICTITIOUS
apologia see APOLOGY
apology, apologia, excuse, plea, pretext, alibi mean matter offered in explanation or defense. **Apology** usu. applies to an expression of regret for a mistake or wrong with implied admission of guilt or fault and with or without reference to palliating circumstances ⟨said by way of *apology* that he would have met them if he could⟩. Sometimes *apology,* like **apologia,** implies not admission of guilt or regret but a desire to make clear the grounds for some course, belief, or position ⟨the speech was an effective *apologia* for his foreign policy⟩. **Excuse** implies an intent to avoid or remove blame or censure ⟨used his illness as an *excuse* for missing the meeting⟩. **Plea** stresses argument or appeal for understanding or sympathy or mercy ⟨her usual *plea* that she was nearsighted⟩. **Pretext** suggests subterfuge and the offering of false reasons or motives in excuse or explanation ⟨used any *pretext* to get out of work⟩. **Alibi** implies a desire to shift blame or evade punishment and imputes plausibility rather than truth to the explanation offered ⟨his *alibi* failed to stand scrutiny⟩.
appall see DISMAY
apparent, illusory, seeming, ostensible mean not actually

being what appearance indicates. **Apparent** suggests appearance to unaided senses that is not or may not be borne out by more rigorous examination or greater knowledge ⟨the *apparent* cause of the train wreck⟩. **Illusory** implies a false impression based on deceptive resemblance or faulty observation, or influenced by emotions that prevent a clear view ⟨vertical stripes will give an *illusory* height to her figure⟩. **Seeming** implies a character in the thing observed that gives it the appearance, sometimes through intent, of something else ⟨the *seeming* simplicity of the story⟩. **Ostensible** suggests a discrepancy between an openly declared or naturally implied aim or reason and the true one ⟨business was the *ostensible* reason for their visit⟩. See in addition EVIDENT.

appease see PACIFY

appetizing see PALATABLE

appliance see IMPLEMENT

applicable see RELEVANT

appoint see FURNISH

apportion see ALLOT

apposite see RELEVANT

appraise see ESTIMATE

appreciable see PERCEPTIBLE

appreciate, value, prize, treasure, cherish mean to hold in high estimation. **Appreciate** often connotes sufficient understanding to enjoy or admire a thing's excellence ⟨*appreciates* fine wine⟩. **Value** implies rating a thing highly for its intrinsic worth ⟨*values* our friendship⟩. **Prize** implies taking a deep pride in something one possesses ⟨Americans *prize* their freedom⟩. **Treasure** emphasizes jealously safeguarding something considered precious ⟨she *treasures* every momento of her youth⟩. **Cherish** implies a special love and care for something ⟨*cherishes* her children above all⟩. See in addition UNDERSTAND.

apprehend see FORESEE

apprehension, foreboding, misgiving, presentiment mean a feeling that something undesirable will or is about to happen. **Apprehension** implies a mind preoccupied with fear and anxiety ⟨approached the dangerous undertaking with great *apprehension*⟩. **Foreboding** suggests fear that is oppressive, unreasoning, or indefinable ⟨the deserted streets filled me with strange *forebodings*⟩. **Misgiving** suggests uneasiness and mistrust ⟨had my *misgivings* about her from the start⟩. **Presentiment** implies a vague or uncanny sense that something is bound to happen ⟨a *presentiment* that some of our group would not survive⟩.

apprehensive see FEARFUL

apprise see INFORM

appropriate *vb* Appropriate, preempt, arrogate, usurp, confiscate mean to seize high-handedly. **Appropriate** suggests making something one's own or converting to one's own use without authority or with questionable right ⟨just *appropriated* the tools meant to be shared by all⟩. **Preempt** implies beforehandedness in taking something desired or needed by others ⟨TV *preempted* much of the programming once broadcast by radio⟩. **Arrogate** implies insolence, presumption, and exclusion of others in seizing rights, powers, or functions ⟨White House staffers *arrogated* powers belonging to cabinet members⟩. **Usurp** implies unlawful or unwarranted intrusion into the place of another and seizure of what is his by custom, right, or law ⟨her new stepmother had *usurped* her status in the household⟩. **Confiscate** always implies seizure through exercise of authority ⟨customs officers *confiscate* all contraband⟩.

appropriate *adj* see FIT

approve, endorse, sanction, accredit, certify mean to have or express a favorable opinion of. **Approve** often implies no more than this but may suggest considerable esteem or admiration ⟨the parents *approve* of the marriage⟩. **Endorse** suggests an explicit statement of support ⟨publicly *endorsed* her for Senator⟩. **Sanction** implies both approval and authorization ⟨the President *sanctioned* covert operations⟩. **Accredit** and **certify** usu. imply official endorsement attesting to conformity to set standards ⟨the board voted to *accredit* the college⟩ ⟨must be *certified* to teach⟩.

apropos see RELEVANT

apt see FIT, QUICK

aptitude see GIFT

arbitrary see ABSOLUTE

archaic see OLD

ardent see IMPASSIONED

ardor see PASSION

arduous see HARD

argot see DIALECT

argue see DISCUSS

arise see SPRING

aristocracy, nobility, gentry, society mean a body of people constituting a socially superior caste. **Aristocracy** usu. refers to those persons of superior birth, breeding, and social station ⟨plantation families constituted the *aristocracy* of the antebellum South⟩. **Nobility** refers to persons of a privileged and titled class that ranks just below royalty ⟨the duke ranks highest in British *nobility*⟩. **Gentry** refers to a class of leisured, well-bred persons who are considered gentlefolk but are without hereditary titles ⟨a private school favored by generations of the *gentry*⟩. **Society** refers to that class of people who are celebrated for their active social life, conspicuous leisure, and fashionable clothes ⟨Newport *society* was famous for its lavish balls⟩.

arm see FURNISH

aroma see SMELL

aromatic see ODOROUS

arrange see ORDER

arrival, advent mean the reaching of a destination. **Arrival** emphasizes the preceding travel or movement ⟨a traffic jam greatly delayed their *arrival*⟩. **Advent** applies to a momentous or conspicuous arrival, an appearance upon a scene esp. for the first time, or a beginning ⟨the *advent* of a new age in space travel⟩.

arrogant see PROUD

arrogate see APPROPRIATE

art, skill, cunning, artifice, craft mean the faculty of executing well what one has devised. **Art** distinctively implies a personal, unanalyzable creative power ⟨an *art* for saying the right thing⟩. **Skill** stresses technical knowledge and proficiency ⟨the *skills* required of a surgeon⟩. **Cunning** suggests ingenuity and subtlety in devising, inventing, or executing ⟨a mystery thriller written with great *cunning*⟩. **Artifice** suggests mechanical skill esp. in imitating things in nature ⟨a painter with much of the *artifice* of Rubens and none of the art⟩. **Craft** may imply expertness in workmanship ⟨a saltcellar wrought with *craft* worthy of Cellini⟩.

artful see SLY

artifice see ART, TRICK

artificial, factitious, synthetic, ersatz mean brought into being not by nature but by art or effort. **Artificial** is applicable to anything that is not the result of natural processes or conditions ⟨the state is an *artificial* society⟩ but esp. to something that has a counterpart in nature ⟨*artificial* teeth⟩. **Factitious** applies chiefly to emotions or states of mind not naturally caused or spontaneously aroused ⟨created a *factitious* demand for the product⟩. **Synthetic** applies esp. to a manufactured substance or to a natural substance so treated that it acquires the appearance or qualities of another and may substitute for it ⟨*synthetic* furs⟩. **Ersatz** often implies the use of an inferior substitute for a natural product ⟨served *ersatz* cream with the coffee⟩.

artless see NATURAL

ascertain see DISCOVER

ascetic see SEVERE

ascribe, attribute, assign, impute, credit mean to lay something to the account of a person or thing. **Ascribe** suggests an inferring or conjecturing of cause, quality, authorship ⟨none of the frivolity commonly *ascribed* to teenagers⟩. **Attribute** suggests less tentativeness than *ascribe,* less definiteness than *assign* ⟨*attribute* the project's failure to poor planning⟩. **Assign** implies ascribing with certainty or after deliberation ⟨an investigatory panel *assigned* blame to top officials⟩. **Impute** suggests ascribing something that brings discredit by way of accusation or blame ⟨tried to *impute* sinister motives to my actions⟩. **Credit** implies ascribing a thing or esp. an action to a person or other thing as its agent, source, or explanation ⟨*credited* his insecurities to an unhappy childhood⟩.

asinine see SIMPLE

ask *vb* Ask, question, interrogate, query, inquire mean to address a person in order to gain information. **Ask** implies no more than the putting of a question ⟨*ask* for directions⟩. **Question** usu. suggests the asking of series of questions ⟨*questioned* them about every detail of the trip⟩. **Interrogate** suggests formal or official systematic questioning ⟨the prosecutor *interrogated* the witness all day⟩. **Query** implies a desire for authoritative information or confirmation ⟨*queried* the reference librarian about the book⟩. **Inquire** implies a searching for facts or for truth often specifically by asking questions ⟨began to *inquire* into the charges of espionage⟩.

ask *vb* **Ask, request, solicit** mean to seek to obtain by making one's wants known. **Ask** implies no more than the statement of the desire ⟨*ask* a favor of a friend⟩. **Request** implies greater formality and courtesy ⟨*requests* the pleasure of your company at the ball⟩. **Solicit** suggests a calling attention to one's wants or desires by public announcement or advertisement ⟨a classified ad that *solicits* a situation as a babysitter⟩.

aspect see PHASE

asperity see ACRIMONY

asperse see MALIGN

aspiration see AMBITION

assail see ATTACK

assassinate see KILL

assault see ATTACK

assemble see GATHER

assent, consent, accede, acquiesce, agree, subscribe mean to concur with what has been proposed. **Assent** implies an act involving the understanding or judgment and applies to propositions or opinions ⟨potential members must *assent* to the organization's credo⟩. **Consent** involves the will or feelings and indicates compliance with what is requested or desired ⟨*consented* to their daughter's going on the trip⟩. **Accede** implies a yielding, often under pressure, of assent or consent ⟨officials *acceded* to every prisoner demand⟩. **Acquiesce** implies tacit acceptance or forbearance of opposition ⟨usually *acquiesces* to his wife's wishes⟩. **Agree** sometimes implies previous difference of opinion or attempts at persuasion ⟨finally *agreed* to give him a raise⟩.

Subscribe implies not only consent or assent but hearty approval and active support ⟨totally *subscribed* to the free enterprise system⟩.

assert, declare, affirm, protest, avow mean to state positively usu. in anticipation of denial or objection. **Assert** implies stating confidently without need for proof or regard for evidence ⟨*asserted* that modern music is just noise⟩. **Declare** stresses open or public statement ⟨the jury *declared* the defendant guilty⟩. **Affirm** implies conviction based on evidence, experience, or faith ⟨*affirmed* the existence of an afterlife⟩. **Protest** emphasizes affirming in the face of denial or doubt ⟨*protested* that he had never had a more splendid meal⟩. **Avow** stresses frank declaration and acknowledgment of personal responsibility for what is declared ⟨*avowed* that all investors would be repaid in full⟩. See in addition MAINTAIN.

assertive see AGGRESSIVE

assess see ESTIMATE

assiduous see BUSY

assign see ALLOT, ASCRIBE

assignment see TASK

assimilate see ABSORB

assist see HELP

associate see JOIN

assuage see RELIEVE

assault see ATTACK

assume, affect, pretend, simulate, feign, counterfeit, sham mean to put on a false or deceptive appearance. **Assume** often implies a justifiable motive rather than an intent to deceive ⟨*assumed* an air of cheerfulness for the sake of the patient⟩. **Affect** implies making a false show of possessing, using, or feeling ⟨willing to *affect* an interest in art in order to impress her⟩. **Pretend** implies an overt and sustained false appearance ⟨*pretended* not to know about her husband's affair⟩. **Simulate** suggests a close imitation of the appearance of something ⟨the training chamber *simulates* a weightless atmosphere⟩. **Feign** implies more artful invention than *pretend,* less specific mimicry than *simulate* ⟨*feigned* sickness in order to stay home from school⟩. **Counterfeit** implies achieving the highest degree of verisimilitude of any of these words ⟨*counterfeited* drunkenness so perfectly that many forgot he was acting⟩. **Sham** implies an obvious falseness that fools only the gullible ⟨*shammed* a most unconvincing limp⟩.

assurance see CERTAINTY, CONFIDENCE

assure see ENSURE

astonish see SURPRISE

astound see SURPRISE

astute see SHREWD

athirst see EAGER

atmosphere, feeling, aura mean an intangible quality that gives something an individual and distinctly recognizable character. **Atmosphere** implies a quality that accrues to something or that pervades it as a whole and that determines the impression given by that thing ⟨a country inn with a warm and friendly *atmosphere*⟩. **Feeling** implies that something has distinctive qualities that create a definite if unanalyzable impression ⟨a Colorado ski resort with an old-world *feeling*⟩. **Aura** suggests an ethereal or mysterious quality that seems to emanate from a person or thing ⟨a movie queen with an unmistakable *aura* of glamour⟩.

atrocious see OUTRAGEOUS

attach see FASTEN

attack, assail, assault, bombard, storm mean to make an onslaught upon. **Attack** implies taking the initiative in a struggle ⟨plan to *attack* at dawn⟩. **Assail** implies attempting to break down resistance by repeated blows or shots ⟨*assailed* the enemy with artillery fire⟩. **Assault** suggests a direct attempt to overpower by suddenness and violence of onslaught ⟨commando troops *assaulted* the building from all sides⟩. **Bombard** applies to attacking with bombs or shells ⟨*bombarded* the city nightly⟩. **Storm** implies attempting to break into a defended position ⟨a fortress that has never been successfully *stormed*⟩.

attainment see ACQUIREMENT

attempt, try, endeavor, essay, strive mean to make an effort to accomplish an end. **Attempt** stresses the initiation or beginning of an effort ⟨will *attempt* to photograph the rare bird⟩. **Try** stresses effort or experiment made in the hope of testing or proving something ⟨*tried* several times to find a solution⟩. **Endeavor** heightens the implications of exertion and difficulty ⟨*endeavored* to find survivors of the crash⟩. **Essay** implies difficulty but also suggests tentative trying or experimenting ⟨had *essayed* dramatic roles on two earlier occasions⟩. **Strive** implies great exertion against great difficulty and specif. suggests persistent effort ⟨continues to *strive* for a lasting peaceful solution⟩.

attend see ACCOMPANY

attest see CERTIFY

attract, allure, charm, captivate, fascinate, enchant mean to draw another by exerting a powerful influence. **Attract** applies to any degree or kind of ability to exert influence over another ⟨a university that *attracts* students from around the world⟩. **Allure** implies an enticing by what is fair, pleasing, or seductive ⟨the excitement of the big city *allures* young people⟩. **Charm** implies the power of casting a spell over the person or thing affected and so compelling a response ⟨*charmed* by the beauty of that serene isle⟩, but it may, like **captivate**, suggest no more than evoking delight or admiration ⟨her grace and beauty *captivated* us all⟩. **Fascinate** suggests a magical influence and tends to stress the ineffectiveness of attempts to resist ⟨a story that continues to *fascinate* children⟩. **Enchant** is perhaps the strongest of these terms in stressing the appeal of the agent and the degree of delight evoked in the subject ⟨hopelessly *enchanted* by his dashing looks and deep voice⟩.

attraction, affinity, sympathy mean the relationship existing between things or persons that are naturally or involuntarily drawn together. **Attraction** implies the possession by one thing of a quality that pulls another to it ⟨a curious *attraction* between people of opposite temperaments⟩. **Affinity** implies a susceptibility or predisposition on the part of the one drawn ⟨a student with an *affinity* for mathematics⟩. **Sympathy** implies a reciprocal or natural relation between two things that are both susceptible to the same influence ⟨there is close *sympathy* between the heart and the lungs⟩.

attribute *vb* see ASCRIBE

attribute *n* see QUALITY

atypical see ABNORMAL

audacity see TEMERITY

augment see INCREASE

aura see ATMOSPHERE

auspicious see FAVORABLE

austere see SEVERE

authentic, genuine, veritable, bona fide mean being actually and exactly what is claimed. **Authentic** implies being fully trustworthy as according with fact or actuality ⟨the *authentic* story⟩. **Genuine** implies accordance with an original or a type without counterfeiting, admixture, or adulteration ⟨*genuine* maple syrup⟩ or it may stress sincerity

⟨*genuine* piety⟩. **Veritable** may stress true existence or actual identity ⟨*veritable* offspring⟩ but more commonly merely asserts the suitability of a metaphor ⟨*veritable* hail of questions⟩. **Bona fide** can apply when sincerity of intention is in question ⟨*bona fide* sale of securities⟩.

authenticate see CONFIRM

authority see INFLUENCE, POWER

autocratic see ABSOLUTE

automatic see SPONTANEOUS

autonomous see FREE

avaricious see COVETOUS

average, mean, median, norm mean something that represents a middle point. **Average** is exactly or approximately the quotient obtained by dividing the sum total of a set of figures by the number of figures ⟨scored an *average* of 85 in a series of five tests⟩. **Mean** may be the simple average or it may represent value midway between two extremes ⟨a high of 70° and a low of 50° give a *mean* of 60°⟩. **Median** applies to the value that represents the point at which there are as many instances above as there are below ⟨*average* of a group of persons earning 3, 4, 5, 8, and 10 dollars a day is 6 dollars, whereas the *median* is 5 dollars⟩. **Norm** means the computed or estimated average of performance of a significantly large group, class, or grade ⟨scores about the *norm* for 5th grade arithmetic⟩

averse see DISINCLINED

avert see PREVENT

avid see EAGER

avoid see ESCAPE

avow see ACKNOWLEDGE, ASSERT

awake see AWARE

award see GRANT

aware, cognizant, conscious, sensible, alive, awake mean having knowledge of something. **Aware** implies vigilance in observing or alertness in drawing inferences from what one experiences ⟨*aware* of a greater number of police officers out and about⟩. **Cognizant** implies having special or certain knowledge as from firsthand sources ⟨as yet, not fully *cognizant* of all the facts⟩. **Conscious** implies that one is focusing one's attention on something or is even preoccupied by it ⟨*conscious* that my heart was pounding away⟩. **Sensible** implies direct or intuitive perceiving esp. of intangibles or of emotional states or qualities ⟨a doctor who was *sensible* of the woman's deep depression⟩. **Alive** adds to *sensible* the implication of acute sensitivity to something ⟨we were fully *alive* to the momentousness of the occasion⟩. **Awake** implies that one has become alive to something and is on the alert ⟨a country not *awake* to the dangers of persistent inflation⟩.

awkward, clumsy, maladroit, inept, gauche mean not marked by ease (as of performance or movement). **Awkward** is widely applicable and may suggest unhandiness, inconvenience, lack of muscular control, embarrassment, or lack of tact ⟨a dinner party marked by periods of *awkward* silence⟩. **Clumsy** implies stiffness and heaviness and so may connote inflexibility, unwieldiness, or lack of ordinary skill ⟨a writer with a persistently *clumsy* style⟩. **Maladroit**\ suggests a tendency to create awkward situations ⟨a *maladroit* handling of a delicate situation⟩. **Inept** often implies complete failure or inadequacy ⟨blamed the conviction on his *inept* defense attorney⟩. **Gauche** implies the effects of shyness, inexperience, or ill breeding ⟨always felt *gauche* and unsophisticated at formal parties⟩.

B

baby see INDULGE

back see RECEDE, SUPPORT

background, setting, environment, milieu, mise-en-scène
mean the place, time, and circumstances in which something occurs. **Background** often refers to the circumstances
or events that precede a phenomenon or development ⟨a
background that prepared her well for the task⟩. **Setting**
suggests looking at real-life situations as though they were
dramatic or literary representations ⟨a social reformer who
was born into the most unlikely social *setting*⟩. **Environment** applies to all the external factors that have a formative influence on one's physical, mental, or moral development ⟨the kind of *environment* that produces junvenile
delinquents⟩. **Milieu** applies esp. to the physical and social
surroundings of a person or group of persons ⟨an intellectual *milieu* conducive to bold experimentation in the arts⟩.
Mise-en-scène strongly suggests the use of properties to
achieve a particular atmosphere or theatrical effect ⟨a tale
of the occult having a carefully crafted *mise-en-scène*⟩.

bad, evil, ill, wicked, naughty mean not morally good. **Bad**
may apply to any degree of reprehensibility ⟨the *bad* guys
in a Western⟩. **Evil** is a stronger term than *bad* and usu.
carries a baleful or sinister connotation ⟨*evil* men who
would even commit murder⟩. **Ill** is a less emphatic synonym of *evil* and may imply malevolence or vice ⟨paid
dearly for his *ill* deeds⟩. **Wicked** usu. connotes malice and
malevolence ⟨a *wicked* woman who delighted in the suffering of others⟩. **Naughty** applies either to trivial mis-

deeds or to matters impolite or amusingly risqué ⟨looked
up all the *naughty* words in the dictionary⟩.

badger see BAIT

baffle see FRUSTRATE

bag see CATCH

bait, badger, heckle, hector, chivy, hound mean to harass by
efforts to break down. **Bait** implies wanton cruelty or delight in persecuting a helpless victim ⟨teenagers *baited* the
chained dog⟩. **Badger** implies pestering so as to drive a
person to confusion or frenzy ⟨*badgered* her father for a
raise in her allowance⟩. **Heckle** implies persistent interrup-
tive questioning of a speaker in order to confuse or discomfit him ⟨drunks *heckled* the stand-up comic⟩. **Hector**
carries an implication of bullying and domineering that
breaks the spirit ⟨as a child he had been *hectored* by his
father⟩. **Chivy** suggests persecution by teasing or nagging
⟨*chivied* her husband to the breaking point⟩. **Hound** implies unrelenting pursuit and harassing ⟨*hounded* on all
sides by creditors⟩.

balance see COMPENSATE

bald see BARE

baleful see SINISTER

balk see FRUSTRATE

balky see CONTRARY

banal see INSIPID

baneful see PERNICIOUS

banish, exile, deport, transport mean to remove by authority from a state or country. **Banish** implies compulsory removal from a country not necessarily one's own ⟨a country that once *banished* the Jesuits⟩. **Exile** may imply
compulsory removal or an enforced or voluntary absence
from one's own country ⟨a writer who *exiled* himself from
South Africa⟩. **Deport** implies sending out of the country

an alien who has illegally entered or whose presence is judged inimical to the public welfare ⟨illegal aliens will be *deported*⟩. **Transport** implies sending a convicted criminal to an overseas penal colony ⟨a convict who was *transported* to Australia⟩.

bankrupt see DEPLETE

barbarous see FIERCE

bare, naked, nude, bald, barren mean deprived of naturally or conventionally appropriate covering. **Bare** implies the removal of what is additional, superfluous, ornamental, or dispensable ⟨a bleak apartment with *bare* walls⟩. **Naked** suggests absence of protective or ornamental covering but may imply a state of nature, of destitution, of defenselessness, of simple beauty ⟨poor, half-*naked* children shivering in the cold⟩. **Nude** applies esp. to the unclothed human figure ⟨a *nude* model posing for art students⟩. **Bald** implies actual or seeming absence of natural covering and may suggest a conspicuous bareness ⟨a *bald* mountain peak⟩. **Barren** often suggests aridity or impoverishment or sterility ⟨*barren* plains with few shrubs and no trees⟩.

barren see BARE

base, low, vile mean deserving of contempt because of the absence of higher values. **Base** stresses the ignoble and may suggest cruelty, treachery, greed, or grossness ⟨real estate developers with *base* motives⟩. **Low** may connote crafty cunning, vulgarity, or immorality and regularly implies an outraging of one's sense of decency or propriety ⟨refused to listen to such *low* talk⟩. **Vile**, the strongest of these words, tends to suggest disgusting depravity or filth ⟨a *vile* remark⟩ ⟨matricide, the *vilest* of crimes⟩.

bashful see SHY

batter see MAIM

bear, suffer, endure, abide, tolerate, stand mean to put up with something trying or painful. **Bear** usu. implies the power to sustain without flinching or breaking ⟨forced to *bear* one personal tragedy after another⟩. **Suffer** often suggests acceptance or passivity rather than courage or patience in bearing ⟨never *suffered* a single insult to go unchallenged⟩. **Endure** implies continuing firm or resolute through trials and difficulties ⟨*endured* years of rejection and neglect⟩. **Abide** suggests acceptance without resistance or protest ⟨I cannot *abide* her chronic rudeness⟩. **Tolerate** suggests overcoming or successfully controlling an impulse to resist, avoid, or resent something injurious or distasteful ⟨*tolerated* his affairs for the sake of the children⟩. **Stand** emphasizes even more strongly the ability to bear without discomposure or flinching ⟨she cannot *stand* teasing⟩. See in addition CARRY.

bearing, deportment, demeanor, mien, manner, carriage mean the outward manifestation of personality or attitude. **Bearing** is the most general of these words but now usu. implies characteristic posture ⟨a woman of regal *bearing*⟩. **Deportment** suggests actions or behavior as formed by breeding or training ⟨a child with atrocious *deportment*⟩. **Demeanor** suggests one's attitude toward others as expressed in outward behavior ⟨the haughty *demeanor* of a head waiter⟩. **Mien** is a literary term referring both to bearing and demeanor ⟨a *mien* of supreme self-satisfaction⟩. **Manner** implies characteristic or customary way of moving and gesturing and addressing others ⟨the imperious *manner* of a man used to giving orders⟩. **Carriage** applies chiefly to habitual posture in standing or walking ⟨the kind of *carriage* learned at elite private schools⟩.

beautiful, lovely, handsome, pretty, comely, fair mean exciting sensuous or aesthetic pleasure. **Beautiful** applies to whatever excites the keenest of pleasure to the senses and stirs emotion through the senses ⟨*beautiful* mountain scenery⟩. **Lovely** is close to *beautiful* but applies to a narrower range of emotional excitation in suggesting the graceful, delicate, or exquisite ⟨a *lovely* melody⟩. **Handsome** suggests aesthetic pleasure due to proportion, symmetry, or elegance ⟨a *handsome* Georgian mansion⟩. **Pretty** applies to superficial or insubstantial attractiveness ⟨a painter of conventionally *pretty* scenes⟩. **Comely** is like *handsome* in suggesting what is coolly approved rather than emotionally responded to ⟨the *comely* grace of a dancer⟩. **Fair** suggests beauty because of purity, flawlessness, or freshness ⟨looking for fashion models with *fair* faces⟩.

beautify see ADORN

beg, entreat, beseech, implore, supplicate, adjure, importune mean to ask urgently. **Beg** suggests earnestness or insistence esp. in asking for a favor ⟨children *begging* to stay up later⟩. **Entreat** implies an effort to persuade or to overcome resistance ⟨*entreated* him to change his mind⟩. **Beseech** implies great eagerness or anxiety ⟨I *beseech* you to have mercy⟩. **Implore** adds to *beseech* a suggestion of greater urgency or anguished appeal ⟨*implored* her not to leave him⟩. **Supplicate** suggests a posture of humility ⟨with bowed heads they *supplicated* their Lord⟩. **Adjure** implies advising as well as pleading and suggests the involving of something sacred ⟨in God's name I *adjure* you to cease⟩. **Importune** suggests an annoying persistence in trying to break down resistance to a request ⟨*importuned* Mother nearly every day to buy him a new bike⟩.

begin, commence, start, initiate, inaugurate mean to take the first step in a course, process, or operation. **Begin** and **commence** are practically identical in meaning but the latter suggests greater formality ⟨*began* taking dancing lessons⟩ ⟨let the games *commence*⟩. **Start,** opposed to *stop,* suggests a getting or setting into motion or setting out on a journey ⟨the procession *started* out slowly⟩. **Initiate** implies the taking of a first step of a process or series that is to continue ⟨*initiated* the custom of annual gift giving⟩. **Inaugurate** implies a ceremonious beginning ⟨the discovery of penicillin *inaugurated* a new medical age⟩.

beguile see DECEIVE

behave, conduct, deport, comport, acquit mean to act or to cause oneself to do something in a certain way. **Behave** may apply to the meeting of a standard of what is proper or decorous ⟨*behaved* very badly throughout the affair⟩. **Conduct** implies action or behavior that shows the extent of one's power to control or direct oneself ⟨*conducted* herself with unfailing good humor⟩. **Deport** implies behaving so as to show how far one conforms to conventional rules of discipline or propriety ⟨an ingenue who *deports* herself in the best musical tradition⟩. **Comport** suggests conduct measured by what is expected or required of one in a certain class or position ⟨*comported* themselves as the gentlemen they were⟩. **Acquit** applies to action under stress that deserves praise or meets expectations ⟨*acquitted* himself well in his first battle⟩.

belief, faith, credence, credit mean to assent to the truth of something offered for acceptance. **Belief** may or may not imply certitude in the believer ⟨my *belief* that I had caught all the errors⟩. **Faith** always does even where there is no evidence or proof ⟨an unshakable *faith* in God⟩. **Credence** suggests intellectual assent without implying anything about grounds for assent ⟨a theory given little *credence* by scientists⟩. **Credit** implies assent on grounds other than direct proof ⟨give no *credit* to idle rumors⟩. See in addition OPINION.

belittle see DECRY

bellicose see BELLIGERENT

belligerent, bellicose, pugnacious, quarrelsome, contentious
mean having an aggressive or fighting attitude. **Belligerent**
implies being actually at war or engaged in hostilities ⟨*belligerent* nations respected the country's neutrality⟩. **Bellicose** suggests a disposition to fight ⟨an intoxicated man in
a *bellicose* mood⟩. **Pugnacious** suggests a disposition that
takes pleasure in personal combat ⟨a *pugnacious* student
always getting into scraps⟩. **Quarrelsome** stresses an ill-natured readiness to fight without good cause ⟨the stifling
heat made us all *quarrelsome*⟩. **Contentious** implies perverse and irritating fondness for arguing and quarreling
⟨wearied by her *contentious* disposition⟩.

bemoan see DEPLORE

bend see CURVE

beneficial, advantageous, profitable mean bringing good or
gain. **Beneficial** implies esp. promoting health or well-
being ⟨legislation that would be *beneficial* to the elderly⟩.
Advantageous stresses a choice or preference that brings
superiority or greater success in attaining an end ⟨a famous surname proved to be *advantageous* in business⟩.
Profitable implies the yielding of useful or lucrative returns ⟨study of the explanatory notes might be *profitable*⟩.

benign see KIND

benignant see KIND

bent see GIFT

berate see SCOLD

beseech see BEG

bestial see BRUTAL

bestow see GIVE

bête noire see ABOMINATION

betray see REVEAL

better see IMPROVE

bewail see DEPLORE

bewilder see PUZZLE

bias *vb* see INCLINE

bias *n* see PREDILECTION

bid see COMMAND

billingsgate see ABUSE

biting see INCISIVE

bizarre see FANTASTIC

blamable see BLAMEWORTHY

blame see CRITICIZE

blameworthy, blamable, guilty, culpable mean deserving reproach or punishment. **Blameworthy** and **blamable** apply to any degree of reprehensibility ⟨conduct adjudged *blameworthy* by a military court⟩ ⟨an accident for which no one is *blamable*⟩. **Guilty** implies responsibility for or consciousness of crime, sin, or, at the least, grave error or misdoing ⟨the defendant was found *guilty*⟩. **Culpable** is weaker than *guilty* and is likely to connote malfeasance or errors of ignorance, omission, or negligence ⟨a clear case of *culpable* neglect on the part of the landlord⟩.

bland see SUAVE

blandish see COAX

blank see EMPTY

blasé see SOPHISTICATED

blatant see VOCIFEROUS

bleak see DISMAL

blemish, defect, flaw mean an imperfection that mars or damages. **Blemish** suggests something that affects only the surface or appearance ⟨fair skin completely devoid of *blemishes*⟩. **Defect** implies a lack, often hidden, of something that is essential to completeness or perfect functioning ⟨the smoke detector failed because of a mechanical *defect*⟩. **Flaw** suggests a small defect in continuity or cohesion that is likely to cause failure under stress ⟨a *flaw* in a pane of glass⟩.

blench see RECOIL

blend see MIX

blithe see MERRY

block see HINDER

bloody, sanguinary, sanguine, gory mean affected by or involving the shedding of blood. **Bloody** is applied esp. to things that are actually covered with blood or are made up of blood ⟨*bloody* hands⟩. **Sanguinary** applies esp. to something attended by, or someone inclined to, bloodshed ⟨the Civil War was America's most *sanguinary* conflict⟩. **Sanguine** is applied specif. to bleeding, bloodthirstiness, or the color of blood ⟨one of the most *sanguine* of the Jacobean revenge tragedies⟩. **Gory** suggests a profusion of blood and slaughter ⟨exceptionally *gory,* even for a teenage horror movie⟩.

blot out see ERASE

bluff, blunt, brusque, curt, crusty, gruff mean abrupt and unceremonious in speech and manner. **Bluff** connotes good-natured outspokenness and unconventionality ⟨a bartender with a *bluff* manner⟩. **Blunt** suggests directness of expression in disregard of others' feelings ⟨a *blunt* appraisal of the performance⟩. **Brusque** applies to a sharpness or ungraciousness ⟨a *brusque* response to a civil question⟩. **Curt** implies disconcerting shortness or rude conciseness ⟨a *curt* comment about the cause of the foul-up⟩. **Crusty** suggests a harsh or surly manner sometimes concealing an inner kindliness ⟨a *crusty* exterior that conceals a heart of gold⟩. **Gruff** suggests a hoarse or husky speech which may imply bad temper but more often implies embarrassment or shyness ⟨puts on a *gruff* pose in front of strangers⟩.

blunder see ERROR

blunt see BLUFF, DULL

boast, brag, vaunt, crow mean to express pride in oneself or one's accomplishments. **Boast** often suggests ostentation and exaggeration ⟨ready to *boast* of every trivial success⟩, but it may imply acclaiming with proper and justifiable pride ⟨the town *boasts* one of the best hospitals in the area⟩. **Brag** suggests crudity and artlessness in glorifying oneself ⟨boys *bragging* to each other⟩. **Vaunt** usu. connotes more pomp and bombast than *boast* and less crudity or naïveté than *brag* ⟨used the occasion to *vaunt* the country's military might⟩. **Crow** usu. implies exultant boasting or bragging ⟨loved to *crow* about his ancestors⟩.

bodily, physical, corporeal, corporal, somatic mean of or relating to the human body. **Bodily** suggests contrasts with *mental* or *spiritual* ⟨an intellectual who also had *bodily* needs⟩. **Physical** suggests more vaguely or less explicitly an organic structure ⟨their ordeal left them at the point of *physical* exhaustion⟩. **Corporeal** suggests the substance of which the body is composed ⟨a divinity who assumed *corporeal* existence⟩. **Corporal** applies chiefly to things that affect or involve the body ⟨a teacher who still used *corporal* punishment⟩. **Somatic** implies contrast with *physical* and is useful as being free of theological and poetic connotations ⟨*somatic* reactions to the drug⟩.

boisterous see VOCIFEROUS

bombard see ATTACK

bona fide see AUTHENTIC

bon vivant see EPICURE

boorish, churlish, loutish, clownish mean uncouth in manners or appearance. **Boorish** implies rudeness of manner due to insensitiveness to others' feelings and unwillingness to be agreeable ⟨your *boorish* behavior at the wedding reception⟩. **Churlish** suggests surliness, unresponsiveness, and ungraciousness ⟨*churlish* remarks made during a television interview⟩. **Loutish** implies bodily awkwardness together with stupidity ⟨her *loutish* boyfriend spoiled the cocktail party⟩. **Clownish** suggests ill-bred awkwardness, ignorance or stupidity, ungainliness, and often a propensity for absurd antics ⟨*clownish* conduct that was out of keeping with the solemn occasion⟩.

boost see LIFT

booty see SPOIL

border, margin, verge, edge, rim, brim, brink mean a line or outer part that marks the limit of something. **Border** denotes the part of a surface that marks its boundary line ⟨the magazine cover's red *border*⟩. **Margin** denotes a border of definite width or distinguishing character ⟨a *margin* of one inch on the page's left side⟩. **Verge** applies to the line marking an extreme limit or termination of something ⟨an empire that extended to the *verge* of the known world⟩. **Edge** denotes the termination line made by two converging surfaces as of a blade or a box ⟨the *edge* of a table⟩. **Rim** applies to an edge of something circular or curving ⟨the *rim* of a wagon wheel⟩. **Brim** applies to the upper inner rim of something hollow ⟨fill the cup to the *brim*⟩. **Brink** denotes the abrupt edge of something that falls away steeply ⟨walked to the *brink* of the cliff⟩.

bother see ANNOY

bountiful see LIBERAL

brag see BOAST

brandish see SWING

breach, infraction, violation, trespass, infringement mean the breaking of a law, duty, or obligation. **Breach** implies failure to keep a promise ⟨sued for *breech* of contract⟩. **Infraction** usu. implies the breaking of a law or promise ⟨an *infraction* of the school rules). **Violation** implies the flagrant disregard of the law or the rights of others and often suggests the exercise of force or violence (the police interference was a *violation* of the right to free assembly). **Trespass** implies an encroachment upon the rights, the comfort, or the property of others (a would-be burglar who was arrested for *trespass*). **Infringement** implies an encroachment upon a legally protected right or privilege (any unauthorized reproduction constitutes an *infringement* of the book's copyright).

break down see ANALYZE

bridle see RESTRAIN

brief, short mean lacking length. **Brief** applies primarily to duration and may imply condensation, conciseness, or occas. intensity (a *brief* speech). **Short** may imply sudden stoppage or incompleteness (the interview was rather *short*).

bright, brilliant, radiant, luminous, lustrous mean shining or glowing with light. **Bright** implies emitting or reflecting a high degree of light (one of the *brightest* stars in the sky). **Brilliant** implies intense often sparkling brightness (*brilliant* diamonds). **Radiant** stresses the emission or seeming emission of rays of light (an imposing figure in *radiant* armor). **Luminous** implies emission of steady, suffused, glowing light by reflection or in surrounding darkness (*luminous* white houses dot the shore). **Lustrous** stresses an even, rich light from a surface that reflects brightly without sparkling or glittering (the *lustrous* sheen of fine satin).

brilliant see BRIGHT

brim see BORDER

brink see BORDER

brisk see AGILE

brittle see FRAGILE

broach see EXPRESS

broad, wide, deep mean having horizontal extent. **Broad** and wide apply to a surface measured or viewed from side to side ⟨a *broad* avenue⟩. **Wide** is more common when units of measurement are mentioned ⟨rugs eight feet *wide*⟩ or applied to unfilled space between limits ⟨*wide* doorway⟩. **Broad** is preferred when full horizontal extent is considered ⟨*broad* shoulders⟩. **Deep** may indicate horizontal extent away from the observer or from a front or peripheral point ⟨a *deep* cupboard⟩ ⟨*deep* woods⟩.

browbeat see INTIMIDATE

brusque see BLUFF

brutal, brutish, bestial, feral mean characteristic of an animal in nature, action, or instinct. **Brutal** applies to people, their acts, or their words and suggests a lack of intelligence, feeling, or humanity ⟨a senseless and *brutal* war⟩. **Brutish** stresses likeness to an animal in low intelligence, in base appetites, and in behavior based on instinct ⟨*brutish* developers were ready to tear down the historic mansion⟩. **Bestial** suggests a depravity or state of degradation unworthy of man and fit only for beasts ⟨decadent Rome carried sexual indulgence to a *bestial* level⟩. **Feral** suggests the savagery or ferocity of wild animals ⟨war had unleashed his *feral* impulses⟩.

brutish see BRUTAL

bucolic see RURAL

bugbear see ABOMINATION

bulge see PROJECTION

bulk, mass, volume mean the aggregate that forms a body or unit. **Bulk** implies an aggregate that is impressively large, heavy, or numerous ⟨the darkened *bulks* of skyscrapers towered over him⟩. **Mass** suggests an aggregate made by piling together things of the same kind ⟨the cave held a *mass* of weapons). **Volume** applies to an aggregate without shape or outline and capable of flowing or fluctuating ⟨a tremendous *volume* of water⟩.

bulldoze see INTIMIDATE

bully see INTIMIDATE

burdensome see ONEROUS

burlesque see CARICATURE

bury see HIDE

business, commerce, trade, industry, traffic mean activity concerned with the supplying and distribution of commodities. **Business** may be an inclusive term but specif. designates the activities of those engaged in the purchase or sale of commodities or in related financial transactions ⟨the *business* section of the newspaper⟩. **Commerce** and **trade** imply the exchange and transportation of commodities ⟨full power to regulate interstate *commerce*⟩ ⟨seek ways to increase foreign *trade*⟩. **Industry** applies to the producing of commodities, esp. by manufacturing or processing, usu. on a large scale ⟨*industry* has overtaken agriculture in the South⟩. **Traffic** applies to the operation and functioning of public carriers of goods and persons ⟨*traffic* managers have rediscovered the railroads⟩. See in addition WORK.

busy, industrious, diligent, assiduous, sedulous mean actively engaged or occupied. **Busy** chiefly stresses activity as opposed to idleness or leisure ⟨too *busy* to spend time with the children⟩. **Industrious** implies characteristic or habitual devotion to work ⟨they are by nature an *industrious* people⟩. **Diligent** suggests earnest application to some specific object or pursuit ⟨very *diligent* in her pursuit of a degree⟩. **Assiduous** stresses careful and unremitting application ⟨mastered the piano only after *assiduous* practice⟩.

Sedulous implies painstaking and persevering application ⟨a *sedulous* reconstruction of the events of that night⟩.

butt in see INTRUDE

C

cabal see PLOT

cajole see COAX

calamity see DISASTER

calculate, compute, estimate, reckon mean to determine something mathematically. **Calculate** is usu. preferred in reference to highly intricate processes and problematical rather than exact or definite results ⟨*calculated* when the comet would next appear⟩. **Compute** is the simpler term for reaching an exact result by simpler arithmetic processes ⟨*computed* the interest at a quarterly rate⟩. **Estimate** applies chiefly to the forecasting of costs or trends and suggests a seeking of usable but tentative and approximate results ⟨the mechanic *estimated* the cost of repairs⟩. **Reckon** usu. suggests the simpler arithmetical processes or rough-and-ready methods ⟨*reckoned* the number of yards of fabric needed⟩.

call see SUMMON

calling see WORK

calm, tranquil, serene, placid, peaceful mean quiet and free from disturbance. **Calm** often implies a contrast with a foregoing or nearby state of agitation or violence ⟨the protests ended, and the streets were *calm* again⟩. **Tranquil** suggests a very deep quietude or composure ⟨the *tranquil* beauty of a formal garden⟩. **Serene** stresses an unclouded and lofty tranquility ⟨a woman of *serene* beauty⟩. **Placid** suggests an undisturbed appearance and often implies a

degree of complacency ⟨led a very *placid* existence⟩.
Peaceful implies a state of repose in contrast with or following strife or turmoil ⟨a former firebrand grown *peaceful* in his old age⟩.

calumniate see MALIGN

cancel see ERASE

candid see FRANK

canon see LAW

cant see DIALECT

capable see ABLE

capacious see SPACIOUS

capitulate see YIELD

caprice, whim, vagary, crotchet mean an irrational or unpredictable idea or desire. **Caprice** stresses lack of apparent motivation and suggests willfulness ⟨by sheer *caprice* she quit her job⟩. **Whim** implies a fantastic, capricious turn of mind or inclination ⟨an odd antique that was bought on a *whim*⟩. **Vagary** stresses the erratic, irresponsible character of the notion or desire ⟨recently he had been prone to strange *vagaries*⟩. **Crotchet** implies an eccentric opinion or preference ⟨a serious scientist equally known for his bizarre *crotchets*⟩.

capricious see INCONSTANT

captious see CRITICAL

captivate see ATTRACT

capture see CATCH

cardinal see ESSENTIAL

care, concern, solicitude, anxiety, worry mean a troubled or engrossed state of mind or the thing that causes this. **Care** implies oppression of the mind weighed down by responsibility or disquieted by apprehension ⟨a face worn by a host of *cares*⟩. **Concern** implies a troubled state of mind because of personal interest, relation, or affection ⟨your happiness is my only *concern*⟩. **Solicitude** implies great concern and connotes either thoughtful or hovering attentiveness toward another ⟨behaved with typical maternal *solicitude*⟩. **Anxiety** stresses anguished uncertainty or fear of misfortune or failure ⟨plagued by *anxiety* and self-doubt⟩. **Worry** suggests fretting over matters that may or may not be real cause for anxiety ⟨a businessman's endless list of *worries*⟩.

careful, meticulous, scrupulous, punctilious mean showing close attention to detail. **Careful** implies attentiveness and cautiousness in avoiding mistakes ⟨a *careful* worker⟩. **Meticulous** may imply either commendable extreme carefulness or a hampering finicky caution over small points ⟨*meticulous* scholarship⟩. **Scrupulous** applies to what is proper or fitting or ethical ⟨*scrupulous* honesty⟩. **Punctilious** implies minute, even excessive attention to fine points ⟨*punctilious* observance of ritual⟩.

caricature, burlesque, parody, travesty mean a comic or grotesque imitation. **Caricature** implies ludicrous exaggeration of the characteristic features of a subject ⟨the movie is a *caricature* of the novel⟩. **Burlesque** implies mockery either through treating a trivial subject in a mock-heroic style or through giving a serious or lofty subject a frivolous treatment ⟨a *burlesque* that treats a petty quarrel as a great battle⟩. **Parody** applies esp. to treatment of a trivial or ludicrous subject in the exactly imitated style of a well-known author or work ⟨a witty *parody* of a popular soap opera⟩. **Travesty** implies that the subject remains unchanged but that the style is extravagant or absurd ⟨this production is a *travesty* of a classic opera⟩.

carnal, fleshly, sensual, animal mean having a relation to the body. **Carnal** may mean only this but more often connotes derogatorily an action or manifestation of man's

lower nature ⟨a woman who was victimized by her own
carnal appetites⟩. **Fleshly** is somewhat less derogatory
than *carnal* ⟨a saint who wrote at length on his *fleshly*
temptations⟩. **Sensual** may apply to any gratification of a
bodily desire or pleasure but commonly implies sexual appetite with absence of the spiritual or intellectual ⟨a place
infamous for providing *sensual* delight⟩. **Animal** stresses a
relation to man's physical as distinguished from his rational nature ⟨led a mindless, *animal* existence⟩.

carping see CRITICAL

carriage see BEARING

carry, bear, convey, transport mean to move something
from one place to another. **Carry** tends to emphasize the
means by which something is moved or the fact of supporting off the ground while moving ⟨*carried* the basket on
her head⟩. **Bear** stresses the effort of sustaining or the importance of what is carried ⟨*bear* the banner aloft⟩. **Convey**
suggests the continuous movement of something in the
mass ⟨the pipeline *conveys* oil for more than a thousand
miles⟩. **Transport** implies the moving of something to its
destination ⟨trucks *transporting* farm produce to market⟩.

case see INSTANCE

cast see DISCARD, THROW

castigate see PUNISH

casual see ACCIDENTAL, RANDOM

cataclysm see DISASTER

catastrophe see DISASTER

catch, capture, trap, snare, entrap, ensnare, bag mean to
come to possess or control by or as if by seizing. **Catch**
implies the seizing of something in motion or in flight or
in hiding ⟨*caught* the dog as it ran by⟩. **Capture** suggests
taking by overcoming resistance or difficulty ⟨*capture* a
stronghold of the enemy⟩. **Trap, snare, entrap, ensnare**

imply seizing by some device that holds the one caught at the mercy of his captor. *Trap* and *snare* apply more commonly to physical seizing ⟨*trap* animals⟩ ⟨*snared* butterflies with a net⟩. *Entrap* and *ensnare* more often are figurative ⟨*entrapped* the witness with a trick question⟩ ⟨a sting operation that *ensnared* burglars⟩. **Bag** implies shooting down a fleeing or distant prey ⟨*bagged* a brace of pheasants⟩.

cause, determinant, antecedent, reason, occasion mean something that produces an effect. **Cause** applies to any event, circumstance, or condition that brings about or helps bring about a result ⟨an icy road was the *cause* of the accident⟩. **Determinant** applies to a cause that fixes the nature of what results ⟨heredity may be a *determinant* of heart disease⟩. **Antecedent** applies to that which has preceded and may therefore be in some degree responsible for what follows ⟨the *antecedents* of the famine⟩. **Reason** applies to a traceable or explainable cause of a known effect ⟨the *reason* I was late was that my car would not start⟩. **Occasion** applies to a particular time or situation at which underlying causes become effective ⟨the assassination was the *occasion* of the war⟩.

caustic, mordant, acrid, scathing mean stingingly incisive. **Caustic** suggests a biting wit ⟨*caustic* comments about her singing ability⟩. **Mordant** suggests a wit that is used with deadly effectiveness ⟨*mordant* reviews put the play out of its misery⟩. **Acrid** implies bitterness and often malevolence ⟨a speech marked by *acrid* invective⟩. **Scathing** implies indignant attacks delivered with fierce severity ⟨a *scathing* satire of corporate life⟩.

cautious, circumspect, wary, chary mean prudently watchful and discreet in the face of danger or risk. **Cautious** implies the exercise of forethought usu. prompted by fear of danger

⟨a *cautious* driver⟩. **Circumspect** suggests less fear and stresses the surveying of all possible consequences before acting or deciding ⟨the panel must be *circumspect* in assigning blame⟩. **Wary** emphasizes suspiciousness and alertness in watching for danger and cunning in escaping it ⟨be *wary* of those claiming to have all the answers⟩. **Chary** implies a cautious reluctance to give, act, or speak freely ⟨I am *chary* of signing papers I have not read⟩.

cease see STOP

celebrate see KEEP

celebrated see FAMOUS

celerity, alacrity mean quickness in movement or action. **Celerity** implies speed in accomplishing work ⟨got dinner ready with remarkable *celerity*⟩. **Alacrity** stresses promptness in response to suggestion or command ⟨the students volunteered with surprising *alacrity*⟩.

censorious see CRITICAL

censure see CRITICIZE

ceremonial, ceremonious, formal, conventional mean marked by attention to or adhering strictly to prescribed forms. **Ceremonial** and **ceremonious** both imply strict attention to what is prescribed by custom or by ritual, but *ceremonial* applies to things that are associated with ceremonies ⟨a *ceremonial* offering⟩, *ceremonious* to persons given to ceremony or to acts attended by ceremony ⟨a *ceremonious* old man⟩. **Formal** applies both to things prescribed by and to persons obedient to custom and may suggest stiff, restrained, or old-fashioned behavior ⟨a *formal* report on the summit meeting⟩ ⟨a *formal* manner⟩. **Conventional** implies accord with general custom and usage and may suggest a stodgy lack of originality or independence ⟨*conventional* courtesy⟩ ⟨*conventional* standards of beauty⟩.

ceremonious see CEREMONIAL

certain see SURE

certainty, certitude, assurance, conviction mean a state of being free from doubt. **Certainty** and **certitude** are very close; *certainty* may stress the existence of objective proof ⟨claims that cannot be confirmed with any scientific *certainty*⟩, while **certitude** may emphasize a faith in something not needing or not capable of proof ⟨believes with all *certitude* in an afterlife⟩. **Assurance** implies confidence rather than intellectual certainty ⟨as much *assurance* as is ever possible where hurricanes are concerned⟩. **Conviction** applies esp. to belief strongly held by an individual ⟨holds firm *convictions* about everything⟩.

certify, attest, witness, vouch mean to testify to the truth or genuineness of something. **Certify** usu. applies to a written statement, esp. one carrying a signature or seal ⟨*certified* that the candidate had met all requirements⟩. **Attest** applies to oral or written testimony usu. from experts or witnesses ⟨*attested* to the authenticity of the document⟩. **Witness** applies to the subscribing of one's own name to a document as evidence of its genuineness ⟨two persons who *witnessed* the signing of the will⟩. **Vouch** applies to one who testifies as a competent authority or a reliable person and who will defend his affirmation ⟨willing to *vouch* for the woman's integrity⟩. See in addition APPROVE.

certitude see CERTAINTY

champion see SUPPORT

change, alter, vary, modify mean to make or become different. **Change** implies making either an essential difference often amounting to a loss of original identity or a substitution of one thing for another ⟨*changed* the shirt for a larger size⟩. **Alter** implies a difference in some particular respect without suggesting loss of identity ⟨slightly *altered* the original design). **Vary** stresses a breaking away from sameness, duplication, or exact repetition ⟨you can *vary* the speed of the conveyor belt⟩. **Modify** suggests a difference that limits, restricts, or adapts to a new purpose ⟨*modified* the building for use by the handicapped⟩.

character see DISPOSITION, QUALITY, TYPE

characteristic, individual, peculiar, distinctive mean indicating a special quality or identity. **Characteristic** applies to something that distinguishes or identifies a person or thing or class ⟨responded with his *characteristic* wit⟩. **Individual** stresses qualities that distinguish one from all other members of the same kind or class ⟨a highly *individual* writing style⟩. **Peculiar** applies to qualities possessed only by a particular individual or class or kind and stresses rarity or uniqueness ⟨an eccentricity that is *peculiar* to the British⟩. **Distinctive** indicates qualities distinguishing and uncommon and often superior or praiseworthy ⟨her *distinctive* aura of grace and elegance⟩.

charge see ACCUSE, COMMAND

charity see MERCY

charm see ATTRACT

charter see HIRE

chary see CAUTIOUS

chase, pursue, follow, trail mean to go after or on the track of something or someone. **Chase** implies going swiftly after and trying to overtake something fleeing or running ⟨a dog *chasing* a cat⟩. **Pursue** suggests a continuing effort to overtake, reach, attain ⟨*pursued* the criminal through the narrow streets⟩. **Follow** puts less emphasis upon speed or intent to overtake ⟨a stray dog *followed* me home⟩. **Trail** may stress a following of tracks or traces rather than a visible object ⟨*trail* deer through deep snow⟩.

chaste, pure, modest, decent mean free from all taint of what is lewd or salacious. **Chaste** primarily implies a refraining from acts or even thoughts or desires that are not virginal or not sanctioned by marriage vows ⟨maintained *chaste* relations until marriage⟩. **Pure** differs from *chaste* in implying innocence and absence of temptation rather than control of one's impulses and actions ⟨the *pure* of heart⟩. **Modest** and **decent** apply esp. to deportment and dress as outward signs of inward chastity or purity ⟨her dress was always *modest*⟩ ⟨*decent* people didn't go to such movies⟩.

chasten see PUNISH

chastise see PUNISH

cheat, cozen, defraud, swindle mean to get something by dishonesty or deception. **Cheat** suggests using trickery that escapes observation ⟨*cheated* in the written examination⟩. **Cozen** implies artful persuading or flattering to attain a thing or a purpose ⟨always able to *cozen* her doting grandfather out of a few dollars⟩. **Defraud** stresses depriving one of his rights and usu. connotes deliberate perversion of the truth ⟨her own lawyer *defrauded* her of her inheritance⟩. **Swindle** implies large-scale cheating by means of misrepresentation or abuse of confidence ⟨widows were *swindled* of their savings by con artists⟩.

check see RESTRAIN

cheek see TEMERITY

cheerless see DISMAL

cherish see APPRECIATE

chide see REPROVE

chimerical see IMAGINARY

chivalrous see CIVIL

chivy see BAIT

choice *n* Choice, option, alternative, preference, selection, election mean the act or opportunity of choosing or the thing chosen. **Choice** suggests the opportunity or privilege

of choosing freely ⟨total freedom of *choice* in the matter⟩.
Option implies a power to choose that is specif. granted or
guaranteed ⟨the *option* of paying now or later⟩. **Alternative**
implies a necessity to choose one and reject another possibility ⟨the *alternatives* were peace with dishonor or war⟩.
Preference suggests the guidance of choice by one's judgment or predilections ⟨stated a *preference* for red-haired
women⟩. **Selection** implies a wide range of choice ⟨a store
offering a varied *selection* of furniture⟩. **Election** implies
an end or purpose which requires exercise of judgment
⟨the careful *election* of college courses⟩.

choice *adj* Choice, exquisite, elegant, rare, dainty, delicate
mean having qualities that appeal to a cultivated taste.
Choice stresses preeminence in quality or kind ⟨a *choice*
bit of gossip⟩. **Exquisite** implies a perfection in workmanship or design that appeals only to very sensitive taste ⟨an
exquisite slender gold bracelet⟩. **Elegant** applies to what is
rich and luxurious but restrained by good taste ⟨the *elegant* dining room boasts genuine French antiques⟩. **Rare**
suggests an uncommon excellence ⟨refuses to drink any
but the *rarest* of wines⟩. **Delicate** implies exquisiteness,
subtlety, fragility ⟨the play's *delicate* charm was lost on
screen⟩. **Dainty** sometimes also suggests smallness and appeal to the eye or palate ⟨precious, *dainty* food that leaves
you hungry⟩.

choleric see IRASCIBLE

chore see TASK

chronic see INVETERATE

churlish see BOORISH

chutzpah see TEMERITY

circumscribe see LIMIT

circumspect see CAUTIOUS

circumstance see OCCURRENCE

circumstantial, minute, particular, detailed mean dealing with a matter fully and usu. point by point. **Circumstantial** implies fullness of detail that fixes something described in time and space ⟨a *circumstantial* account of our visit⟩. **Minute** implies close and searching attention to the smallest details ⟨a *minute* examination of a fossil⟩. **Particular** implies a precise attention to every detail ⟨a *particular* description of the scene of the crime⟩. **Detailed** stresses abundance or completeness of detail ⟨a *detailed* analysis of the event⟩.

circumvent see FRUSTRATE

citation see ENCOMIUM

cite see SUMMON

citizen, subject, national mean a person owing allegiance to and entitled to the protection of a sovereign state. **Citizen** is preferred for one owing allegiance to a state in which sovereign power is retained by the people and sharing in the political rights of those people ⟨the inalienable rights of a free *citizen*⟩. **Subject** implies allegiance to a personal sovereign such as a monarch ⟨the king enjoys the loyalty of his *subjects*⟩. **National** designates one who may claim the protection of a state and applies esp. to one living or traveling outside that state ⟨American *nationals* currently in Libya⟩.

civil, polite, courteous, gallant, chivalrous mean observant of the forms required by good breeding. **Civil** often suggests little more than the avoidance of overt rudeness ⟨a *civil* reply that showed a lack of real enthusiasm⟩. **Polite** commonly implies polish of speech and manners and sometimes suggests an absence of cordiality ⟨the minister's conversation was as *polite* as it was condescending⟩. **Courteous** implies more actively considerate or dignified politeness ⟨clerks who were unfailingly *courteous* to cus-

tomers⟩. **Gallant** and **chivalrous** imply courteous attentiveness esp. to women. *Gallant* suggests spirited and
dashing behavior and ornate expressions of courtesy ⟨a
gallant suitor of the old school⟩. *Chivalrous* suggests high-
minded and self-sacrificing behavior ⟨a *chivalrous* display
of duty⟩.

claim see DEMAND

clamorous see VOCIFEROUS

clandestine see SECRET

clear *adj* Clear, transparent, translucent, limpid mean capable of being seen through. **Clear** implies absence of
cloudiness, haziness, or muddiness ⟨*clear* water⟩. **Transparent** implies being so clear that objects can be seen distinctly ⟨a *transparent* sheet of film⟩. **Translucent** implies
the passage of light but not a clear view of what lies beyond
⟨*translucent* frosted glass⟩. **Limpid** suggests the soft clear-
ness of pure water ⟨pale *limpid* blue eyes⟩.

clear *adj* Clear, perspicuous, lucid mean quickly and easily
understood. **Clear** implies freedom from obscurity, ambiguity, or undue complexity ⟨the instructions were perfectly
clear⟩. **Perspicuous** applies to a style that is simple and elegant as well as clear ⟨the *perspicuous* beauty of Shakespeare's sonnets⟩. **Lucid** suggests a clear logical coherence
and evident order of arrangement ⟨an amazingly *lucid* description of nuclear physics⟩. See in addition EVIDENT.

clear-cut see INCISIVE

cleave see STICK, TEAR

clemency see MERCY

clever, adroit, cunning, ingenious mean having or showing
practical wit or skill in contriving. **Clever** stresses physical
or mental quickness, deftness, or great aptitude ⟨a person
clever with horses⟩. **Adroit** often implies a skillful use of
expedients to achieve one's purpose in spite of difficulties

⟨an *adroit* negotiator of business deals⟩. **Cunning** implies great skill in constructing or creating ⟨a writer who is *cunning* in his manipulation of the reader⟩. **Ingenious** suggests the power of inventing or discovering a new way of accomplishing something ⟨an *ingenious* computer engineer keeping pace with ever-changing technology⟩. See in addition INTELLIGENT.

climax see SUMMIT

cling see STICK

cloak see DISGUISE

clog see HAMPER

close *vb* Close, end, conclude, finish, complete, terminate mean to bring or come to a stopping point or limit. **Close** usu. implies that something has been in some way open as well as unfinished ⟨*close* a debate⟩. **End** conveys a strong sense of finality ⟨*ended* his life⟩. **Conclude** may imply a formal closing (as of a meeting) ⟨the service *concluded* with a blessing⟩. **Finish** may stress completion of a final step in a process ⟨after it is painted, the house will be *finished*⟩. **Complete** implies the removal of all deficiencies or a successful finishing of what has been undertaken ⟨the resolving of this last issue *completes* the agreement⟩. **Terminate** implies the setting of a limit in time or space ⟨your employment *terminates* after three months⟩.

close *adj* Close, dense, compact, thick mean massed tightly together. **Close** implies the least possible space or interval between elements without actual pressure or loss of individual identity ⟨the paintings are hung *close* together⟩. **Dense** implies compression of parts or elements so great as to be almost impenetrable ⟨the *dense* growth in a tropical rain forest⟩. **Compact** suggests a firm union or consolidation of parts within a small compass ⟨a lithe, *compact*, muscular body⟩. **Thick** implies a concentrated abundance

of parts or units ⟨a *thick* head of hair⟩. See in addition
STINGY.

clownish see BOORISH

cloy see SATIATE

clumsy see AWKWARD

clutch see TAKE

coalesce see MIX

coalition see ALLIANCE

coarse, vulgar, gross, obscene, ribald mean offensive to good
taste or morals. **Coarse** implies roughness, rudeness, or
crudeness of spirit, behavior, or language ⟨found the
coarse humor of her coworkers offensive⟩. **Vulgar** often
implies boorishness or ill-breeding ⟨a loud *vulgar* laugh⟩.
Gross implies extreme coarseness and insensitiveness
⟨*gross* eating habits make others lose their appetites⟩. **Obscene** applies to anything strongly repulsive to the sense of
decency and propriety esp. in sexual matters ⟨*obscene* language that violated the broadcasters' code⟩. **Ribald** applies
to what is amusingly or picturesquely vulgar or irreverent
or mildly indecent ⟨entertained the campers with *ribald*
folk songs⟩.

coax, cajole, wheedle, blandish mean to influence or gently
urge by caressing or flattering. **Coax** suggests an artful
pleading or teasing in an attempt to gain one's ends
⟨*coaxed* their friends into staying for dinner⟩. **Cajole** usu.
suggests an ingratiating artfulness in attempting to persuade ⟨*cajoled* by his wife into trying the exotic dish⟩.
Wheedle stresses the use of soft words, artful flattery, or
seductive appeal ⟨a pretty young thing *wheedled* the old
man out of his money⟩. **Blandish** suggests open flattery
and the obvious use of charm in an effort to win over ⟨a
salesclerk not above shameless *blandishing* in order to
make a sale⟩.

cocksure see SURE
coerce see FORCE
coeval see CONTEMPORARY
cogent see VALID
cogitate see THINK
cognizant see AWARE
cohere see STICK
coincide see AGREE
coincident see CONTEMPORARY
collate see COMPARE
colleague see CONFEDERATE
collect see GATHER
collected see COOL
colossal see ENORMOUS
combat see OPPOSE
combine see JOIN
comely see BEAUTIFUL
comfort, console, solace mean to offer help in relieving suffering or sorrow. **Comfort** implies imparting cheer, strength, or encouragement as well as lessening pain ⟨a message intended to *comfort* the grieving family⟩. **Console** emphasizes the alleviating of grief or mitigating the sense of loss rather than distinct or full relief ⟨*consoled* herself by remembering the good times⟩. **Solace** suggests a lifting of spirits often from loneliness or boredom as well as from pain or grief ⟨*solaced* himself by reading books and writing poetry⟩.
comfortable, cozy, snug, easy, restful mean enjoying or providing a position of contentment and security. **Comfortable** applies to anything that encourages serenity, well-being, or complacency as well as physical ease ⟨began to feel *comfortable* in her new surroundings⟩. **Cozy** suggests warmth, shelter, assured ease, and friendliness ⟨a *cozy*

neighborhood coffee shop⟩. **Snug** suggests having just enough space for comfort and safety but no more ⟨a *snug* little cottage⟩. **Easy** implies relief from or absence of anything likely to cause physical or mental discomfort or constraint ⟨our host had a warm, *easy* manner⟩. **Restful** applies to whatever induces or contributes to rest or relaxation ⟨a quiet *restful* inn where indolence is encouraged⟩.

comic see LAUGHABLE

comical see LAUGHABLE

command *vb* Command, order, bid, enjoin, direct, instruct, charge mean to issue orders. **Command** and **order** imply authority and usu. some degree of formality and impersonality. *Command* stresses official exercise of authority ⟨when his superior *commands*, a soldier obeys⟩. *Order* may suggest peremptory or arbitrary exercise ⟨*ordered* his men about like slaves⟩. **Bid** suggests giving orders peremptorily (as to children or servants) ⟨*bade* her fix a drink for him⟩. **Enjoin** implies giving an order or direction authoritatively and urgently and often with admonition or solicitude ⟨our guide *enjoined* us to be quiet in the cathedral⟩. **Direct** and **instruct** both connote expectation of obedience and usu. concern specific points of procedure or method, *instruct* sometimes implying greater explicitness or formality ⟨*directed* her assistant to hold all calls⟩ ⟨the judge *instructed* the jury to ignore the remark⟩. **Charge** adds to *enjoin* an implication of imposing as a duty or responsibility ⟨*charged* by the President with a covert mission⟩.

command *n* see POWER

commemorate see KEEP

commence see BEGIN

commensurable see PROPORTIONAL

commensurate see PROPORTIONAL

commerce see BUSINESS
commingle see MIX
commisseration see PITY
commit, entrust, confide, consign, relegate mean to assign to
a person or place esp. for safekeeping. **Commit** may express
the general idea of delivering into another's charge or the
special sense of transferring to a superior power or to a special place of custody ⟨*committed* the person to prison⟩.
Entrust implies committing with trust and confidence ⟨the
president is *entrusted* with broad powers⟩. **Confide** implies
entrusting with assurance or reliance ⟨*confided* all power
over my financial affairs to an attorney⟩. **Consign** suggests
transferring to remove from one's control with formality
or finality ⟨*consigned* my paintings to a gallery for sale⟩.
Relegate implies a consigning to a particular class or
sphere often with a suggestion of getting rid of ⟨*relegated*
to an obscure position in the company⟩.
commodious see SPACIOUS
common, ordinary, plain, familiar, popular, vulgar mean
generally met with and not in any way special, strange, or
unusual. **Common** implies usual everyday quality or frequency of occurrence ⟨a *common* error⟩ ⟨lacked *common*
honesty⟩ and may additionally suggest inferiority or
coarseness ⟨his *common* manners shocked her family⟩.
Ordinary stresses conformance in quality or kind with the
regular order of things ⟨an *ordinary* pleasant summer day⟩
⟨a very *ordinary* sort of man⟩. **Plain** is likely to suggest
homely simplicity ⟨she comes from *plain,* hard-working
stock⟩. **Familiar** stresses the fact of being generally known
and easily recognized ⟨a *familiar* melody⟩. **Popular** applies
to what is accepted by or prevalent among people in general sometimes in contrast to upper classes or special
groups ⟨a hero typically found in *popular* fiction⟩. **Vulgar,**

otherwise similar to *popular,* is likely to carry derogatory connotations (as of inferiority or coarseness) ⟨goods designed to appeal to the *vulgar* taste⟩. See in addition RECIPROCAL.

common sense see SENSE

commotion, tumult, turmoil, upheaval mean great physical, mental, or emotional excitement. **Commotion** suggests disturbing sometimes violent bustle or hubbub ⟨the unexpected dinner guests caused quite a *commotion*⟩. **Tumult** suggests a shaking up or stirring up that is accompanied by uproar, din, or great disorder ⟨the town was in a *tumult* over the war news⟩. **Turmoil** suggests a state devoid of calm and seething with excitement ⟨a well-ordered life that was suddenly thrown into great *turmoil*⟩. **Upheaval** suggests a violent and forceful thrusting that results in a heaving up or an overthrowing ⟨a nation in need of peace after years of *upheaval*⟩.

compact see CLOSE

compare, contrast, collate mean to set side by side in order to show differences and likenesses. **Compare** implies an aim of showing relative values or excellences by bringing out characteristic qualities whether similar or divergent ⟨wanted to *compare* the convention facilities of the two cities⟩. **Contrast** implies an emphasis on differences ⟨*contrasted* the computerized system with the old filing cards⟩. **Collate** implies minute and critical inspection in order to note points of agreement or divergence ⟨data from police districts across the country will be *collated*⟩.

compass see RANGE

compassion see PITY

compatible see CONSONANT

compel see FORCE

compendious see CONCISE

compendium, syllabus, digest, survey, sketch, précis, aperçu mean a brief treatment of a subject. A **compendium** gathers together and presents in concise or in outline form all the essential facts and details of a subject ⟨a *compendium* of computer technology to date⟩. A **syllabus** gives the material necessary for a comprehensive view of a whole subject often in the form of a series of heads or propositions ⟨a *syllabus* for a college history course⟩. A **digest** presents material gathered from many sources and arranged for ready reference ⟨a *digest* of world opinion on the Central America question⟩. A **survey** is a brief but comprehensive treatment presented often as a preliminary to further study or discussion ⟨a *survey* of current trends in higher education⟩. A **sketch** is a similar but slighter and more tentative treatment ⟨a *sketch* of the president's first year in office⟩. A **précis** is a concise statement of essential facts or points ⟨a *précis* precedes the full medical report⟩. An **aperçu** ignores details and gives a quick impression of the whole ⟨the magazine article is an *aperçu* of current cancer research⟩.

compensate, countervail, balance, offset mean to make up for what is excessive or deficient, helpful or harmful in another. **Compensate** implies making up a lack or making amends for loss or injury ⟨*compensated* for an injury on the job⟩. **Countervail** suggests counteracting a bad or harmful influence or the damage suffered through it ⟨a compassionate heart *countervails* his short temper⟩. **Balance** implies the equalizing or adjusting of two or more things that are contrary or opposed so that no one outweighs the other or others in effect ⟨in sentencing prisoners, the judge *balanced* justice and mercy⟩. **Offset** implies neutralizing one thing's good or evil effect by something that exerts a contrary effect ⟨overeating will *offset* the benefits of exercise⟩. See in addition PAY.

competent see ABLE, SUFFICIENT

complaisant see AMIABLE

complete *vb* see CLOSE

complete *adj* see FULL

complex, complicated, intricate, involved, knotty mean having confusingly interrelated parts. **Complex** suggests the unavoidable result of a necessary combining and does not imply a fault or failure ⟨a *complex* problem that calls for a *complex* solution⟩. **Complicated** applies to what offers great difficulty in understanding, solving, or explaining ⟨baffled by the *complicated* budgetary procedures⟩. **Intricate** suggests such interlacing of parts as to make it nearly impossible to follow or grasp them separately ⟨the *intricate* balance of power among nations⟩. **Involved** implies extreme complication and often disorder ⟨an *involved* explanation that clarified nothing⟩. **Knotty** suggests complication and entanglement that make solution or understanding improbable ⟨*knotty* questions concerning free expression and censorship⟩.

complicated see COMPLEX

component see ELEMENT

comport see BEHAVE

composed see COOL

composure see EQUANIMITY

comprehend see INCLUDE, UNDERSTAND

compress see CONTRACT

compunction see PENITENCE, QUALM

compute see CALCULATE

conceal see HIDE

concede see GRANT

conceive see THINK

concept see IDEA
conception see IDEA
concern see CARE
conciliate see PACIFY
concise, terse, succinct, laconic, summary, pithy, compendious mean very brief in statement or expression. **Concise** suggests the removal of all that is superfluous or elaborative ⟨a *concise* study of the situation⟩. **Terse** implies pointed conciseness ⟨a *terse* reply that ended the conversation⟩. **Succinct** implies the greatest possible compression ⟨a *succinct* letter of resignation⟩. **Laconic** implies brevity to the point of seeming rude, indifferent, or mysterious ⟨a *laconic* people who are cold to strangers⟩. **Summary** suggests the statement of main points with no elaboration or explanation ⟨a *summary* listing of the year's main events⟩. **Pithy** adds to *succinct* or *terse* the implication of richness of meaning or substance ⟨the play's dialogue is studded with *pithy* one-liners⟩. **Compendious** applies to a treatment at once full in scope and brief and concise in treatment ⟨a *compendious* report giving all that is known about the disease⟩.
conclude see CLOSE, INFER
conclusive, decisive, determinative, definitive mean bringing to an end. **Conclusive** applies to reasoning or logical proof that puts an end to debate or questioning ⟨*conclusive* evidence of criminal guilt⟩. **Decisive** may apply to something that ends a controversy, a contest, or any uncertainty ⟨the *decisive* battle of the war⟩. **Determinative** adds an implication of giving a fixed course or direction ⟨the *determinative* influence in her life⟩. **Definitive** applies to what is put forth as final and permanent ⟨the *definitive* biography of Jefferson⟩.
concord see HARMONY

concur see AGREE

condemn see CRITICIZE

condense see CONTRACT

condescend see STOOP

condolence see PITY

condone see EXCUSE

conduct, manage, control, direct mean to use one's powers to lead, guide, or dominate. **Conduct** implies taking responsibility for the acts and achievements of a group ⟨in charge of *conducting* the negotiations⟩. **Manage** implies direct handling and manipulating or maneuvering toward a desired result ⟨*manages* the financial affairs of the company⟩. **Control** implies a regulating or restraining in order to keep within bounds or on a course ⟨try to *control* the number of people using the park⟩. **Direct** implies constant guiding and regulating so as to achieve smooth operation ⟨*directs* the day-to-day running of the store⟩. See in addition BEHAVE.

confederate, partner, copartner, colleague, ally mean one who acts in association with another. **Confederate** implies an entering into a close or permanent union esp. for solidarity ⟨*confederates* in crime⟩. **Partner** implies a business association or an association of two ⟨looking for a woman to be his lifelong *partner*⟩. **Copartner** may stress the equality of the partnership ⟨management and labor are *copartners* in this endeavor⟩. **Colleague** implies a professional association ⟨admired by her *colleagues* in the dance world⟩. **Ally** implies an often temporary association in a common cause or in affairs of policy or statecraft ⟨a joint statement by the *allies* condemning the raid⟩.

confederation see ALLIANCE

confer, consult, advise, parley mean to engage in discussion in order to reach a decision or settlement. **Confer** implies

comparison of views or opinions and usu. an equality between participants ⟨the executives *confer* weekly about
current business problems⟩. **Consult** adds to *confer* the implication of seeking or taking counsel ⟨before acting, the
president *consulted* with his aides⟩. **Advise** applies esp. to
the seeking of opinions regarding personal matters ⟨before
deciding to run, he *advised* with friends⟩. **Parley** implies a
conference for the sake of settling differences ⟨the government refusing to *parley* with the rebels⟩.

confer see GIVE

confess see ACKNOWLEDGE

confide see COMMIT

confidence, assurance, self-possession, aplomb mean a state
of mind or a manner marked by easy coolness and freedom from uncertainty, diffidence, or embarrassment. **Confidence** stresses faith in oneself and one's powers without
any suggestion of conceit or arrogance ⟨had the *confidence*
that comes only from long experience⟩. **Assurance** carries
a stronger implication of certainty and may suggest arrogance or lack of objectivity in assessing one's own powers
⟨had an exaggerated *assurance* of his own worth⟩. **Self-
possession** implies an ease or coolness under stress that reflects perfect self-control and command of one's powers
⟨she answered the insolent question with complete *self-
possession*⟩. **Aplomb** implies a manifest self-possession in
trying or challenging situations ⟨handled the horde of reporters with great *aplomb*⟩.

configuration see FORM

confine see LIMIT

**confirm, corroborate, substantiate, verify, authenticate, val-
idate** mean to attest to the truth or validity of something.
Confirm implies the removing of doubts by an authoritative statement or indisputable fact ⟨*confirmed* reports of

troop movments). **Corroborate** suggests the strengthening of what is already partly established ⟨witnesses *corroborated* his story⟩. **Substantiate** implies the offering of evidence that sustains the contention ⟨claims that have yet to be *substantiated*⟩. **Verify** implies the establishing of correspondence of actual facts or details with those proposed or guessed at ⟨all statements of fact in the article have been *verified*⟩. **Authenticate** implies establishing genuineness by adducing legal or official documents or expert opinion ⟨handwriting experts *authenticated* the diaries⟩. **Validate** implies establishing validity by authoritative affirmation or by factual proof ⟨*validate* a passport⟩.

confirmed see INVETERATE

confiscate see APPROPRIATE

conflict see DISCORD

conform see ADAPT

conformation see FORM

confound see PUZZLE

confute see DISPROVE

congenial see CONSONANT

congenital see INNATE

congregate see GATHER

congruous see CONSONANT

conjecture, surmise, guess mean to draw an inference from slight evidence. **Conjecture** implies forming an opinion or judgment upon evidence insufficient for definite knowledge ⟨scientists could only *conjecture* about the animal's breeding cycle⟩. **Surmise** implies even slighter evidence and suggests the influence of imagination or suspicion ⟨*surmised* the real reason for the generous gift⟩. **Guess** stresses a hitting upon a conclusion either wholly at random or from very uncertain evidence ⟨you would never *guess* that they were wealthy⟩.

conjugal see MATRIMONIAL

connect see JOIN

connubial see MATRIMONIAL

conquer, vanquish, defeat, subdue, reduce, overcome, overthrow mean to get the better of by force or strategy. **Conquer** implies gaining mastery of ⟨*conquer* your fear of flying⟩. **Vanquish** implies a complete overpowering ⟨*vanquished* the rebels in a decisive battle⟩. **Defeat** does not imply the finality or completeness of *vanquish* which it otherwise equals ⟨have *defeated* the Miami team on several occasions⟩. **Subdue** implies a defeating and suppression ⟨*subdued* the native tribes after years of fighting⟩. **Reduce** implies a forcing to capitulate or surrender ⟨the city was *reduced* after a month-long siege⟩. **Overcome** suggests getting the better of with difficulty or after hard struggle ⟨*overcame* a host of legal and bureaucratic troubles⟩. **Overthrow** stresses the bringing down or destruction of enemy power ⟨violently *overthrew* the established government⟩.

conscientious see UPRIGHT

conscious see AWARE

consecrate see DEVOTE

consent see ASSENT

consequence see EFFECT, IMPORTANCE

consider, study, contemplate, weigh mean to think about in order to arrive at a judgment or decision. **Consider** may suggest giving thought to in order to reach a suitable conclusion, opinion, or decision ⟨refused to even *consider* my proposal⟩. **Study** implies sustained purposeful concentration and attention to details and minutiae ⟨*study* the budget before making sweeping cuts⟩. **Contemplate** stresses focusing one's thoughts on something but does not imply coming to a conclusion or decision ⟨*contemplate* the consequences of such a decision). **Weigh** implies attempting to reach the truth or arrive at a decision by balancing conflicting claims or evidence ⟨*weigh* the pros and cons of the case⟩.

consign see COMMIT

consistent see CONSONANT

console see COMFORT

consonant, consistent, compatible, congruous, congenial, sympathetic mean being in agreement one with another or agreeable one to another. **Consonant** implies the absence of elements making for discord or difficulty ⟨a spokesperson *consonant* with the company's philosophy⟩. **Consistent** may also imply this or it may stress absence of contradiction between things or between details of the same thing ⟨behavior that is not *consistent* with her general character⟩. **Compatible** suggests having a capacity for existing or functioning together without disagreement, discord, or mutual interference ⟨looking for a *compatible* roommate⟩. **Congruous** is more positive in suggesting a pleasing effect resulting from fitness or appropriateness of component elements ⟨modern furniture is not *congruous* with a colonial house⟩. **Congenial** implies a generally satisfying harmony between personalities or a fitness to one's personal taste ⟨did not find the atmosphere of the bar *congenial*⟩. **Sympathetic** suggests a more subtle or quieter kind of harmony than *congenial* ⟨a music critic not very *sympathetic* to rock⟩.

conspectus see ABRIDGMENT

conspicuous see NOTICEABLE

conspiracy see PLOT

constant see CONTINUAL, FAITHFUL

constituent see ELEMENT

constrain see FORCE

constrict see CONTRACT

consult see CONFER

contain, hold, accommodate mean to have or be capable of having within. **Contain** implies the actual presence of a specified substance or quantity within something ⟨the can *contains* about a quart of oil⟩. **Hold** implies the capacity of containing or the usual or permanent function of containing or keeping ⟨the container will *hold* a gallon of liquid⟩. **Accommodate** stresses holding without crowding or inconvenience ⟨the banquet hall can *accommodate* 500 diners⟩.

contaminate, taint, pollute, defile mean to make impure or unclean. **Contaminate** implies intrusion of or contact with dirt or foulness from an outside source ⟨water *contaminated* by industrial wastes⟩ ⟨the bigotry of elders that may *contaminate* young minds⟩. **Taint** stresses the loss of purity or cleanliness that follows contamination ⟨*tainted* meat⟩ ⟨the scandal *tainted* the rest of his political career⟩. **Pollute,** sometimes interchangeable with *contaminate,* distinctively may imply that the process which begins with contamination is complete and that what was pure or clean has been made foul, poisoned, or filthy ⟨the *polluted* waters of the lake, in parts no better than an open cesspool⟩. **Defile** implies befouling of what could or should have been kept clean and pure or held sacred and commonly suggests violation or desecration ⟨*defile* a hero's memory with slanderous innuendo⟩.

contemn see DESPISE

contemplate see CONSIDER

contemporaneous see CONTEMPORARY

contemporary, contemporaneous, coeval, synchronous, simultaneous, coincident mean existing or occurring at the same time. **Contemporary** is likely to apply to people and what relates to them ⟨Abraham Lincoln was *contemporary* with Charles Darwin⟩. **Contemporaneous** applies to events ⟨Victoria's reign was *contemporaneous* with British hegemony⟩. **Coeval** refers usu. to periods, ages, eras, eons ⟨the rise of the leisure class was *coeval* with the flowering of the arts⟩. **Synchronous** implies exact correspondence in time and esp. in periodic intervals ⟨the movements of the two pendulums are *synchronous*⟩. **Simultaneous** implies correspondence in a moment of time ⟨a *simultaneous* ringing of church bells miles apart⟩. **Coincident** is applied to events and may be used in order to avoid implication of causal relationship ⟨the end of World War II was *coincident* with a great vintage year⟩.

contemptible, despicable, pitiable, sorry, scurvy mean arousing or deserving scorn. **Contemptible** may imply any quality provoking scorn or a low standing in any scale of values ⟨a *contemptible* bigot and liar⟩. **Despicable** may imply utter worthlessness and usu. suggests arousing an attitude of moral indignation ⟨the *despicable* crime of child abuse⟩. **Pitiable** applies to what inspires mixed contempt and pity ⟨the play is his *pitiable* attempt at tragedy⟩. **Sorry** may stress pitiable inadequacy or may suggest wretchedness or sordidness ⟨the orphanage was the *sorriest* of places⟩. **Scurvy** adds to *despicable* an implication of arousing disgust ⟨the offer of help turned out to be a *scurvy* trick⟩.

contention see DISCORD

contentious see BELLIGERENT

contiguous see ADJACENT

contingency see JUNCTURE

contingent see ACCIDENTAL

continual, continuous, constant, incessant, perpetual, perennial mean characterized by continued occurrence or recurrence. **Continual** implies a close prolonged succession or recurrence ⟨*continual* showers the whole weekend⟩. **Continuous** usu. implies an uninterrupted flow or spatial extension ⟨the *continuous* roar of the falls⟩. **Constant** implies uniform or persistent occurrence or recurrence ⟨lived in *constant* pain⟩. **Incessant** implies ceaseless or uninterrupted activity ⟨the *incessant* quarreling frayed her nerves⟩. **Perpetual** suggests unfailing repetition or lasting duration ⟨the fear of *perpetual* torment after death⟩. **Perennial** implies enduring existence often through constant renewal ⟨a *perennial* source of controversy⟩.

continue, last, endure, abide, persist mean to exist over a period of time or indefinitely. **Continue** applies to a process going on without ending ⟨the stock market will *continue* to rise⟩. **Last**, esp. when unqualified, may stress existing beyond what is normal or expected ⟨buy shoes that will *last*⟩. **Endure** adds an implication of resisting destructive forces or agencies ⟨in spite of everything, her faith *endured*⟩. **Abide** implies stable and constant existing esp. as opposed to mutability ⟨through 40 years of marriage, their love *abided*⟩. **Persist** suggests outlasting the normal or appointed time and often connotes obstinacy or doggedness ⟨the sense of guilt *persisted*⟩.

continuous see CONTINUAL

contort see DEFORM

contour see OUTLINE

contract, shrink, condense, compress, constrict, deflate mean to decrease in bulk or volume. **Contract** applies to a drawing together of surfaces or particles or a reduction of area or length ⟨caused his muscles to *contract*⟩. **Shrink** implies a contracting or a loss of material and stresses a falling short of original dimensions ⟨the sweater will *shrink* if washed improperly⟩. **Condense** implies a reducing of something homogeneous to greater compactness without significant loss of content ⟨*condense* the report to five pages⟩. **Compress** implies a pressing into a small compass and definite shape usu. against resistance ⟨*compressed* the comforter to fit the box⟩. **Constrict** implies a tightening that reduces diameter ⟨the throat is *constricted* by too tight a collar⟩. **Deflate** implies a contracting by reducing the internal pressure of contained air or gas ⟨*deflate* the balloon⟩.

contradict see DENY

contradictory see OPPOSITE

contrary, perverse, restive, balky, wayward mean inclined to resist authority or control. **Contrary** implies a temperamental unwillingness to accept orders or advice ⟨the most *contrary* child in my class⟩. **Perverse** may imply wrongheaded, determined, or cranky opposition to what is reasonable or normal ⟨offered the most *perverse* argument for declaring war⟩. **Restive** suggests unwillingness or inability to submit to discipline or follow orders ⟨*restive* individuals who had no place in the army⟩. **Balky** suggests a refusing to proceed in a desired direction or course of action ⟨workers became *balky* when asked to accept pay cuts⟩. **Wayward** suggests strong-willed capriciousness and irregularity in behavior ⟨*wayward* inmates are isolated from the others⟩. See in addition OPPOSITE.

contrast see COMPARE

contravene see DENY

contrition see PENITENCE

control *vb* see CONDUCT

control *n* see POWER

controvert see DISPROVE

conundrum see MYSTERY

convene see SUMMON

conventional see CEREMONIAL
convert see TRANSFORM
convey see CARRY
conviction see CERTAINTY, OPINION
convincing see VALID
convoke see SUMMON
convulse see SHAKE
convulsive see FITFUL
cool, composed, collected, unruffled, imperturbable, nonchalant mean free from agitation or excitement. **Cool** may imply calmness, deliberateness, or dispassionateness ⟨kept a *cool* head during the emergency⟩. **Composed** implies freedom from agitation as a result of self-discipline or a sedate disposition ⟨the *composed* pianist gave a flawless concert⟩. **Collected** implies a concentration of mind that eliminates distractions esp. in moments of crisis ⟨even in heated debate she remains very *collected*⟩. **Unruffled** suggests apparent serenity and poise in the face of setbacks or in the midst of exitement ⟨his mother remained *unruffled* during the wedding⟩. **Imperturbable** implies coolness or assurance even under severe provocation ⟨a guest speaker who maintained an air of *imperturbable* civility⟩. **Nonchalant** stresses an easy coolness of manner or casualness that suggests indifference or unconcern ⟨*nonchalant* as ever, she was oblivious to the crying baby⟩.
copartner see CONFEDERATE
copious see PLENTIFUL
copy *vb* Copy, imitate, mimic, ape, mock mean to make something so that it resembles an existing thing. **Copy** suggests duplicating an original as nearly as possible ⟨*copied* the painting and sold the fake as an original⟩. **Imitate** suggests following a model or a pattern but may allow for some variation ⟨*imitate* a poet's style⟩. **Mimic** implies a

close copying (as of voice or mannerism) often for fun, ridicule, or lifelike imitation ⟨pupils *mimicking* their
teacher⟩. **Ape** may suggest presumptuous, slavish, or inept
imitating of a superior original ⟨American fashion design-
ers *aped* their European colleagues⟩. **Mock** usu. implies
imitation with derision ⟨*mocking* a vain man's manner⟩.

copy *n* see REPRODUCTION

coquet see TRIFLE

cordial see GRACIOUS

corporal see BODILY

corporeal see BODILY, MATERIAL

correct *vb* Correct, rectify, emend, remedy, redress, amend,
reform, revise mean to make right what is wrong. **Correct**
implies taking action to remove errors, faults, deviations,
defects ⟨*corrected* all her spelling errors⟩. **Rectify** implies a
more essential changing to make something right, just, or
properly controlled or directed ⟨a major error in judgment
that should be *rectified* at once⟩. **Emend** specif. implies
correction of a text or manuscript ⟨*emend* the text to
match the first edition⟩. **Remedy** implies removing or
making harmless a cause of trouble, harm, or evil ⟨set out
to *remedy* the evils of the world⟩. **Redress** implies making
compensation or reparation for an unfairness, injustice, or
imbalance ⟨we must *redress* past social injustices⟩.
Amend, reform, revise imply an improving by making corrective changes, *amend* usu. suggesting slight changes ⟨a
law that needs to be *amended*⟩, *reform* implying drastic
change ⟨plans to *reform* the entire court system⟩, and *revise* suggesting a careful examination of something and the
making of necessary changes ⟨forced to *revise* the production schedule⟩. See in addition PUNISH.

correct *adj* Correct, accurate, exact, precise, nice, right mean
conforming to fact, standard, or truth. **Correct** usu. implies

freedom from fault or error ⟨*correct* answers⟩ ⟨socially *correct* dress⟩. **Accurate** implies fidelity to fact or truth attained by exercise of care ⟨an *accurate* description of the whole situation⟩. **Exact** stresses a very strict agreement with fact, standard, or truth ⟨a suit tailored to *exact* measurements⟩. **Precise** adds to *exact* an emphasis on sharpness of definition or delimitation ⟨the *precise* terms of the contract⟩. **Nice** stresses great precision and delicacy of adjustment or discrimination ⟨makes *nice* distinctions between freedom and license⟩. **Right** is close to *correct* but has a stronger positive emphasis on conformity to fact or truth rather than mere absence of error or fault ⟨the *right* thing to do⟩.

corroborate see CONFIRM

corrupt *vb* see DEBASE

corrupt *adj* see VICIOUS

costly, expensive, dear, valuable, precious, invaluable, priceless mean having a high esp. monetary value. **Costly** implies high price and may suggest sumptuousness, luxury, or rarity ⟨the *costliest* of delicacies grace her table⟩. **Expensive** may further imply a price beyond the thing's value or the buyer's means ⟨the resort's shops seemed rather *expensive*⟩. **Dear** implies a relatively high or exorbitant price usu. due to factors other than the thing's intrinsic value ⟨coffee was *dear* during the war⟩. **Valuable** may suggest worth measured in usefulness as well as in market value ⟨iron ore was a *valuable* commodity⟩. **Precious** applies to what is of great or even incalculable value because scarce or irreplaceable ⟨our *precious* natural resources⟩. **Invaluable** and **priceless** imply such great worth as to make valuation nearly impossible ⟨a good education is *invaluable*⟩ ⟨a bon mot that was *priceless*⟩.

counsel see ADVICE

countenance see FACE
counter see ADVERSE
counteractive see ADVERSE
counterfeit *vb* see ASSUME
counterfeit *n* see IMPOSTURE
countervail see COMPENSATE
courage, mettle, spirit, resolution, tenacity mean mental or moral strength to resist opposition, danger, or hardship. **Courage** implies firmness of mind and will in the face of danger or extreme difficulty ⟨the *courage* to support unpopular causes⟩. **Mettle** suggests an ingrained capacity for meeting strain or difficulty with fortitude and resilience ⟨a challenge that will test your *mettle*⟩. **Spirit** also suggests a quality of temperament enabling one to hold one's own or keep up one's morale when opposed or threatened ⟨too many failures had broken the *spirit* of the man⟩. **Resolution** stresses firm determination to achieve one's ends ⟨the strong *resolution* of the pioneer women⟩. **Tenacity** adds to *resolution* implications of stubborn persistence and unwillingness to admit defeat ⟨the *tenacity* to continue when all others doubted⟩.
court see INVITE
courteous see CIVIL
covert see SECRET
covet see DESIRE
covetous, greedy, acquisitive, grasping, avaricious mean having or showing a strong desire for material possessions. **Covetous** implies inordinate desire often for another's possessions ⟨*covetous* of his brother's success⟩. **Greedy** stresses lack of restraint and often of discrimination in desire ⟨soldiers *greedy* for glory⟩. **Acquisitive** implies both eagerness to possess and ability to acquire and keep ⟨mansions that were the pride of the *acquisitive* class⟩. **Grasping**

adds to *covetous* and *greedy* an implication of selfishness and often suggests unfair or ruthless means ⟨*grasping* developers defrauded the homesteaders⟩. **Avaricious** implies obsessive acquisitiveness esp. of money and strongly suggests stinginess ⟨*avaricious* capitalists detested the social programs⟩.

cow see INTIMATE

cowardly, pusillanimous, craven, dastardly mean having or showing a lack of courage. **Cowardly** implies a weak or ignoble lack of courage ⟨the *cowardly* retreat of the army⟩. **Pusillanimous** suggests a contemptible lack of courage ⟨*pusillanimous* politicians feared crossing him⟩. **Craven** suggests extreme defeatism and complete lack of resistance ⟨secretly despised the *craven* toadies around her⟩. **Dastardly** implies behavior that is both cowardly and treacherous or skulking or outrageous ⟨a *dastardly* attack on unarmed civilians⟩.

cower see FAWN

coy see SHY

cozen see CHEAT

cozy see COMFORTABLE

crabbed see SULLEN

craft see ART

crafty see SLY

cranky see IRASCIBLE

crave see DESIRE

craven see COWARDLY

craze see FASHION

create see INVENT

credence see BELIEF

credit *vb* see ASCRIBE

credit *n* see BELIEF, INFLUENCE

crime see OFFENSE

cringe see FAWN
cripple see MAIM, WEAKEN
crisis see JUNCTURE
crisp see FRAGILE, INCISIVE
criterion see STANDARD
critical, hypercritical, faultfinding, captious, carping, censorious mean inclined to look for and point out faults and defects. **Critical** may also imply an effort to see a thing clearly and truly in order to judge it fairly ⟨a *critical* essay on modern drama⟩. **Hypercritical** suggests a tendency to judge by unreasonably strict standards ⟨petty, *hypercritical* disparagement of other people's success⟩. **Faultfinding** implies a querulous or exacting temperament ⟨a *faultfinding* theater reviewer⟩. **Captious** suggests a readiness to detect trivial faults or raise objections on trivial grounds ⟨no point is too minute for this *captious* critic to overlook⟩. **Carping** implies an ill-natured or perverse picking of flaws ⟨the *carping* editorial writer soon wearied readers⟩. **Censorious** implies a disposition to be severely critical and condemnatory ⟨the *censorious* tone of the papal encyclical⟩. See in addition ACUTE.
criticize, reprehend, blame, censure, reprobate, condemn, denounce mean to find fault with openly. **Criticize** implies finding fault esp. with methods or policies or intentions ⟨*criticized* the police for using violence⟩. **Reprehend** implies both criticism and severe rebuking ⟨*reprehends* the self-centeredness of today's students⟩. **Blame** may imply simply the opposite of *praise* but more often suggests the placing of responsibility for something bad or unfortunate ⟨*blames* herself for the accident⟩. **Censure** carries a stronger suggestion of authority and of reprimanding than *blame* ⟨a Senator formally *censured* by his peers⟩. **Reprobate** implies strong disapproval or firm refusal to sanction

⟨*reprobated* his son's adulterous adventures⟩. **Condemn** usu. suggests an unqualified and final unfavorable judgment ⟨*condemn* the government's racial policies⟩. **Denounce** adds to *condemn* the implication of a public declaration ⟨bishops have *denounced* abortion⟩.

cross see IRASCIBLE, STUPID

crotchet see CAPRICE

crow see BOAST

crowd, throng, crush, mob, horde mean an assembled multitude usu. of people. **Crowd** implies a close gathering and pressing together ⟨a small *crowd* greeted the returning athletes⟩. **Throng** strongly suggests movement and pushing ⟨a *throng* of reporters followed the President⟩. **Crush** emphasizes the compactness of the group, the difficulty of individual movement, and the attendant discomfort ⟨a *crush* of fans waited outside the theater⟩. **Mob** implies a disorderly crowd with the potential for violence ⟨heard an angry *mob* outside the jail⟩. **Horde** suggests a rushing or tumultuous crowd ⟨a *horde* of shoppers looking for bargains⟩.

crucial see ACUTE

crude see RUDE

cruel see FIERCE

crush *vb* **Crush, quell, extinguish, suppress, quash** mean to bring to an end by destroying or defeating. **Crush** implies a force that destroys all opposition or brings an operation to a halt ⟨a rebellion that was brutally *crushed*⟩. **Quell** means to overwhelmn completely and to reduce to submission, inactivity, or passivity ⟨statements intended to *quell* the fears of the people⟩. **Extinguish** suggests ending something as abruptly and completely as putting out a flame ⟨a promising life *extinguished* by a single bullet⟩. **Suppress** implies a conscious determination to subdue

⟨the government *suppressed* all opposition newspapers⟩. **Quash** implies a sudden and summary extinction ⟨the rejection *quashed* all their hopes for a better life⟩.

crush *n* see CROWD

crusty see BLUFF

cryptic see OBSCURE

culmination see SUMMIT

culpable see BLAMEWORTHY

cumbersome see HEAVY

cumbrous see HEAVY

cumulative, accumulative, additive, summative mean increasing or produced by the addition of new material of the same kind. **Cumulative** implies a constant increase (as in amount or power) by a series of additions, accretions, or repetitions ⟨the *cumulative* effect of taking a drug for many months⟩. **Accumulative** may distinctively imply that something has reached its maximum or greatest magnitude through many additions ⟨the *accumulative* impact of a well-ordered sales presentation⟩. **Additive** implies that something is capable of assimilating or incorporating new material ⟨as new art forms arise, we develop an *additive* notion of what is art⟩. **Summative** implies that something is capable of association or combination with others so as to create a total effect ⟨the *summative* effect of the show's music, dancing, and staging⟩.

cunning *n* see ART

cunning *adj* see CLEVER, SLY

curb see RESTRAIN

cure, heal, remedy mean to rectify an unhealthy or undesirable condition. **Cure** implies restoration to health after disease ⟨searched for new medications to *cure* the dread disease⟩. **Heal** may also apply to this but commonly suggests restoring to soundness after a wound or sore ⟨his wounds were slow to *heal*⟩. **Remedy** suggests correction or relief of a morbid or evil condition ⟨vainly searched for something to *remedy* her arthritis⟩.

curious, inquisitive, prying mean interested in what is not one's personal or proper concern. **Curious,** a neutral term, basically connotes an active desire to learn or to know ⟨children are *curious* about everything⟩. **Inquisitive** suggests impertinent and habitual curiosity and persistent quizzing ⟨dreaded the visits of their *inquisitive* relatives⟩. **Prying** implies busy meddling and officiousness ⟨*prying* neighbors who refuse to mind their own business⟩.

current *adj* see PREVAILING

current *n* see TENDENCY

curse see EXECRATE

cursory see SUPERFICIAL

curt see BLUFF

curtail see SHORTEN

curve, bend, turn, twist mean to swerve or cause to swerve from a straight line. **Curve** implies following or producing a line suggesting the arc of a circle or ellipse ⟨the road *curves* sharply to the left⟩. **Bend** suggests a yielding to force and usu. implies a distortion from normal or desirable straightness ⟨metal rods *bending* under the immense weight⟩. **Turn** implies change of direction essentially by rotation and not usu. as a result of force ⟨the comet will *turn* closer towards the earth⟩. **Twist** implies the influence of irresistible force having a spiral effect throughout the object or course involved ⟨the *twisted* wreckage of the spacecraft⟩.

custom see HABIT

customary see USUAL

cutting see INCISIVE

cynical, misanthropic, pessimistic, misogynistic mean

deeply distrustful. **Cynical** implies having a sneering disbelief in sincerity or integrity ⟨always *cynical* about other people's motives⟩. **Misanthropic** suggests a rooted distrust and dislike of human beings and their society ⟨a zoologist who had grown *misanthropic* in recent years⟩. **Pessimistic** implies having a gloomy, distrustful view of life ⟨a philosopher *pessimistic* about the future of the human race⟩. **Misogynistic** applies to a man having a deep-seated distrust of and aversion to women ⟨a *misogynistic* scientist more at home in his laboratory⟩.

D

dabbler see AMATEUR
dainty see CHOICE, NICE
dally see DELAY, TRIFLE
damage see INJURE
damn see EXECRATE
damp see WET
dangerous, hazardous, precarious, perilous, risky mean bringing or involving the chance of loss or injury. **Dangerous** applies to something that may cause harm or loss unless dealt with carefully ⟨soldiers on a *dangerous* mission⟩. **Hazardous** implies great and continuous risk of harm or failure and small chance of successfully avoiding disaster ⟨claims that smoking is *hazardous* to your health⟩. **Precarious** suggests both insecurity and uncertainty ⟨has only a *precarious* hold on reality⟩. **Perilous** strongly implies the immediacy of danger ⟨the situation at the foreign embassy has grown *perilous*⟩. **Risky** often applies to a known and accepted danger ⟨shy away from *risky* investments⟩.
dank see WET

daredevil see ADVENTUROUS

daring see ADVENTUROUS

dark, dim, dusky, murky, gloomy mean more or less deficient in light. **Dark**, the general term, implies utter or virtual lack of illumination ⟨a *dark* cave⟩. **Dim** suggests too weak a light for things to be seen clearly or distinctly ⟨a clandestine meeting in a *dim* bar⟩. **Dusky** suggests deep twilight and close approach to darkness ⟨trudging through *dusky* woods at day's end⟩. **Murky** implies a heavy darkness such as that caused by smoke, fog, or dust in air or mud in water. ⟨fish cannot live in the river's *murky* waters⟩. **Gloomy** implies serious interference with normal light and connotes cheerlessness and pessimism ⟨a *gloomy* room in the basement of the house⟩. See in addition OBSCURE.

dastardly see COWARDLY

daunt see DISMAY

dawdle see DELAY

dead, defunct, deceased, departed, late mean devoid of life. **Dead** applies literally to what is deprived of vital force but is used figuratively of anything that has lost any attribute (as energy, activity, radiance) suggesting life ⟨a *dead* engine⟩. **Defunct** stresses cessation of active existence or operation ⟨a *defunct* television series⟩. **Deceased, departed,** and **late** apply to persons who have died recently, *deceased* occurring esp. in legal use ⟨the rights of the *deceased* must be acknowledged⟩, *departed* usu. as a euphemism ⟨pray for our *departed* mother⟩, and *late* esp. with reference to a person in a specific relation or status ⟨the *late* president of the company⟩.

deadly, mortal, fatal, lethal mean causing or capable of causing death. **Deadly** applies to an established or very likely cause of death ⟨a *deadly* disease⟩. **Mortal** implies that death has occurred or is inevitable ⟨a *mortal* wound⟩. **Fatal** stresses the inevitability of what has in fact resulted in death or destruction ⟨*fatal* consequences⟩. **Lethal** applies only to something that is bound to cause death or exists for the destruction of life ⟨*lethal* gas⟩.

deal see DISTRIBUTE

dear see COSTLY

debar see EXCLUDE

debase, vitiate, deprave, corrupt, debauch, pervert mean to cause deterioration or lowering in quality or character. **Debase** implies a loss of position, worth, value, or dignity ⟨commercialism has *debased* the holiday⟩. **Vitiate** implies a destruction of purity, validity, or effectiveness by allowing entrance of a fault or defect ⟨partisanship and factionalism *vitiated* our foreign policy⟩. **Deprave** implies moral deterioration by evil thoughts or influences ⟨accused of *depraving* the children⟩. **Corrupt** implies loss of soundness, purity, or integrity ⟨believes that bureaucratese *corrupts* the language⟩. **Debauch** implies a debasing through sensual indulgence ⟨led a *debauched* life after the divorce⟩. **Pervert** implies a twisting or distorting from what is natural or normal ⟨*perverted* the original goals of the institute⟩. See in addition ABASE.

debate see DISCUSS

debauch see DEBASE

debilitate see WEAKEN

decadence see DETERIORATION

decay, decompose, rot, putrefy, spoil mean to undergo destructive dissolution. **Decay** implies a slow change from a state of soundness or perfection ⟨a *decaying* Southern mansion⟩. **Decompose** stresses a breaking down by chemical change and when applied to organic matter a corruption ⟨the body was badly *decomposed*⟩. **Rot** is a close synonym of *decompose* and often connotes foulness ⟨grain was left to *rot* in warehouses⟩. **Putrefy** implies the rotting of animal matter and offensiveness to sight and smell ⟨corpses *putrefying* on the battlefield⟩. **Spoil** applies chiefly to the decomposition of foods ⟨be on guard against *spoiled* mayonnaise⟩.

deceased see DEAD

deceitful see DISHONEST

deceive, mislead, delude, beguile mean to lead astray or frustrate usu. by underhandedness. **Deceive** implies imposing a false idea or belief that causes ignorance, bewilderment, or helplessness ⟨the salesman tried to *deceive* me about the car⟩. **Mislead** implies a leading astray that may or may not be intentional ⟨I was *mislead* by the confusing sign⟩. **Delude** implies deceiving so thoroughly as to obscure the truth ⟨we were *deluded* into thinking we were safe⟩. **Beguile** stresses the use of charm and persuasion in deceiving ⟨his ingratiating ways *beguiled* us all⟩.

decency see DECORUM

decent see CHASTE

deception, fraud, double-dealing, subterfuge, trickery mean the acts or practices of one who deliberately deceives. **Deception** may or may not imply blameworthiness, since it may suggest cheating or merely tactical resource ⟨magicians are masters of *deception*⟩. **Fraud** always implies guilt and often criminality in act or practice ⟨indicted for *fraud*⟩. **Double-dealing** suggests treachery or at least action contrary to a professed attitude ⟨the guerillas accused the go-between of *double-dealing*⟩. **Subterfuge** suggests the adoption of a stratagem or the telling of a lie in order to escape guilt or to gain an end ⟨obtained the papers by *subterfuge*⟩. **Trickery** implies ingenious acts intended to dupe or cheat ⟨will resort to any *trickery* to gain her ends⟩.

decide, determine, settle, rule, resolve mean to come or cause to come to a conclusion. **Decide** implies previous consideration of a matter causing doubt, wavering, debate, or controversy ⟨will *decide* tonight where to build the school⟩. **Determine** implies fixing the identity, character, scope, or direction of something ⟨*determined* the cause of the problem⟩. **Settle** implies a decision reached by someone with power to end all dispute or uncertainty ⟨the court's decision *settles* the matter⟩. **Rule** implies a determination by judicial or administrative authority ⟨the judge *ruled* that the evidence was inadmissible⟩. **Resolve** implies an expressed or clear decision or determination to do or refrain from doing something ⟨both nations *resolved* to stop terrorism⟩.

declare, announce, publish, proclaim, promulgate mean to make known publicly. **Declare** implies explicitness and usu. formality in making known ⟨the referee *declared* the contest a draw⟩. **Announce** implies the declaration for the first time of something that is of interest or has created speculation ⟨*announced* their engagement at a party⟩. **Publish** implies making public through print ⟨*published* the list of winners in the paper⟩. **Proclaim** implies declaring clearly, forcefully, and authoritatively ⟨the president *proclaimed* a national day of mourning⟩. **Promulgate** implies the proclaiming of a dogma, doctrine, or law ⟨*promulgated* an edict of religious toleration⟩. See in addition ASSERT.

decisive see CONCLUSIVE

deck see ADORN

decline *vb* Decline, refuse, reject, repudiate, spurn mean to turn away by not accepting, receiving, or considering. **Decline** often implies courteous refusal esp. of offers or invitations ⟨*declined* the invitation to dinner⟩. **Refuse** suggests more positiveness or ungraciousness and often implies the denial of something asked for ⟨*refused* them the loan they needed⟩. **Reject** implies a peremptory refusal by sending away or discarding ⟨*rejected* the plan as unworkable⟩. **Repudiate** implies a casting off or disowning as untrue, unauthorized, or unworthy of acceptance ⟨*repudiated* the values of their parents⟩. **Spurn** stresses contempt or disdain in rejection or repudiation ⟨*spurned* his amorous advances⟩.

decline *n* see DETERIORATION

decompose see DECAY

decorate see ADORN

decorum, decency, propriety, dignity, etiquette mean observance of the rules governing proper conduct. **Decorum** suggests conduct according with good taste, often formally prescribed ⟨had violated the *decorum* expected of an army officer⟩. **Decency** implies behavior according with normal self-respect or humane feeling for others, or with what is fitting to a particular profession or condition in life ⟨maintained a strict *decency* in dress⟩. **Propriety** suggests an artificial standard of what is correct in conduct or speech ⟨regarded the *propriety* expected of a society matron as stifling⟩. **Dignity** implies reserve or restraint in conduct prompted less by obedience to a code than by a sense of personal integrity or of social importance ⟨conveyed a quiet *dignity* and sincerity that won him respect⟩. **Etiquette** is the usual term for the detailed rules governing manners and conduct and for the observance of these rules ⟨the *etiquette* peculiar to the U.S. Senate⟩.

decoy see LURE

decrease, lessen, diminish, reduce, abate, dwindle mean to grow or make less. **Decrease** suggests a progressive decline in size, amount, numbers, or intensity ⟨slowly *decreased* the amount of pressure⟩. **Lessen** suggests a decline in amount rather than in number ⟨has been unable to *lessen* her debt at all⟩. **Diminish** emphasizes a perceptible loss and implies its subtraction from a total ⟨his muscular strength has *diminished* with age⟩. **Reduce** implies a bringing down or lowering ⟨*reduce* your caloric intake⟩. **Abate** implies a reducing of something excessive or oppressive in force or amount ⟨the storm *abated* in the afternoon⟩. **Dwindle** implies progressive lessening and is applied to things growing visibly smaller ⟨their provisions *dwindled* slowly but surely⟩.

decree see DICTATE

decrepit see WEAK

decry, depreciate, disparage, belittle, minimize mean to express a low opinion of. **Decry** implies open condemnation with intent to discredit ⟨*decried* their do-nothing attitude⟩. **Depreciate** implies a representing as being of less value than commonly believed ⟨critics *depreciate* his plays for being unabashedly sentimental⟩. **Disparage** implies depreciation by indirect means such as slighting or invidious comparison ⟨*disparaged* golf as recreation for the middle-aged⟩. **Belittle** and **minimize** imply depreciation, *belittle* suggesting usu. a contemptuous or envious attitude ⟨inclined to *belittle* the achievements of others⟩, *minimize* connoting less personal animus ⟨do not try to *minimize* the danger involved⟩.

dedicate see DEVOTE

deduce see INFER

deep see BROAD

deep-rooted see INVETERATE

deep-seated see INVETERATE

defame see MALIGN

defeat see CONQUER

defect see BLEMISH

defend, protect, shield, guard, safeguard mean to keep secure from danger or against attack. **Defend** denotes warding off actual or threatened attack ⟨a large army needed to *defend* the country⟩. **Protect** implies the use of something (as a covering) as a bar to the admission or impact of what may attack or injure ⟨*protect* one's eyes from the sun with dark glasses⟩. **Shield** suggests protective intervention in imminent danger or actual attack ⟨tried to *shield* her child from the real world⟩. **Guard** implies protecting with vigilance and force against expected danger ⟨all White House entrances are well *guarded*⟩. **Safeguard** implies taking precautionary protective measures against merely possible danger ⟨individual rights must be *safeguarded* whatever the cost⟩. See in addition MAINTAIN.

defer, postpone, suspend, stay mean to delay an action or proceeding. **Defer** implies a deliberate putting off to a later time ⟨*deferred* buying a car until next spring⟩. **Postpone** implies an intentional deferring usu. to a definite time ⟨the game was *postponed* until Saturday⟩. **Suspend** implies temporary stoppage with an added suggestion of waiting until some condition is satisfied ⟨all business has been *suspended* while repairs are being made⟩. **Stay** suggests the stopping or checking by an intervening agency or authority ⟨measures intended to *stay* the soaring rate of inflation⟩. See in addition YIELD.

deference see HONOR

defile see CONTAMINATE

definite see EXPLICIT

definitive see CONCLUSIVE

deflate see CONTRACT

deform, distort, contort, warp mean to mar or spoil by or as if by twisting. **Deform** may imply a change of shape through stress, injury, or some accident of growth ⟨relentless winds *deformed* the pines into bizarre shapes⟩. **Distort** and **contort** both imply a wrenching from the natural, normal or justly proportioned, but *contort* suggests a more involved twisting and a more grotesque and painful result ⟨the odd camera angle *distorts* his face in the photograph⟩ ⟨a degenerative bone disease had painfully *contorted* her body⟩. **Warp** indicates physically an uneven shrinking that bends or twists out of a flat plane ⟨*warped* floorboards⟩.

defraud see CHEAT

deft see DEXTEROUS

defunct see DEAD

degenerate see VICIOUS

degeneration see DETERIORATION

degrade see ABASE

deign see STOOP

dejected see DOWNCAST

dejection see SADNESS

delay *vb* Delay, retard, slow, slacken, detain mean to cause to be late or behind in movement or progress. **Delay** implies a holding back, usu. by interference, from completion or arrival ⟨bad weather *delayed* our arrival⟩. **Retard** applies chiefly to motion and suggests reduction of speed without actual stopping ⟨language barriers *retarded* their rate of learning⟩. **Slow** and **slacken** both imply also a reduction of speed, *slow* often suggesting deliberate intention ⟨the engineer *slowed* the train⟩, *slacken* an easing up or relaxing of power or effort ⟨he needs to *slacken* his pace if he intends to finish the race⟩. **Detain** implies a holding back beyond a reasonable or appointed time ⟨unexpected business had *detained* her⟩.

delay *vb* Delay, procrastinate, lag, loiter, dawdle, dally mean to move or act slowly so as to fall behind. **Delay** usu. implies a putting off (as a beginning or departure) ⟨a tight schedule means we cannot *delay* any longer⟩. **Procrastinate** implies blameworthy delay esp. through laziness or apathy ⟨*procrastinates* about making every decision⟩. **Lag** implies failure to maintain a speed set by others ⟨we *lag* behind other countries in shoe production⟩. **Loiter** and **dawdle** imply delay while in progress, esp. in walking, but *dawdle* more clearly suggests an aimless wasting of time ⟨*loitered* at several store windows before going to church⟩ ⟨children *dawdling* on their way home from school⟩. **Dally** suggests delay through trifling or vacillation when promptness is necessary ⟨stop *dallying* and get to work⟩.

delete see ERASE

deleterious see PERNICIOUS

deliberate *vb* see THINK

deliberate *adj* see VOLUNTARY

delicate see CHOICE

deliver see RESCUE

delude see DECEIVE

demand, claim, require, exact mean to ask or call for something as due or as necessary. **Demand** implies peremptoriness and insistence and often the right to make requests that are to be regarded as commands ⟨the physician *demanded* payment of her bill⟩. **Claim** implies a demand for the delivery or concession of something due as one's own or one's right ⟨*claimed* to be the first to describe the disease⟩. **Require** suggests the imperativeness that arises from inner necessity, compulsion of law or regulation, or the exigencies of the situation ⟨the patient *requires* constant attention⟩. **Exact** implies not only demanding but getting what one demands ⟨the president *exacts* absolute loyalty from his aides⟩.

demean see ABASE

demeanor see BEARING

demented see INSANE
demonstrate see SHOW
demur see QUALM
denounce see CRITICIZE
dense see CLOSE, STUPID

deny, gainsay, contradict, contravene mean to refuse to accept as true or valid. **Deny** implies a firm refusal to accept as true, to grant or concede, or to acknowledge the existence or claims of ⟨tried to *deny* the charges⟩. **Gainsay** implies disputing the truth of what another has said ⟨no one can *gainsay* that everything I've said is a fact⟩. **Contradict** implies an open or flat denial ⟨her report *contradicts* every point of his statement to the police⟩. **Contravene** implies not so much an intentional opposition as some inherent incompatibility ⟨laws against whaling that *contravene* Eskimo tradition⟩.

depart see SWERVE

departed see DEAD

deplete, drain, exhaust, impoverish, bankrupt mean to deprive of something essential to existence or potency. **Deplete** implies a reduction in number or quantity so as to endanger the ability to function ⟨we cannot afford to *deplete* our natural resources⟩. **Drain** implies a gradual withdrawal and ultimate deprivation of what is necessary to a thing's existence ⟨a series of personal tragedies *drained* him of hope⟩. **Exhaust** stresses a complete emptying or evacuation ⟨a theme that can never be *exhausted*⟩. **Impoverish** suggests a deprivation of something essential to vigorous well-being ⟨without the arts we would lead an *impoverished* existence⟩. **Bankrupt** suggests impoverishment to the point of imminent collapse ⟨war had *bankrupted* the nation of manpower and resources⟩.

deplore, lament, bewail, bemoan mean to express grief or sorrow for something. **Deplore** implies regret for the loss or impairment of something of value ⟨*deplores* the bad manners of today's young people⟩. **Lament** implies a profound or demonstrative expression of sorrow ⟨never stopped *lamenting* the loss of their only son⟩. **Bewail** and **bemoan** imply sorrow, disappointment, or protest finding outlet in words or cries, *bewail* commonly suggesting loudness, and *bemoan* lugubriousness, in uttering complaints or expressing regret ⟨fans *bewailed* the thunderous defeat of the home team⟩ ⟨purists continually *bemoan* the corruption of the language⟩.

deport see BANISH, BEHAVE

deportment see BEARING

deprave see DEBASE

depreciate see DECRY

depreciatory see DEROGATORY

depressed see DOWNCAST

depression see SADNESS

deranged see INSANE

deride see RIDICULE

derive see SPRING

derogatory, depreciatory, disparaging, slighting, pejorative mean designed or tending to belittle. **Derogatory** often applies to expressions or modes of expression that are intended to detract or belittle ⟨does not consider the word "politician" a *derogatory* term⟩. **Depreciatory** is often applied to writing or speech that tends to lower a thing in value or status ⟨her habit of referring to the human body in the most *depreciatory* of ways⟩. **Disparaging** implies an intent to depreciate by the use of oblique or indirect methods ⟨a *disparaging* look at some popular heroes⟩. **Slighting** may imply mild disparagement, indifference, or even scorn ⟨made brief but *slighting* references to the other candidates in the race). **Pejorative** is applied esp. to words whose basic meaning is depreciated either by a suffix or by semantic application or association ⟨"egghead" is a *pejorative* term for an intellectual⟩.

description see TYPE

desert see ABANDON

design see INTENTION, PLAN

desire, wish, want, crave, covet mean to have a longing for. **Desire** stresses the strength of feeling and often implies strong intention or aim ⟨*desires* to start a new life in another state⟩. **Wish** sometimes implies a general or transient longing esp. for the unattainable ⟨she *wished* that there were some way she could help⟩. **Want** specif. suggests a felt need or lack ⟨*want* to have a family⟩. **Crave** stresses the force of physical appetite or emotional need ⟨*crave* constantly for sweets⟩. **Covet** implies strong envious desire ⟨one of the most *coveted* honors in the sports world⟩.

desist see STOP

desolate see ALONE, DISMAL

despairing see DESPONDENT

desperate see DESPONDENT

despicable see CONTEMPTIBLE

despise, contemn, scorn, disdain, scout mean to regard as unworthy of one's notice or consideration. **Despise** may suggest an emotional response ranging from strong dislike to loathing ⟨*despises* those who show any sign of weakness⟩. **Contemn** implies a vehement condemnation of a person or thing as low, vile, feeble, or ignominious ⟨*contemns* the image of women promoted by advertisers⟩. **Scorn** implies a ready or indignant contempt ⟨*scorns* the very thought of retirement⟩. **Disdain** implies an arrogant or supercilious aversion to what is regarded as unworthy

despoil 102

⟨*disdained* all manner of popular music⟩. **Scout** suggests abrupt rejection or dismissal ⟨*scouted* any suggestion that their son was other than angelic⟩.

despoil see RAVAGE

despondent, despairing, desperate, hopeless mean having lost all or nearly all hope. **Despondent** implies a deep dejection arising from a conviction of the uselessness of further effort ⟨*despondent* over the death of her father⟩. **Despairing** suggests the slipping away of all hope and often despondency ⟨*despairing* appeals for the return of the kidnapped boy⟩. **Desperate** implies despair that prompts reckless action or violence in the face of defeat or frustration ⟨one last *desperate* attempt to turn the tide of the war⟩. **Hopeless** suggests despair and the cessation of effort or resistance and often implies acceptance or resignation ⟨the situation of the trapped miners is *hopeless*⟩.

despotic see ABSOLUTE

destiny see FATE

destitution see POVERTY

desultory see RANDOM

detached see INDIFFERENT

detail see ITEM

detailed see CIRCUMSTANTIAL

detain see DELAY, KEEP

deterioration, degeneration, decadence, decline mean the falling from a higher to a lower level in quality, character, or vitality. **Deterioration** implies impairment of vigor, resilience, or usefulness ⟨the *deterioration* of her memory in recent years⟩. **Degeneration** stresses physical, intellectual, or esp. moral retrogression ⟨the *degeneration* of his youthful idealism to cynicism⟩. **Decadence** presupposes a reaching and passing the peak of development and implies a turn downward with a consequent loss in vitality or energy

⟨cited rock music as a sign of cultural *decadence*⟩. **Decline** differs from *decadence* in suggesting a more markedly downward direction and greater momentum as well as more obvious evidence of deterioration ⟨the meteoric rise and *decline* of his career⟩.

determinant see CAUSE

determinative see CONCLUSIVE

determine see DECIDE, DISCOVER

detest see HATE

detestable see HATEFUL

detrimental see PERNICIOUS

devastate see RAVAGE

deviate see SWERVE

devote, dedicate, consecrate, hallow mean to set apart for a special and often higher end. **Devote** is likely to imply compelling motives and often attachment to an objective ⟨*devoted* his evenings to study⟩. **Dedicate** implies solemn and exclusive devotion to a sacred or serious use or purpose ⟨*dedicated* her life to medical research⟩. **Consecrate** stresses investment with a solemn or sacred quality ⟨*consecrate* a church to the worship of God⟩. **Hallow,** often differing little from *dedicate* or *consecrate,* may distinctively imply an attribution of intrinsic sanctity ⟨battleground *hallowed* by the blood of patriots⟩.

devotion see FIDELITY

devout, pious, religious, pietistic, sanctimonious mean showing fervor in the practice of religion. **Devout** stresses a mental attitude that leads to frequent and sincere though not always outwardly evident prayer and worship ⟨a pilgrimage that is the goal of *devout* Christians⟩. **Pious** applies to the faithful performance of religious duties and maintenance of outwardly religious attitudes ⟨a *pious* family that faithfully observes the Sabbath⟩. **Religious** may imply devoutness and piety but it emphasizes faith in a deity and adherence to a way of life in keeping with that faith ⟨a basically *religious* man, although not a regular churchgoer⟩. **Pietistic** implies an insistence on the emotional as opposed to the intellectual aspects of religion ⟨regarded religious articles as *pietistic* excess⟩. **Sanctimonious** implies pretensions to holiness or smug appearance of piety ⟨a *sanctimonious* preacher without mercy or human kindness⟩.

dexterous, adroit, deft mean ready and skilled in physical movement. **Dexterous** implies expertness with consequent facility and quickness in manipulation ⟨a *dexterous* handling of a volatile situation⟩. **Adroit** implies dexterity but may also stress resourcefulness or artfulness or inventiveness ⟨the *adroit* host of a radio call-in show⟩ **Deft** emphasizes lightness, neatness, and sureness of touch or handling ⟨a *deft* interweaving of the novel's several subplots⟩.

dialect, vernacular, lingo, jargon, cant, argot, slang mean a form of language that is not recognized as standard. **Dialect** applies commonly to a form of language found regionally or among the uneducated ⟨the *dialect* of the Cajuns in Louisiana⟩. **Vernacular** applies to the everyday speech of the people in contrast to that of the learned ⟨the doctor used the *vernacular* in describing the disease⟩. **Lingo** is a mildly contemptuous term for any language not readily understood ⟨foreign tourists speaking some strange *lingo*⟩. **Jargon** applies to a technical or esoteric language used by a profession, trade, or cult ⟨educationese is the *jargon* of educational theorists⟩. **Cant** is applied derogatorily to language that is both peculiar to a group or class and marked by hackneyed expressions ⟨the *cant* of TV sportscasters⟩. **Argot** is applied to a peculiar language of a clique or other closely knit group ⟨the *argot* of narcotics smugglers⟩.

Slang designates a class of mostly recently coined and frequently short-lived terms or usages informally preferred to standard language as being forceful, novel, or voguish ⟨the ever-changing *slang* of college students⟩.

dictate, prescribe, ordain, decree, impose mean to issue something to be followed, observed, obeyed, or accepted. **Dictate** implies an authoritative directive given orally or as if orally ⟨in matters of love, do as the heart *dictates*⟩. **Prescribe** implies an authoritative pronouncement that is clear and definite ⟨the *prescribed* procedure for requesting new supplies⟩. **Ordain** implies institution, establishment, or enactment by a supreme or unquestioned authority ⟨nature has *ordained* that we humans either swelter or shiver⟩. **Decree** implies a formal pronouncement esp. by one of great or absolute authority ⟨the Pope *decreed* that next year will be a Holy Year⟩. **Impose** implies a subjecting to what must be borne, endured, or submitted to ⟨morality cannot be *imposed* by law⟩.

dictatorial, magisterial, dogmatic, doctrinaire, oracular mean imposing one's will or opinions on others. **Dictatorial** stresses autocratic, high-handed methods and a domineering manner ⟨a *dictatorial* manner that alienates her colleagues⟩. **Magisterial** stresses assumption or use of prerogatives appropriate to a magistrate or schoolmaster in forcing acceptance of one's opinions ⟨the *magisterial* tone of his arguments imply that only a fool would disagree⟩. **Dogmatic** implies being unduly and offensively positive in laying down principles and expressing opinions ⟨very *dogmatic* about deciding what is art and what is not⟩. **Doctrinaire** implies a disposition to follow abstract theories in framing laws or policies affecting people ⟨a *doctrinaire* conservative unable to deal with complex realities⟩. **Oracular** implies the manner of one who delivers opinions in cryptic phrases or with pompous dogmatism ⟨for three decades she was the *oracular* voice of fashion⟩.

different, diverse, divergent, disparate, various mean unlike in kind or character. **Different** may imply little more than separateness but it may also imply contrast or contrariness ⟨*different* foods⟩. **Diverse** implies both distinctness and marked contrast ⟨such *diverse* interests as dancing and football⟩. **Divergent** implies movement away from each other and unlikelihood of ultimate meeting or reconciliation ⟨went on to pursue two very *divergent* careers⟩. **Disparate** emphasizes incongruity or incompatibility ⟨*disparate* notions of freedom⟩. **Various** stresses the number of sorts or kinds ⟨*various* methods have been tried⟩.

difficult see HARD

diffident see SHY

diffuse see WORDY

digest see COMPENDIUM

dignity see DECORUM

digress see SWERVE

dilate see EXPAND

dilemma see PREDICAMENT

dilettante see AMATEUR

diligent see BUSY

dim see DARK

diminish see DECREASE

diminutive see SMALL

diplomatic see SUAVE

direct see COMMAND, CONDUCT

dirty, filthy, foul, nasty, squalid mean conspicuously unclean or impure. **Dirty** emphasizes the presence of dirt more than an emotional reaction to it ⟨children *dirty* from play⟩ ⟨a *dirty* littered street⟩. **Filthy** carries a strong suggestion of offensiveness and typically of gradually accu-

mulated dirt that begrimes and besmears ⟨a stained greasy
floor, utterly *filthy*⟩. **Foul** implies extreme offensiveness
and an accumulation of what is rotten or stinking ⟨a *foul*-
smelling open sewer⟩. **Nasty** applies to what is actually
foul or is repugnant to one used to or expecting freshness,
cleanliness, or sweetness ⟨it's a *nasty* job to clean up after
a sick cat⟩. In practice, *nasty* is often weakened to the
point of being no more than a synonym of *unpleasant* or
disagreeable ⟨had a *nasty* fall⟩ ⟨his answer gave her a *nasty*
shock⟩. **Squalid** adds to the idea of dirtiness and filth that
of slovenly neglect ⟨living in *squalid* poverty⟩ ⟨*squalid*
slums⟩. All these terms are applicable to moral unclean-
ness or baseness or obscenity. **Dirty** then stresses meanness
or despicableness ⟨don't ask me to do your *dirty* work⟩,
while **filthy** and **foul** describe disgusting obscenity or loath-
some behavior ⟨*filthy* language⟩ ⟨a *foul* story of lust and
greed⟩, and **nasty** implies a peculiarly offensive unpleasantness ⟨his comedy always has a *nasty* ring to it⟩. Distinctively **squalid** implies sordidness as well as baseness
and dirtiness ⟨her life was a series of *squalid* affairs⟩.

disable see WEAKEN

disaffect see ESTRANGE

disallow see DISCLAIM

disaster, catastrophe, calamity, cataclysm mean an event or
situation that is a terrible misfortune. **Disaster** is an unforeseen, ruinous, and often sudden misfortune that happens either through lack of foresight or through some hostile external agency ⟨the war proved to be a *disaster* for the
country⟩. **Catastrophe** implies a disastrous conclusion emphasizing finality ⟨speculation about the *catastrophe* that
befell Atlantis⟩. **Calamity** stresses a great personal or public loss ⟨the father's sudden death was a *calamity* for the
family⟩. **Cataclysm,** orig. a deluge or geological convul-

sion, applies to an event or situation that produces an upheaval or complete reversal ⟨the French Revolution ranks
as one of the *cataclysms* of the modern era⟩.

disavow see DISCLAIM

discard, cast, shed, slough, scrap, junk mean to get rid of.
Discard implies the letting go or throwing away of something that has become useless or superfluous though often
not intrinsically valueless ⟨*discard* any clothes you are unlikely to wear again⟩. **Cast,** esp. when used with *off, away,*
and *out* implies a forceful rejection or repudiation ⟨*cast* off
her friends when they grew tiresome⟩. **Shed** and **slough**
imply a throwing off of something both useless and encumbering and often suggest a consequent renewal of vitality
or luster ⟨the willpower needed to *shed* a bad habit⟩ ⟨fi-
nally *sloughed* her air of jaded worldliness⟩. **Scrap** and
junk imply throwing away or breaking up as worthless in
existent form ⟨all the old ideas of warfare had to be
scrapped⟩ ⟨those who would *junk* our entire educational
system⟩.

**discernment, discrimination, perception, penetration, in-
sight, acumen** mean a power to see what is not evident to
the average mind. **Discernment** stresses accuracy (as in
reading character or motives or appreciating art) ⟨had not
the *discernment* to know who her friends really were⟩. **Discrimination** stresses the power to distinguish and select
what is true or appropriate or excellent ⟨acquire *discrimination* by looking at a lot of art⟩. **Perception** implies quick
and often sympathetic discernment (as of shades of feeling) ⟨a novelist of keen *perception*⟩. **Penetration** implies a
searching mind that goes beyond what is obvious or superficial ⟨has not the *penetration* to see beneath their deceptive facade⟩. **Insight** suggests depth of discernment
coupled with understanding sympathy ⟨a documentary

providing *insight* into the plight of the homeless⟩. **Acumen** implies characteristic penetration combined with keen practical judgment ⟨a theater director of reliable critical *acumen*⟩.

discharge see PERFORM

disciple see FOLLOWER

discipline see PUNISH, TEACH

disclaim, disavow, repudiate, disown, disallow mean to refuse to admit, accept, or approve. **Disclaim** implies a refusal to accept either a rightful claim or an imputation made by another ⟨*disclaimed* in equal measure the virtues and vices attributed to her⟩. **Disavow** implies a vigorous denial of personal responsibility, acceptance, or approval ⟨the radical group *disavowed* any responsibility for the bombing⟩. **Repudiate** implies a rejection or denial of something that had been previously acknowledged, recognized, or accepted ⟨*repudiated* the socialist views of his college days⟩. **Disown** implies a vigorous rejection or denial of something with which one formerly had a close relationship ⟨*disowned* his allegiance to the country of his birth⟩. **Disallow** implies the withholding of sanction or approval and sometimes suggests complete rejection or condemnation ⟨IRS auditors *disallowed* that deduction⟩.

disclose see REVEAL

discomfit see EMBARRASS

discompose, disquiet, disturb, perturb, agitate, upset, fluster mean to destroy capacity for collected thought or decisive action. **Discompose** implies some degree of loss of self-control or self-confidence esp. through emotional stress ⟨*discomposed* by the loss of his beloved wife⟩. **Disquiet** suggests loss of sense of security or peace of mind ⟨the *disquieting* news of a tragic accident⟩. **Disturb** implies interference with one's mental processes caused by worry, perplexity, or interruption ⟨the puzzling discrepancy *disturbed* me⟩. **Perturb** implies deep disturbance of mind and emotions ⟨*perturbed* by her husband's strange behavior⟩. **Agitate** suggests obvious external signs of nervous or emotional excitement ⟨in his *agitated* state he was unfit to go to work⟩. **Upset** implies the disturbance of normal or habitual functioning by disappointment, distress, or grief ⟨constant bickering that greatly *upsets* their son⟩. **Fluster** suggests bewildered agitation ⟨his amorous advances completely *flustered* her⟩.

disconcert see EMBARRASS

disconsolate see DOWNCAST

discontinue see STOP

discord, strife, conflict, contention, dissension, variance mean a state or condition marked by a lack of agreement or harmony. **Discord** implies an intrinsic or essential lack of harmony producing quarreling, factiousness, or antagonism ⟨years of *discord* had left its mark on the political party⟩. **Strife** emphasizes a struggle for superiority rather than the incongruity or incompatibility of the persons or things involved ⟨during his reign the empire was free of *strife*⟩. **Conflict** usu. stresses the action of forces in opposition but in static applications implies an irreconcilability as of duties or desires ⟨a *conflict* of professional interests⟩. **Contention** applies to strife or competition that shows itself in quarreling, disputing, or controversy ⟨several points of *contention* between the two sides⟩. **Dissension** implies strife or discord and stresses a division into factions ⟨religious *dissensions* threatened to split the colony⟩. **Variance** implies a clash between persons or things owing to a difference in nature, opinion, or interest ⟨cultural *variances* delayed the process of national unification⟩.

discover, ascertain, determine, unearth, learn mean to find out what one did not previously know. **Discover** may apply to something requiring exploration or investigation or to a chance encounter ⟨*discovered* the source of the river⟩. **Ascertain** implies effort to find the facts or the truth proceeding from awareness of ignorance or uncertainty ⟨will try to *ascertain* the population of the region⟩. **Determine** emphasizes the intent to establish the facts definitely or precisely ⟨unable to *determine* the exact etiology of the disease⟩. **Unearth** implies bringing to light something forgotten or hidden ⟨*unearth* old records⟩. **Learn** may imply acquiring knowledge with little effort or conscious intention (as by simply being told) or it may imply study and practice ⟨I *learned* her name only today⟩ ⟨spent years *learning* Greek⟩. See in addition INVENT, REVEAL.

discrete see DISTINCT

discrimination see DISCERNMENT

discuss, argue, debate, dispute mean to discourse about in order to reach conclusions or to convince. **Discuss** implies a sifting of possibilities esp. by presenting considerations pro and con ⟨*discussed* the need for widening the expressway⟩. **Argue** implies the offering of reasons or evidence in support of convictions already held ⟨*argued* that the project would be too costly⟩. **Debate** suggests formal or public argument between opposing parties ⟨*debated* the merits of the proposed constitutional amendment⟩; it may also apply to deliberation with oneself ⟨I'm *debating* whether I should go⟩. **Dispute** implies contentious or heated argument ⟨scientists *dispute* the reasons for the extinction of the dinosaurs⟩.

disdain see DESPISE

disdainful see PROUD

disembarrass see EXTRICATE

disencumber see EXTRICATE

disentangle see EXTRICATE

disgrace, dishonor, disrepute, infamy, ignominy mean the
state or condition of suffering loss of esteem and of enduring reproach. **Disgrace** often implies complete humiliation
and sometimes ostracism ⟨his conviction for bribery
brought *disgrace* upon his family⟩. **Dishonor** emphasizes
the loss of honor that one has enjoyed or the loss of self-
esteem ⟨prefer death to life with *dishonor*⟩. **Disrepute**
stresses loss of one's good name or the acquiring of a bad
reputation ⟨a once-proud name now fallen into *disrepute*⟩.
Infamy usu. implies notoriety as well as exceeding shame
⟨a gangster whose name retains an enduring *infamy*⟩. **Ignominy** stresses the almost unendurable contemptibility or
despicableness of the disgrace ⟨suffered the *ignominy* of
being brought back in irons⟩.

disguise, cloak, mask, dissemble mean to alter the dress or
appearance so as to conceal the identity or true nature.
Disguise implies a change in appearance or behavior that
misleads by presenting a different apparent identity ⟨*dis-
guised* himself as a peasant to escape detection⟩. **Cloak**
suggests a means of hiding a movement or an intention
completely ⟨*cloaks* her greed and self-interest in the rhet-
oric of philosophy⟩. **Mask** suggests some usu. obvious
means of preventing recognition and does not always
imply deception or pretense ⟨a smiling front that *masks* a
will of iron⟩. **Dissemble** stresses simulation for the purpose of deceiving ⟨*dissembled* madness to survive the intrigues at court⟩.

dishonest, deceitful, mendacious, lying, untruthful mean unworthy of trust or belief. **Dishonest** implies a willful perversion of truth in order to deceive, cheat, or defraud ⟨a
swindle usually involves two *dishonest* people⟩. **Deceitful**
usu. implies an intent to mislead and commonly suggests

a false appearance or double-dealing ⟨learned of the secret affairs of his *deceitful* wife⟩. **Mendacious** is less forthright than *lying,* may suggest bland or even harmlessly mischievous deceit, and used of people often suggests a habit of telling untruths ⟨his sea stories became increasingly *mendacious*⟩. **Lying** implies a specific act or instance rather than a habit or tendency ⟨a conviction based upon testimony of a *lying* witness⟩. **Untruthful** is a less brutal term than *lying* and in application to accounts or description stresses a discrepancy between what is said and fact or reality rather than an intent to deceive ⟨the version given in her memoirs is *untruthful* in several respects⟩.

dishonor see DISGRACE

disinclined, hesitant, reluctant, loath, averse mean lacking the will or desire to do something indicated. **Disinclined** implies lack of taste for or inclination toward and often active disapproval of the thing suggested ⟨*disinclined* to believe their story⟩. **Hesitant** implies a holding back through fear, uncertainty, or disinclination ⟨*hesitant* about asking her for a date⟩. **Reluctant** implies a holding back through unwillingness ⟨I'm *reluctant* to blame anyone just now⟩. **Loath** implies hesitancy because of conflict with one's opinions, predilections, or liking ⟨*loath* to believe that he could do anything right⟩. **Averse** implies a holding back from or avoiding because of distaste or repugnance ⟨seems *averse* to anything requiring work⟩.

disinterested see INDIFFERENT

disloyal see FAITHLESS

dismal, dreary, cheerless, dispiriting, bleak, desolate mean devoid of all that is cheerful and comfortable. **Dismal** may imply extreme gloominess or somberness that is utterly depressing ⟨a *dismal* day of unrelenting rain⟩. **Dreary** implies a sustained gloom, dullness, or tiresomeness that discourages or enervates ⟨spent her days alone in a *dreary* apartment⟩. **Cheerless** stresses a pervasive, disheartening joylessness or hopelessness ⟨faced a *cheerless* life as a drudge⟩. **Dispiriting** implies a lessening of morale or determination ⟨problems that made for a *dispiriting* start for their new venture⟩. **Bleak** implies a chilly, dull barrenness ⟨a *bleak,* windswept landscape offering no refuge for the wayward traveler⟩. **Desolate** implies that something disheartens by being utterly barren, lifeless, uninhabitable, or abandoned ⟨the long trek into the country's *desolate* interior⟩.

dismay, appall, horrify, daunt mean to unnerve or deter by arousing fear, apprehension, or aversion. **Dismay** implies that one is balked and perplexed or at a loss as to how to deal with something ⟨*dismayed* to find herself the center of attention⟩. **Appall** implies that one is faced with that which perturbs, confounds, or shocks ⟨*appalled* by your utter lack of concern⟩. **Horrify** stresses a reaction of horror or revulsion ⟨the scope of the famine is quite *horrifying*⟩. **Daunt** suggests a cowing, subduing, disheartening, or frightening in a venture requiring courage ⟨problems that would *daunt* even the most intrepid of reformers⟩.

dismiss see EJECT
disown see DISCLAIM
disparage see DECRY
disparaging see DEROGATORY
disparate see DIFFERENT
dispassionate see FAIR
dispatch *n* see HASTE
dispatch *vb* see KILL
dispel see SCATTER
dispense see DISTRIBUTE
disperse see SCATTER

dispirited see DOWNCAST
dispiriting see DISMAL
displace see REPLACE
display see SHOW
dispose see INCLINE
disposition, temperament, temper, character, personality
mean the dominant quality or qualities distinguishing a
person or group. **Disposition** implies customary moods
and attitude toward the life around one ⟨a boy of cheerful
disposition⟩. **Temperament** implies a pattern of innate
characteristics associated with one's specific physical and
nervous organization ⟨an artistic *temperament* inherited
from his mother⟩. **Temper** implies the qualities acquired
through experience that determine how a person or group
meets difficulties or handles situations ⟨the national *temper* has always been one of optimism⟩. **Character** applies
to the aggregate of moral qualities by which a person is
judged apart from his intelligence, competence, or special
talents ⟨a woman of iron-willed *character*⟩. **Personality**
applies to an aggregate of qualities that distinguish one as
a person ⟨a somber *personality* not to everyone's liking⟩.
disprove, refute, confute, rebut, controvert mean to show or
try to show by presenting evidence that something is not
true. **Disprove** implies the demonstration by any method
of the falseness or invalidity of a claim or argument ⟨the
view that one can neither prove nor *disprove* the existence
of God⟩. **Refute** stresses a logical method of disproving
⟨*refuted* every piece of his argument⟩. **Confute** implies reducing an opponent to silence by an overwhelming argument ⟨a triumphal flight that *confuted* all of the doubters⟩.
Rebut suggests formality in the act of answering an argument and does not necessarily imply success in disproving
⟨give the opposing side time to *rebut*⟩. **Controvert** stresses

the act of opposing with denial or an answering argument ⟨a thesis that withstood every attempt to *controvert* it⟩.

dispute see DISCUSS

disquiet see DISCOMPOSE

disregard see NEGLECT

disrepute see DISGRACE

dissect see ANALYZE

dissemble see DISGUISE

dissension see DISCORD

dissipate see SCATTER

distasteful see REPUGNANT

distend see EXPAND

distinct, separate, several, discrete mean not being each and every one the same. **Distinct** indicates that something is distinguished by the mind or eye as being apart or different from others ⟨each and every bowl is hand-decorated and *distinct*⟩. **Separate** often stresses lack of connection or a difference in identity between two things ⟨the two schools are *separate* and unequal⟩. **Several** indicates distinctness, difference, or separation from similar items ⟨a survey of the *several* opinions of the new building⟩. **Discrete** strongly emphasizes individuality and lack of physical connection despite apparent similarity or seeming continuity ⟨two *discrete* issues are being confused here⟩. See in addition EVIDENT.

distinctive see CHARACTERISTIC

distinguished see FAMOUS

distort see DEFORM

distract see PUZZLE

distress, suffering, misery, agony mean the state of being in great trouble. **Distress** implies an external and usu. temporary cause of great physical or mental strain and stress ⟨news of the hurricane put everyone in great *distress*⟩. **Suf-**

fering implies conscious endurance of pain or distress ⟨the *suffering* of earthquake victims⟩. **Misery** stresses the unhappiness attending esp. sickness, poverty, or loss ⟨the poor live with *misery* every day⟩. **Agony** suggests pain too intense to be borne ⟨in *agony* over their daughter's suicide⟩.

distribute, dispense, divide, deal, dole mean to give out, usu. in shares, to each member of a group. **Distribute** implies an apportioning by separation of something into parts, units, or amounts ⟨*distributed* the work to all employees⟩. **Dispense** suggests the giving of a carefully weighed or measured portion to each of a group according to due or need ⟨*dispensed* medicine during the epidemic⟩. **Divide** stresses the separation of a whole into parts and implies that the parts are equal ⟨three charitable groups *divided* the proceeds⟩. **Deal** emphasizes the allotment of something piece by piece ⟨*deal* out equipment and supplies to each soldier⟩. **Dole** implies a carefully measured portion that is often scant or niggardly ⟨*doled* out the little food there was⟩.

disturb see DISCOMPOSE
diverge see SWERVE
divergent see DIFFERENT
diverse see DIFFERENT
divert see AMUSE
divide see DISTRIBUTE, SEPARATE
divine see FORESEE
division see PART
divorce see SEPARATE
divulge see REVEAL
docile see OBEDIENT
doctrinaire see DICTATORIAL
dogged see OBSTINATE

dogmatic see DICTATORIAL
dole see DISTRIBUTE
dominant, predominant, paramount, preponderant, sovereign mean superior to all others in power, influence, or importance. **Dominant** applies to something that is uppermost because ruling or controlling ⟨a *dominant* social class⟩. **Predominant** applies to something that exerts, often temporarily, the most marked influence ⟨at the time fear was my *predominant* emotion⟩. **Paramount** implies supremacy in importance, rank, or jurisdiction ⟨inflation was the *paramount* issue in the campaign⟩. **Preponderant** applies to an element or factor that outweighs all others in influence or effect ⟨*preponderant* evidence in his favor⟩. **Sovereign** indicates quality or rank to which everything else is clearly subordinate or inferior ⟨the *sovereign* power resides in the people⟩.
domineering see MASTERFUL
dominion see POWER
donate see GIVE
doom see FATE
dormant see LATENT
double-dealing see DECEPTION
double entendre see AMBIGUITY
doubt see UNCERTAINTY
doubtful, dubious, problematic, questionable mean not affording assurance of the worth, soundness, or certainty of something. **Doubtful** implies little more than a lack of conviction or certainty ⟨still *doubtful* about the cause of the explosion⟩. **Dubious** stresses suspicion, mistrust, or hesitation ⟨*dubious* about the practicality of the scheme⟩. **Problematic** applies esp. to things whose existence, meaning, fulfillment, or realization is highly uncertain ⟨whether the project will ever be finished is *problematic*⟩. **Question-**

able may imply no more than the existence of doubt but usu. suggests that the suspicions are well-grounded ⟨a real estate agent of *questionable* honesty⟩.

downcast, dispirited, dejected, depressed, disconsolate, woebegone mean affected by or showing very low spirits. **Downcast** implies an overwhelming shame, mortification, or loss of confidence ⟨negative reviews left all of the actors feeling *downcast*⟩. **Dispirited** implies extreme low-spiritedness resulting from failure ⟨*dispirited,* the doomed explorers resigned themselves to failure⟩. **Dejected** implies a sudden but often temporary loss of hope, courage, or vigor ⟨a crushing defeat that left the team in a *dejected* mood⟩. **Depressed** may imply either a temporary or a chronic low-spiritedness ⟨*depressed* by his failures to the point of suicide⟩. **Disconsolate** implies being inconsolable or very uncomfortable ⟨*disconsolate* motorists leaning against their disabled car⟩. **Woebegone** suggests a defeated, spiritless condition ⟨a rundown, *woebegone* motel on an empty back road⟩.

drag see PULL

drain see DEPLETE

dramatic, theatrical, histrionic, melodramatic mean having a character or an effect like that of acted plays. **Dramatic** applies to situations in life and literature that stir the imagination and emotions deeply ⟨a *dramatic* meeting of world leaders⟩. **Theatrical** implies a crude appeal through artificiality or exaggeration in gesture or vocal expression ⟨a *theatrical* oration⟩. **Histrionic** applies to tones, gestures, and motions and suggests a deliberate affectation or staginess ⟨a *histrionic* show of grief⟩. **Melodramatic** suggests an exaggerated emotionalism or an inappropriate theatricalism ⟨making a *melodramatic* scene in public⟩.

draw see PULL

dread see FEAR

dreary see DISMAL

drench see SOAK

drift see TENDENCY

drive see MOVE

drudgery see WORK

drunk, drunken, intoxicated, inebriated, tipsy, tight mean considerably affected by alcohol. **Drunk** and **drunken** are the plainspoken, direct, and inclusive terms ⟨arrived at the party already *drunk*⟩ ⟨a *drunken* man stumbled out of the bar⟩. **Intoxicated** is a more formal term and likely to be used in legal or medical contexts ⟨arrested for driving while *intoxicated*⟩. **Inebriated** stresses the hilarious or noisy aspects of drunkenness ⟨the *inebriated* revelers bellowed out songs⟩. **Tipsy** may imply only slight drunkenness ⟨a *tipsy* patron began making unwelcome amorous advances⟩. **Tight** usu. suggests obvious drunkenness ⟨at midnight he returned, *tight* as a drum⟩.

drunken see DRUNK

dubiety see UNCERTAINTY

dubious see DOUBTFUL

ductile see PLASTIC

dudgeon see OFFENSE

dull, blunt, obtuse mean not sharp, keen, or acute. **Dull** suggests a lack or loss of keenness, zest, or pungency ⟨a *dull* pain⟩ ⟨a *dull* mind⟩. **Blunt** suggests an inherent lack of sharpness or quickness of feeling or perception ⟨even a person of his *blunt* sensibility was moved⟩. **Obtuse** implies such bluntness as makes one insensitive in perception or imagination ⟨too *obtuse* to realize that she had deeply hurt us⟩. See in addition STUPID.

dumb see STUPID

dumbfound see PUZZLE

dupe, gull, trick, hoax mean to deceive by underhanded means. **Dupe** suggests unwariness in the person deluded ⟨*duped* us into buying a lemon of a car⟩. **Gull** stresses credulousness or readiness to be imposed on (as through greed) on the part of the victim ⟨are you so easily *gulled* by these contest promoters⟩. **Trick** implies an intent to delude by means of a ruse or fraud but does not always imply a vicious intent ⟨special effects can *trick* moviegoers into believing anything⟩. **Hoax** implies the contriving of an elaborate or adroit imposture in order to deceive ⟨*hoaxed* the public by broadcasting news of a Martian invasion⟩.

duplicate see REPRODUCTION

durable see LASTING

dusky see DARK

duty see FUNCTION, TASK

dwindle see DECREASE

E

eager, avid, keen, anxious, athirst mean moved by a strong and urgent desire or interest. **Eager** implies ardor and enthusiasm and sometimes impatience at delay or restraint ⟨*eager* to get started on the trip⟩. **Avid** adds to *eager* the implication of insatiability or greed ⟨young pleasure-seekers *avid* for the next thrill⟩. **Keen** suggests intensity of interest and quick responsiveness in action ⟨very *keen* on the latest styles and fashions⟩. **Anxious** emphasizes fear of frustration or failure or disappointment ⟨*anxious* to know that they got home safely⟩. **Athirst** stresses yearning but not necessarily readiness for action ⟨*athirst* for adventure on her first trip to India⟩.

earn see GET

earnest see SERIOUS

earsplitting see LOUD

earthly, mundane, worldly mean belonging to or characteristic of the earth. **Earthly** often implies a contrast with what is heavenly or spiritual ⟨abandoned *earthly* concerns and entered a convent⟩. **Worldly** and **mundane** both imply a relation to the immediate concerns and activities of human beings, *worldly* suggesting tangible personal gain or gratification ⟨a philosopher with no interest in *worldly* goods⟩, and *mundane* suggesting reference to the immediate and practical ⟨a *mundane* discussion of finances⟩.

easy, facile, simple, light, effortless, smooth mean not demanding effort or involving difficulty. **Easy** is applicable either to persons or things imposing tasks or to activity required by such tasks ⟨an *easy* college course requiring little work⟩. **Facile** often adds to *easy* the connotation of undue haste or shallowness ⟨offers only *facile* solutions to complex problems⟩. **Simple** stresses ease in understanding or dealing with because complication is absent ⟨a *simple* problem in arithmetic⟩. **Light** stresses freedom from what is burdensome, and often suggests quickness of movement ⟨her novels are pretty *light* stuff⟩. **Effortless** stresses the appearance of ease and usu. implies the prior attainment of artistry or expertness ⟨a champion figure skater moving with *effortless* grace⟩. **Smooth** stresses the absence or removal of all difficulties, hardships, or obstacles ⟨appliances make life for working mothers a little *smoother*⟩. See in addition COMFORTABLE.

ebb see ABATE

eccentric see STRANGE

economical see SPARING

ecstasy, rapture, transport mean intense exaltation of mind and feelings. **Ecstasy** may apply to any strong emotion (as joy, fear, rage, adoration) ⟨the sculptor was in *ecstasy* when his work was unveiled⟩. **Rapture** usu. implies intense bliss or beatitude ⟨in speechless *rapture* during the entire wedding⟩. **Transport** applies to any powerful emotion that lifts one out of oneself and usu. provokes vehement expression or frenzied action ⟨in a *transport* of rage after reading the article⟩.

edge see BORDER

educate see TEACH

educe, evoke, elicit, extract, extort mean to draw out something hidden, latent, or reserved. **Educe** implies the bringing out of something potential or latent ⟨a teacher who can *educe* the best in her students⟩. **Evoke** implies a strong stimulus that arouses an emotion or an interest or recalls an image or memory ⟨a song that *evokes* many memories⟩. **Elicit** usu. implies some effort or skill in drawing forth a response ⟨unable to *elicit* a straight answer from the candidate⟩. **Extract** implies the use of force or pressure in obtaining answers or information ⟨*extract* testimony from a hostile witness⟩. **Extort** suggests a wringing or wresting from one who resists strongly ⟨*extorted* the money from his father-in-law⟩.

eerie see WEIRD

efface see ERASE

effect *n* **Effect, consequence, result, issue, outcome** mean a condition or occurrence traceable to a cause. **Effect** designates something that necessarily and directly follows or occurs by reason of a cause ⟨the *effects* of radiation on the body⟩. **Consequence** implies a looser or remoter connection with a cause and usu. implies that the cause is no longer operating ⟨a single act that had far-reaching *consequences*⟩. **Result** applies often to the last in a series of effects ⟨the end *result* was a growth in business⟩. **Issue** applies to a result that ends or solves a difficulty ⟨a successful *issue* that rendered all the controversy moot⟩. **Outcome** suggests the final result of complex or conflicting causes or forces ⟨the *outcome* of generations of controlled breeding⟩.

effect *vb* see PERFORM

effective, effectual, efficient, efficacious mean producing or capable of producing a result. **Effective** stresses the actual production of or the power to produce an effect ⟨an *effective* rebuttal⟩. **Effectual** suggests the accomplishment of a desired result esp. as viewed after the fact ⟨the measures to halt crime proved *effectual*⟩. **Efficient** suggests an acting or a potential for action or use in such a way as to avoid loss or waste of energy in effecting, producing, or functioning ⟨an *efficient* small car⟩. **Efficacious** suggests possession of a special quality or virtue that gives effective power ⟨a detergent that is *efficacious* in removing grease⟩.

effectual see EFFECTIVE

efficacious see EFFECTIVE

efficient see EFFECTIVE

effort, exertion, pains, trouble mean the active use of energy in producing a result. **Effort** often suggests a single action or attempt and implies the calling up or directing of energy by the conscious will ⟨made the supreme *effort* and crossed the finish line first⟩. **Exertion** may describe the bringing into effect of any power of mind or body or it may suggest laborious and exhausting effort ⟨a job not requiring much physical *exertion*⟩. **Pains** implies toilsome or solicitous effort ⟨take *pains* to do the job well⟩. **Trouble** implies effort that inconveniences or slows down ⟨went through a lot of *trouble* to get the right equipment⟩.

effortless see EASY

effrontery see TEMERITY

eject, expel, oust, evict, dismiss mean to drive or force out. **Eject** carries an esp. strong implication of throwing or thrusting out from within as a physical action ⟨*ejected* the obnoxious patron from the bar⟩. **Expel** stresses a thrusting out or driving away esp. permanently which need not be physical ⟨a student *expelled* from college⟩. **Oust** implies removal or dispossession by power of the law or by compulsion of necessity ⟨issued a general order *ousting* all foreigners⟩. **Evict** chiefly applies to turning out of house and home ⟨they were *evicted* for nonpayment of rent⟩. **Dismiss** implies a getting rid of something unpleasant or troublesome simply by refusing to consider it further ⟨simply *dismissed* the quarrel from her mind⟩.

elastic, resilient, springy, flexible, supple mean able to endure strain without being permanently injured. **Elastic** implies the property of resisting deformation by stretching ⟨slacks that come with an *elastic* waistband⟩. **Resilient** im-

plies the ability to recover shape quickly when the deform-
ing force or pressure is removed ⟨a good running shoe has
a *resilient* innersole⟩. **Springy** stresses both the ease with
which something yields to pressure and the quickness of
its return to original shape ⟨the cake is done when the top
is *springy*⟩. **Flexible** applies to something which may or
may not be resilient or elastic but which can be bent or
folded without breaking ⟨*flexible* plastic tubing⟩. **Supple**
applies to something that can be readily bent, twisted, or
folded without any sign of injury ⟨shoes made of luxurious, *supple* leather⟩.

election see CHOICE

elegant see CHOICE

element, component, constituent, ingredient, factor mean
one of the parts of a compound or complex whole. **Element** applies to any such part and often connotes irreduc-
ible simplicity ⟨the basic *elements* of the gothic novel⟩.
Component and **constituent** may designate any of the substances (whether elements or compounds) or the qualities
that enter into the makeup of a complex product; *component* stresses its separate entity or distinguishable character
⟨able to identify every *component* of his firearm⟩; *constituent* stresses its essential and formative character ⟨ana-
lyzed the *constituents* of the compound⟩. **Ingredient** applies to any of the substances which when combined form
a particular mixture (as a medicine or alloy) ⟨the *ingredients* of a cocktail⟩. **Factor** applies to any constituent or element whose presence helps actively to perform a certain
kind of work or produce a definite result ⟨price was a *factor* in her decision to buy⟩.

elevate see LIFT

elevation see HEIGHT

elicit see EDUCE

eliminate see EXCLUDE
elucidate see EXPLAIN
elude see ESCAPE
emanate see SPRING
emancipate see FREE
emasculate see UNNERVE
embarrass, discomfit, abash, disconcert, rattle mean to distress by confusing or confounding. **Embarrass** implies some influence that impedes thought, speech, or action ⟨*embarrassed* to admit that she liked the movie⟩. **Discomfit** implies a hampering or frustrating accompanied by confusion ⟨persistent heckling *discomfited* the speaker⟩. **Abash** presupposes some initial self-confidence that receives a sudden check by something that produces shyness, shame, or a conviction of inferiority ⟨completely *abashed* by her swift and cutting retort⟩. **Disconcert** implies an upsetting of equanimity or assurance producing uncertainty or hesitancy ⟨*disconcerted* by the sight of the large audience⟩. **Rattle** implies an agitation that impairs thought and judgment ⟨a tennis player not at all *rattled* by television cameras⟩.
embellish see ADORN
embolden see ENCOURAGE
embrace see ADOPT, INCLUDE
emend see CORRECT
emergency see JUNCTURE
eminent see FAMOUS
emotion see FEELING
employ see USE
employment see WORK
empty, vacant, blank, void, vacuous mean lacking contents which could or should be present. **Empty** suggests a complete absence of contents ⟨an *empty* bucket⟩. **Vacant** sug-

gests an absence of appropriate contents or occupants ⟨a *vacant* apartment⟩. **Blank** stresses the absence of any significant, relieving, or intelligible features on a surface ⟨a *blank* wall⟩. **Void** suggests absolute emptiness as far as the mind or senses can determine ⟨a statement *void* of meaning⟩. **Vacuous** suggests the emptiness of a vacuum and esp. the lack of intelligence or significance ⟨a *vacuous* facial expression⟩. See in addition VAIN.

enchant see ATTRACT

encomium, eulogy, panegyric, tribute, citation mean a formal expression of praise. **Encomium** implies enthusiasm and warmth in praising a person or a thing ⟨the subject of several spirited *encomiums* at the banquet⟩. **Eulogy** applies to a prepared speech or writing extolling the virtues and services of a person ⟨delivered the *eulogy* at the funeral⟩. **Panegyric** suggests an elaborate often poetic compliment ⟨coronations once inspired *panegyrics*⟩. **Tribute** implies deeply felt praise conveyed either through words or through a significant act ⟨a page of *tributes* marking his fifty years of service⟩. **Citation** applies to the formal praise accompanying the mention of a person in a military dispatch or in awarding an honorary degree ⟨a *citation* noting her lasting contribution to biology⟩.

encourage, inspirit, hearten, embolden mean to fill with courage or strength of purpose. **Encourage** suggests the raising of one's confidence esp. by an external agency ⟨the teacher's praise *encouraged* the student to try even harder⟩. **Inspirit** implies instilling life, energy, courage, or vigor into something ⟨pioneers *inspirited* by the stirring accounts of the explorers⟩. **Hearten** implies a dispiritedness or despondency that is lifted by an infusion of fresh courage or zeal ⟨a hospital patient *heartened* by the display of moral support⟩. **Embolden** implies the giving of courage sufficient to overcome timidity or reluctance ⟨a successful climb *emboldened* her to try more difficult ones⟩.

encroach see TRESPASS

end *n* End, termination, ending, terminus mean the point or line beyond which something does not or cannot go. **End** is the inclusive term, implying the final limit in time or space, in extent of influence, or range of possibility ⟨the report put an *end* to all speculation⟩. **Termination** and **ending** apply to the end of something having predetermined limits or being complete or finished ⟨the *termination* of a lease⟩ ⟨the *ending* of a search⟩. *Ending* often includes the portion leading to the actual final point ⟨a film marred by a contrived *ending*⟩. **Terminus** applies commonly to the point to which one moves or progresses ⟨Chicago is the *terminus* for many air routes⟩. See in addition INTENTION.

end *vb* see CLOSE

endeavor see ATTEMPT

endemic see NATIVE

ending see END

endorse see APPROVE

endure see BEAR, CONTINUE

energetic see VIGOROUS

energy see POWER

enervate see UNNERVE

enfeeble see WEAKEN

engineer see GUIDE

enhance see INTENSIFY

enigma see MYSTERY

enigmatic see OBSCURE

enjoin see COMMAND

enlarge see INCREASE

enliven see QUICKEN

enmity, hostility, antipathy, antagonism, animosity, rancor,

animus mean deep-seated dislike or ill will. **Enmity** suggests positive hatred which may be open or concealed ⟨an unspoken *enmity* seethed between the two⟩. **Hostility** suggests an enmity showing itself in attacks or aggression ⟨a history of *hostility* between the two nations⟩. **Antipathy** and **antagonism** imply a natural or logical basis for one's hatred or dislike, *antipathy* suggesting repugnance, a desire to avoid or reject, and *antagonism* suggesting a clash of temperaments leading readily to hostility ⟨a natural *antipathy* for self-important upstarts⟩ ⟨a long-standing *antagonism* between the banker and his prodigal son⟩. **Animosity** suggests intense ill will and vindictiveness that threaten to kindle hostility ⟨*animosity* that eventually led to revenge⟩. **Rancor** esp. is applied to bitter brooding over a wrong ⟨*rancor* filled every line of his letters⟩. **Animus** implies strong prejudice ⟨my objections are devoid of any personal *animus*⟩.

enormous, immense, huge, vast, gigantic, colossal, mammoth mean exceedingly large. **Enormous** and **immense** both suggest an exceeding of all ordinary bounds in size or amount or degree, but *enormous* often adds an implication of abnormality or monstrousness ⟨the *enormous* expense of the program⟩ ⟨the *immense* size of the new shopping mall⟩. **Huge** commonly suggests an immensity of bulk or amount ⟨quickly incurred a *huge* debt⟩. **Vast** usu. suggests immensity of extent ⟨the *vast* Russian steppes⟩. **Gigantic** stresses the contrast with the size of others of the same kind ⟨a *gigantic* sports stadium⟩. **Colossal** applies esp. to a human creation of stupendous or incredible dimensions ⟨a *colossal* statue of Lincoln⟩. **Mammoth** suggests both hugeness and ponderousness of bulk ⟨a *mammoth* boulder⟩.

enough see SUFFICIENT

ensnare see CATCH

ensue see FOLLOW

ensure, insure, assure, secure mean to make a thing or person sure. **Ensure** implies a virtual guarantee ⟨the government has *ensured* the safety of the foreign minister⟩. **Insure** sometimes stresses the taking of necessary measures beforehand ⟨careful planning should *insure* the success of the party⟩. **Assure** distinctively implies the removal of doubt and suspense from a person's mind ⟨I *assure* you that no one will be harmed⟩. **Secure** implies action taken to guard against attack or loss ⟨made a reservation in order to *secure* a table⟩.

enter, penetrate, pierce, probe mean to make way into something. **Enter** is the most general of these and may imply either going in or forcing a way in ⟨*entered* the city in triumph⟩. **Penetrate** carries a strong implication of an impelling force or compelling power that achieves entrance ⟨no bullet has ever *penetrated* a vest of that material⟩. **Pierce** adds to *penetrate* a clear implication of an entering point ⟨a fracture in which the bone *pierces* the skin⟩. **Probe** implies penetration to investigate or explore something hidden from sight or knowledge ⟨*probed* the depths of the sea⟩.

entertain see AMUSE

enthusiasm see PASSION

entice see LURE

entire see PERFECT, WHOLE

entrap see CATCH

entreat see BEG

entrench see TRESPASS

entrust see COMMIT

environment see BACKGROUND

envisage see THINK

envision see THINK

ephemeral see TRANSIENT

epicure, gourmet, gastronome, bon vivant mean one who takes pleasure in eating and drinking. **Epicure** implies fastidiousness and voluptuousness of taste ⟨a delicacy that only an *epicure* would appreciate⟩. **Gourmet** implies being a connoisseur in food and drink and the discriminating enjoyment of them ⟨*gourmets* rate the restaurant highly⟩. **Gastronome** implies that one has studied extensively the history and rituals of haute cuisine ⟨an annual banquet that attracts *gastronomes* from all over⟩. **Bon vivant** stresses the enjoyment of fine food and drink in company ⟨*bon vivants* rang in the New Year in style⟩.

episode see OCCURRENCE

epitome see ABRIDGMENT

epoch see PERIOD

equable see STEADY

equal see SAME

equanimity, composure, sangfroid, phlegm mean evenness of mind under stress. **Equanimity** suggests a habit of mind that is only rarely disturbed under great strain ⟨accepted fortune's slings and arrows with resigned *equanimity*⟩. **Composure** implies the controlling of emotional or mental agitation by an effort of will or as a matter of habit ⟨maintained his *composure* even under hostile questioning⟩. **Sangfroid** implies great coolness and steadiness under strain ⟨an Olympian diver of remarkable *sangfroid*⟩. **Phlegm** implies insensitiveness and suggests apathy rather than self-control ⟨good news and bad news alike had no effect on her *phlegm*⟩.

equip see FURNISH

equitable see FAIR

equivalent see SAME

equivocal see OBSCURE
equivocate see LIE
equivocation see AMBIGUITY
era see PERIOD
eradicate see EXTERMINATE
erase, expunge, cancel, efface, obliterate, blot out, delete
mean to remove something so that it no longer has any
effect or existence. **Erase** implies the act of rubbing or wip-
ing out (letters or impressions) often in preparation for
correction or new matter ⟨*erase* what you wrote and start
over⟩. **Expunge** stresses a removal or destruction that
leaves no trace ⟨*expunged* all references to the deposed
leader⟩. **Cancel** implies an action (as marking, revoking, or
neutralizing) that makes a thing no longer effective or usable ⟨a crime that *cancelled* out all her good deeds⟩. **Efface**
implies the removal of an impression by damage to or
wearing off of the surface ⟨the subway sign had been badly
effaced⟩. **Obliterate** and **blot out** both imply a covering up
or smearing over that removes all traces of a thing's existence ⟨an outdoor mural almost *obliterated* by graffiti⟩
⟨*blotted* out the offensive passage with black ink⟩. **Delete**
implies a deliberate exclusion, or a marking to direct exclusion, of written matter ⟨his editor *deleted* all unflatter-
ing references to others⟩.
erratic see STRANGE
error, mistake, slip, blunder, lapse mean a departure from
what is true, right, or proper. **Error** suggests the existence
of a standard or guide and a straying from the right course
through failure to make effective use of this ⟨one *error* in
judgment lost the battle⟩. **Mistake** implies misconception
or inadvertence and usu. expresses less criticism than *error*
⟨dialed the wrong number by *mistake*⟩. **Blunder** regularly
imputes stupidity or ignorance as a cause and connotes

some degree of blame ⟨a political campaign noted mostly for its series of *blunders*⟩. **Slip** stresses inadvertence or accident and applies esp. to trivial but embarrassing mistakes ⟨during the speech I made several *slips*⟩. **Lapse** stresses forgetfulness, weakness, or inattention as a cause ⟨apart from a few grammatical *lapses*, the paper is good⟩.

ersatz see ARTIFICIAL

erudition see KNOWLEDGE

escape, avoid, evade, elude, shun, eschew mean to get away or keep away from something. **Escape** stresses the fact of getting away or being passed by not necessarily through effort or by conscious intent ⟨nothing *escapes* her sharp eyes⟩. **Avoid** stresses forethought and caution in keeping clear of danger or difficulty ⟨with careful planning we can *avoid* the fate of previous attempts⟩. **Evade** implies adroitness, ingenuity, or lack of scruple in escaping or avoiding ⟨*evaded* the question by changing the subject⟩. **Elude** implies a slippery or baffling quality in the person or thing that escapes ⟨what she sees in him *eludes* me⟩. **Shun** often implies an avoiding as a matter of habitual practice or policy and may imply repugnance or abhorrence ⟨you have *shunned* your responsibilities⟩. **Eschew** implies an avoiding or abstaining from as unwise or distasteful ⟨a playwright who *eschews* melodrama and claptrap⟩.

eschew see ESCAPE

escort see ACCOMPANY

especial see SPECIAL

espouse see ADOPT

essay see ATTEMPT

essential, fundamental, vital, cardinal mean so important as to be indispensable. **Essential** implies belonging to the very nature of a thing and therefore being incapable of removal without destroying the thing itself or its character

⟨conflict is an *essential* element in drama⟩. **Fundamental** applies to something that is a foundation without which an entire system or complex whole would collapse ⟨the *fundamental* principles of democracy⟩. **Vital** suggests something that is necessary to a thing's continued existence or operation ⟨air bases that are *vital* to our national security⟩. **Cardinal** suggests something on which an outcome turns or depends ⟨one of the *cardinal* events of the Civil War⟩.

esteem see REGARD

estimate, appraise, evaluate, value, rate, assess mean to judge something with respect to its worth or significance. **Estimate** implies a judgment, considered or casual, that precedes or takes the place of actual measuring or counting or testing out ⟨*estimated* that there were a hundred people there⟩. **Appraise** commonly implies the fixing by an expert of the monetary worth of a thing, but it may be used of any critical judgment ⟨a real estate agent *appraised* the house⟩. **Evaluate** suggests an attempt to determine either the relative or intrinsic worth of something in terms other than monetary ⟨instructors will *evaluate* all students' work⟩. **Value** equals *appraise* but without implying expertness of judgment ⟨a watercolor *valued* by the donor at $500⟩. **Rate** adds to *estimate* the notion of placing a thing according to a scale of values ⟨an actress who is *rated* highly by her peers⟩. **Assess** implies a critical appraisal for the purpose of understanding or interpreting, or as a guide in taking action ⟨officials are still trying to *assess* the damage⟩.

estimate see CALCULATE

estrange, alienate, disaffect, wean mean to cause one to break a bond of affection or loyalty. **Estrange** implies the development of indifference or hostility with consequent separation or divorcement ⟨a chance meeting with his *es-*

tranged wife). **Alienate** may or may not suggest separation but always implies loss of affection or interest ⟨managed to *alienate* all her coworkers with her arrogance⟩. **Disaffect** refers esp. to those from whom loyalty is expected and stresses the effects (as rebellion or discontent) of alienation without actual separation ⟨overly strict parents who *disaffect* their children⟩. **Wean** implies separation from something having a strong hold on one ⟨willpower is needed to *wean* yourself from a bad habit⟩.

ethical see MORAL

etiquette see DECORUM

eulogy see ENCOMIUM

evade see ESCAPE

evaluate see ESTIMATE

evanescent see TRANSIENT

even see LEVEL, STEADY

event see OCCURRENCE

eventual see LAST

evict see EJECT

evidence see SHOW

evident, manifest, patent, distinct, obvious, apparent, plain, clear mean readily perceived or apprehended. **Evident** implies presence of visible signs that lead one to a definite conclusion ⟨an *evident* fondness for the company of beautiful women⟩. **Manifest** implies an external display so evident that little or no inference is required ⟨her *manifest* joy upon receiving the award⟩. **Patent** applies to a cause, effect, or significant feature that is clear and unmistakable once attention has been directed to it ⟨*patent* defects in the item when sold⟩. **Distinct** implies such sharpness of outline or definition that no unusual effort to see or hear or comprehend is required ⟨my offer met with a *distinct* refusal⟩. **Obvious** implies such ease in discovering or accounting for that it often suggests conspicuousness or little need for perspicacity in the observer ⟨the motives are *obvious* to all but the most obtuse⟩. **Apparent** is very close to *evident* except that it may imply more conscious exercise of inference ⟨the absurdity of the charge is *apparent* to all who know him⟩. **Plain** implies lack of intricacy, complexity, or elaboration ⟨her feelings about him are quite *plain*⟩. **Clear** implies an absence of anything that confuses the mind or obscures the pattern ⟨it's *clear* now what's been going on⟩.

evil see BAD

evince see SHOW

evoke see EDUCE

exact *adj* see CORRECT

exact *vb* see DEMAND

exacting see ONEROUS

examine see SCRUTINIZE

example see INSTANCE, MODEL

exasperate see IRRITATE

exceed, surpass, transcend, excel, outdo, outstrip mean to go or be beyond a stated or implied limit, measure, or degree. **Exceed** implies going beyond a limit set by authority or established by custom or by prior achievement ⟨*exceed* the speed limit⟩. **Surpass** suggests superiority in quality, merit, or skill ⟨the book *surpassed* our expectations⟩. **Transcend** implies a rising or extending notably above or beyond ordinary limits ⟨*transcended* the values of their culture⟩. **Excel** implies preeminence in achievement or quality and may suggest superiority to all others ⟨*excels* in mathematics⟩. **Outdo** applies to a bettering or exceeding what has been done before ⟨*outdid* herself this time⟩. **Outstrip** suggests surpassing in a race or competition ⟨*outstripped* other firms in selling the new plastic⟩.

excel see EXCEED

excessive, immoderate, inordinate, extravagant, exorbitant, extreme mean going beyond a normal limit. **Excessive** implies an amount or degree too great to be reasonable or acceptable ⟨punishment that was deemed *excessive*⟩. **Immoderate** implies lack of desirable or necessary restraint ⟨an *immoderate* amount of time spent on grooming⟩. **Inordinate** implies an exceeding of the limits dictated by reason or good judgment ⟨an *inordinate* portion of their budget goes to entertainment⟩. **Extravagant** implies an indifference to restraints imposed by truth, prudence, or good taste ⟨*extravagant* claims for the product⟩. **Exorbitant** implies a departure from accepted standards regarding amount or degree ⟨a menu with *exorbitant* prices⟩. **Extreme** may imply an approach to the farthest limit possible or conceivable but commonly means only to a notably high degree ⟨views concerning marriage that are a bit *extreme*⟩.

excite see PROVOKE

exclude, debar, eliminate, suspend mean to shut or put out. **Exclude** implies keeping out what is already outside ⟨children under 17 are *excluded* from seeing the movie⟩. **Debar** implies setting up a barrier that is effectual in excluding a person or class from what is open or accessible to others ⟨arbitrary standards that effectively *debar* most female candidates⟩. **Eliminate** implies the getting rid of what is already within esp. as a constituent part or element ⟨a company's plans to *eliminate* a fourth of its work force⟩. **Suspend** implies temporary and commonly disciplinary removal from membership in a school or organization ⟨a student *suspended* for possession of drugs⟩.

exculpate, absolve, exonerate, acquit, vindicate mean to free from a charge. **Exculpate** implies a clearing from blame or fault often in a matter of small importance ⟨I cannot *exculpate* myself of the charge of overenthusiasm⟩. **Absolve** implies a release either from an obligation that binds the conscience or from the consequences of disobeying the law or committing a sin ⟨*absolved* the subject from his oath of allegiance⟩. **Exonerate** implies a complete clearance from an accusation or charge and from any attendant suspicion of blame or guilt ⟨a committee *exonerated* the governor of bribery⟩. **Acquit** implies a formal decision in one's favor with respect to a definite charge ⟨*acquitted* by a jury of murder⟩. **Vindicate** may refer to things as well as persons that have been subjected to critical attack or imputation of guilt, weakness, or folly, and implies a clearing effected by proving the unfairness of such criticism or blame ⟨an investigation *vindicated* the senator on all counts⟩.

excuse, condone, pardon, forgive mean to exact neither punishment nor redress. **Excuse** may refer to specific acts esp. in social or conventional situations or to the person responsible for these ⟨*excuse* an interruption⟩ ⟨*excused* her for interrupting⟩. Often the term implies extenuating circumstances ⟨injustice *excuses* strong responses⟩. **Condone** implies that one overlooks without censure behavior (as dishonesty or violence) that involves a serious breach of a moral, ethical, or legal code, and the term may refer to the behavior or to the agent responsible for it ⟨a society that *condones* alcohol but not drugs⟩. **Pardon** implies that one remits a penalty due for an admitted or established offense ⟨*pardon* a criminal⟩ ⟨*pardon* the noisy enthusiasm of a child⟩. **Forgive** implies that one gives up all claim to requital and to resentment or vengeful feelings ⟨*forgave* her husband for his infidelities⟩.

excuse *n* see APOLOGY

execrate, curse, damn, anathematize mean to denounce violently. **Execrate** implies intense loathing and usu. passionate fury ⟨*execrated* the men who had molested his family⟩. **Curse** and **damn** imply angry denunciation by blasphemous oaths or profane imprecations ⟨a drunken wino *cursing* passersby⟩ ⟨*damns* the city council for not anticipating the problem⟩. **Anathematize** implies solemn denunciation of an evil or an injustice ⟨preachers *anathematizing* pornography⟩.

execute, administer mean to carry out the declared intent of another. **Execute** stresses the enforcing of the specific provisions of a law, will, commission, or a command ⟨charged with failing to *execute* the order⟩. **Administer** implies the continuing exercise of delegated authority in pursuance of only generally indicated goals rather than specif. prescribed means of attaining them ⟨the agency in charge of *administering* Indian affairs⟩. See in addition KILL, PERFORM.

exemplar see MODEL

exertion see EFFORT

exhaust see DEPLETE, TIRE

exhibit see SHOW

exigency see JUNCTURE

exile see BANISH

exonerate see EXCULPATE

exorbitant see EXCESSIVE

expand, amplify, swell, distend, inflate, dilate mean to increase in size or volume. **Expand** may apply whether the increase comes from within or without and regardless of manner (as growth, unfolding, addition of parts) ⟨our business has *expanded* with every passing year⟩. **Amplify** implies the extension or enlargement of something inadequate ⟨*amplify* the statement with some details⟩. **Swell** implies gradual expansion beyond a thing's original or normal limits ⟨the bureaucracy *swelled* to unmanageable proportions⟩. **Distend** implies outward extension caused by pressure from within ⟨a stomach *distended* by gas⟩. **Inflate** implies expanding by introduction of air or something insubstantial and suggests a resulting vulnerability and liability to sudden collapse ⟨*inflate* a balloon⟩ ⟨an *inflated* ego⟩. **Dilate** applies esp. to expansion of circumference ⟨dim light causes the pupils of the eyes to *dilate*⟩.

expect, hope, look mean to await some occurrence or outcome. **Expect** implies a high degree of certainty and usu. involves the idea of preparing or envisioning ⟨I *expect* to be finished by Tuesday⟩. **Hope** implies little certainty but suggests confidence or assurance in the possibility that what one desires or longs for will happen ⟨she *hopes* to find a job soon⟩. **Look** suggests a degree of expectancy and watchfulness rather than confidence or certainty ⟨we *look* to the day when peace will be universal⟩.

expedient *adj* **Expedient, politic, advisable** mean dictated by practical or prudent motives. **Expedient** usu. implies what is immediately advantageous without regard for ethics or consistent principles ⟨a truce was the *expedient* answer⟩. **Politic** stresses judiciousness and tactical value but usu. implies some lack of candor or sincerity ⟨converted to Catholicism when it was *politic* to do so⟩. **Advisable** applies to what is practical, prudent, or advantageous but lacks the derogatory implication of *expedient* and *politic* ⟨it's *advisable* to say nothing at all⟩.

expedient *n* see RESOURCE
expedition see HASTE
expeditious see FAST
expel see EJECT
expensive see COSTLY
expert see PROFICIENT

explain, expound, explicate, elucidate, interpret mean to make something clear or understandable. **Explain** implies a making plain or intelligible what is not immediately obvious or entirely known ⟨the doctor *explained* what the operation would entail⟩. **Expound** implies a careful often elaborate explanation ⟨a professor *expounding* the theory of relativity⟩. **Explicate** adds the idea of a developed or detailed analysis ⟨a passage that critics have been inspired to *explicate* at length⟩. **Elucidate** stresses the throwing of light upon as by offering details or motives previously obscure or only implicit ⟨a newspaper report that tries to *elucidate* the reasons for the crime⟩. **Interpret** adds to *explain* the need for imagination or sympathy or special knowledge in dealing with something ⟨*interprets* the play as an allegory about good and evil⟩.

explicate see EXPLAIN

explicit, definite, express, specific mean perfectly clear in meaning. **Explicit** implies such verbal plainness and distinctness that there is no need for inference and no room for difficulty in understanding ⟨the dress code is very *explicit*⟩. **Definite** stresses precise, clear statement or arrangement that leaves no doubt or indecision ⟨the law is *definite* regarding such cases⟩. **Express** implies both explicitness and direct and positive utterance ⟨her *express* wish was to be cremated⟩. **Specific** applies to what is precisely and fully treated in detail or particular ⟨two *specific* criticisms of the proposal⟩.

exploit see FEAT

expose see SHOW

exposed see LIABLE

expostulate see OBJECT

expound see EXPLAIN

express *vb* Express, vent, utter, voice, broach, air mean to make known what one thinks or feels. **Express** suggests an impulse to reveal in words, gestures, or actions, or through what one creates or produces ⟨paintings that *express* the artist's loneliness⟩. **Vent** stresses a strong inner compulsion to express esp. in words ⟨her stories *vent* the frustrations of black women⟩. **Utter** implies the use of the voice not necessarily in articulate speech ⟨would occasionally *utter* words of encouragement⟩. **Voice** does not necessarily imply vocal utterance but does imply expression or formulation in words ⟨an editorial *voicing the concerns of many*⟩. **Broach** adds the implication of disclosing for the first time something long thought over or reserved for a suitable occasion ⟨*broached* the subject of a divorce⟩. **Air** implies an exposing or parading of one's views often in order to gain relief or sympathy or attention ⟨cabinet members publicly *airing* their differences⟩.

express *adj* see EXPLICIT

expunge see ERASE

exquisite see CHOICE

extemporaneous, improvised, impromptu, offhand, unpremeditated mean done or devised on the spur of the moment and not beforehand. **Extemporaneous** stresses the demands imposed by the occasion or situation and may imply a certain sketchiness or roughness ⟨an *extemporaneous* shelter prompted by the sudden storm⟩. **Improvised** implies the constructing or devising of something without advance knowledge, thought, or preparation and often without the proper equipment ⟨*improvised* a barbecue pit at the campground⟩. **Impromptu** stresses the immediacy and the spontaneity of the thing composed or devised ⟨an *impromptu* speech at an awards ceremony⟩. **Offhand** strongly implies casualness, carelessness, or indifference ⟨his *offhand* remarks often got him into trouble⟩. **Unpre-**

meditated suggests some strong often suddenly provoked emotion that impels one to action ⟨*unpremeditated* murder⟩.

extend, lengthen, prolong, protract mean to draw out or add to so as to increase in length. **Extend** and **lengthen** imply a drawing out in space or time but *extend* may also imply increase in width, scope, area, or range ⟨*extend* a vacation⟩ ⟨*extend* welfare services⟩ ⟨*lengthen* a skirt⟩ ⟨*lengthen* the workweek⟩. **Prolong** suggests chiefly increase in duration esp. beyond usual limits ⟨*prolonged* illness⟩. **Protract** adds to *prolong* implications of needlessness, vexation, or indefiniteness ⟨*protracted* litigation⟩.

exterminate, extirpate, eradicate, uproot mean to effect the destruction or abolition of something. **Exterminate** implies complete and immediate extinction by killing off all individuals ⟨failed attempts to *exterminate* the mosquitoes⟩. **Extirpate** implies extinction of a race, family, species, or sometimes an idea or doctrine by destruction or removal of its means of propagation ⟨disease more than anything else *extirpated* the Native Americans⟩. **Eradicate** implies the driving out or elimination of something that has established itself ⟨polio had virtually been *eradicated*⟩. **Uproot** implies a forcible or violent removal and stresses displacement or dislodgment rather than immediate destruction ⟨the war had *uprooted* thousands⟩.

extinguish see CRUSH

extirpate see EXTERMINATE

extort see EDUCE

extract see EDUCE

extraneous see EXTRINSIC

extravagant see EXCESSIVE

extreme see EXCESSIVE

extricate, disentangle, untangle, disencumber, disembarrass

mean to free from what binds or holds back. **Extricate** implies the use of care or ingenuity in freeing from a difficult position or situation ⟨a knack for *extricating* himself from damaging political rows⟩. **Disentangle** and **untangle** suggest painstaking separation of a thing from other things ⟨a biography that *disentangles* the myth from the man⟩ ⟨*untangled* a web of deceit⟩. **Disencumber** implies a release from something that clogs or weighs down ⟨a science article *disencumbered* of scientific jargon⟩. **Disembarrass** suggests a release from something that impedes or hinders ⟨*disembarrassed* herself of her frivolous companions⟩.

extrinsic, extraneous, foreign, alien mean external to a thing, its essential nature, or its original character. **Extrinsic** applies to what is distinctly outside the thing in question or is not contained in or derived from its essential nature ⟨sentimental attachment that is *extrinsic* to the house's market value⟩. **Extraneous** applies to what is on or comes from the outside and may or may not be capable of becoming an essential part ⟨*extraneous* arguments that obscure the real issue⟩. **Foreign** applies to what is so different as to be rejected or repelled or, if admitted, to be incapable of becoming identified or assimilated by the thing in question ⟨inflammation resulting from a *foreign* body in the eye⟩. **Alien** is stronger than *foreign* in suggesting opposition, repugnance, or irreconcilability ⟨a practice that is totally *alien* to our democratic principles⟩.

exuberant see PROFUSE

F

fabricate see MAKE

fabulous see FICTITIOUS

face, countenance, visage, physiognomy mean the front part of the head from forehead to chin. **Face** is the simple, direct, and also the inclusive term ⟨a strikingly handsome *face*⟩. **Countenance** applies to a face as seen and as revealing a mood or attitude ⟨the benign *countenance* of my grandmother⟩. **Visage** suggests attention to shape and proportions and sometimes expression ⟨a penetrating gaze and an aquiline nose gave him a birdlike *visage*⟩. **Physiognomy** suggests attention to the contours and characteristic expression as indicative of race, temperament, or qualities of mind or character ⟨a youth with the *physiognomy* of a warrior⟩.

facet see PHASE

facetious see WITTY

facile see EASY

facsimile see REPRODUCTION

factitious see ARTIFICIAL

factor see ELEMENT

faculty see GIFT

fad see FASHION

fag see TIRE

failing see FAULT

fair, just, equitable, impartial, unbiased, dispassionate, objective mean free from favor toward either or any side. **Fair** implies an elimination of one's own feelings, prejudices, and desires so as to achieve a proper balance of conflicting interests ⟨a *fair* decision by a judge⟩. **Just** implies an exact following of a standard of what is right and proper ⟨a *just* settlement of territorial claims⟩. **Equitable** implies a less rigorous standard than *just* and usu. suggests equal treatment of all concerned ⟨provides for the *equitable* distribution of his property⟩. **Impartial** stresses an absence of favor or prejudice ⟨arbitration by an *impartial* third party⟩. **Unbiased** implies even more strongly an absence of all prejudice ⟨your *unbiased* opinion of the whole affair⟩. **Dispassionate** suggests freedom from the influence of strong feeling and often implies cool or even cold judgment ⟨a *dispassionate* summation of the facts⟩. **Objective** stresses a tendency to view events or persons as apart from oneself and one's own interest or feelings ⟨it's impossible for me to be *objective* about my own child⟩. See in addition BEAUTIFUL.

faith see BELIEF

faithful, loyal, constant, staunch, steadfast, resolute mean firm in adherence to whatever one owes allegiance. **Faithful** implies unswerving adherence to a person or thing or to the oath or promise by which a tie was contracted ⟨*faithful* to her marriage vows⟩. **Loyal** implies a firm resistance to any temptation to desert or betray ⟨the army remained *loyal* to the czar⟩. **Constant** stresses continuing firmness of emotional attachment without necessarily implying strict obedience to promises or vows ⟨*constant* lovers⟩. **Staunch** suggests fortitude and resolution in adherence and imperviousness to influences that would weaken it ⟨a *staunch* defender of free speech⟩. **Steadfast** implies a steady and unwavering course in love, allegiance, or conviction ⟨*steadfast* in their support of democratic principles⟩. **Resolute** implies firm determination to adhere to a cause or purpose ⟨*resolute* in his determination to see justice done⟩.

faithless, false, disloyal, traitorous, treacherous, perfidious
mean untrue to what should command one's fidelity or allegiance. **Faithless** applies to any failure to keep a promise
or pledge or any breach of allegiance or loyalty ⟨*faithless*
allies refused to support the sanctions⟩. **False** stresses the
fact of failing to be true in any manner ranging from fickleness to cold treachery ⟨betrayed by *false* friends⟩. **Disloyal** implies a lack of complete faithfulness in thought or
words or actions to a friend, cause, leader, or country ⟨ac-
cused the hostages of being *disloyal* to their country⟩. **Traitorous** implies either actual treason or a serious betrayal of
trust ⟨*traitorous* acts punishable by death⟩. **Treacherous**
implies readiness to betray trust or confidence ⟨the victim
of *treacherous* allies. **Perfidious** adds to *faithless* the implication of an incapacity for fidelity or reliability ⟨repeated
and *perfidious* violations of the treaty⟩.

fake see IMPOSTURE

false see FAITHLESS

falter see HESITATE

familiar, intimate mean closely acquainted. **Familiar** suggests the ease, informality, absence of reserve or constraint
natural among members of a family or acquaintances of
long standing ⟨resent being addressed by strangers in a *familiar* tone⟩. **Intimate** stresses the closeness and intensity
rather than the mere frequency of personal association and
suggests either deep mutual understanding or the sharing
of deeply personal thoughts and feelings ⟨their love letters
became increasingly *intimate*⟩. See in addition COMMON.

**famous, renowned, celebrated, noted, notorious, distin-
guished, eminent, illustrious** mean known far and wide.
Famous implies little more than the fact of being, sometimes briefly, widely and popularly known ⟨a *famous* television actress⟩. **Renowned** implies more glory and accla-

mation ⟨one of the most *renowned* figures in sports history⟩. **Celebrated** implies notice and attention esp. in print ⟨the most *celebrated* beauty of her day⟩. **Noted** suggests well-deserved public attention ⟨the *noted* mystery writer⟩. **Notorious** frequently adds to *famous* an implication of questionableness or evil ⟨a *notorious* gangster⟩. **Distinguished** implies acknowledged excellence or superiority ⟨a *distinguished* scientist who recently won the Nobel Prize⟩. **Eminent** implies even greater conspicuousness for outstanding quality or character ⟨a conference of the country's most *eminent* writers⟩. **Illustrious** stresses enduring honor and glory attached to a deed or person ⟨the *illustrious* deeds of national heroes⟩.

fanciful see IMAGINARY

fancy see THINK

fantastic, bizarre, grotesque mean conceived, made, or carried out without adherence to truth or reality. **Fantastic** may connote unrestrained extravagance in conception or merely ingenuity of decorative invention ⟨*fantastic* theories about the origins of life⟩. **Bizarre** applies to the sensationally queer or strange and implies violence of contrast or incongruity of combination ⟨a *bizarre* pseudo-medieval castle⟩. **Grotesque** may apply to what is conventionally ugly but artistically effective or it may connote ludicrous awkwardness or incongruity often with sinister or tragic overtones ⟨*grotesque* statues adorn the cathedral⟩ ⟨*grotesque* attempts at operatic roles⟩. See in addition IMAGINARY.

fascinate see ATTRACT

fashion *n* Fashion, style, mode, vogue, fad, rage, craze mean the usage accepted by those who want to be up-to-date. **Fashion** is the most general term and applies to any way of dressing, behaving, writing, or performing that is favored at any one time or place ⟨the current *fashion* for Russian ballet dancers⟩. **Style** often implies a distinctive fashion adopted by people of wealth or taste ⟨a media mogul used to traveling in *style*⟩. **Mode** suggests the fashion of the moment among those anxious to appear elegant and sophisticated ⟨sleek, tanned bodies are the *mode* at such resorts⟩. **Vogue** stresses the wide acceptance of a fashion ⟨a novelist who is no longer much in *vogue*⟩. **Fad** suggests caprice in taking up or in dropping a fashion ⟨nothing is more dated than last year's *fad*⟩. **Rage** and **craze** stress intense enthusiasm in adopting a fad ⟨Cajun food was quite the *rage*⟩ ⟨a sport that is more than a passing *craze*⟩. See in addition METHOD.

fashion *vb* see MAKE

fast, rapid, swift, fleet, quick, speedy, hasty, expeditious mean moving, proceeding, or acting with celerity. **Fast** and **rapid** are very close in meaning, but *fast* applies particularly to the thing that moves ⟨*fast* horse⟩ and *rapid* to the movement itself ⟨*rapid* current⟩. **Swift** suggests great rapidity coupled with ease of movement ⟨returned the ball with one *swift* stroke⟩. **Fleet** adds the implication of lightness and nimbleness ⟨*fleet* runners⟩. **Quick** suggests promptness and the taking of little time ⟨a *quick* wit⟩. **Speedy** implies quickness of successful accomplishment ⟨*speedy* delivery of the mail⟩ and may also suggest unusual velocity. **Hasty** suggests hurry and precipitousness and often connotes carelessness ⟨a *hasty* inspection⟩. **Expeditious** suggests efficiency together with rapidity of accomplishment ⟨an *expeditious* processing of a merchandise order⟩.

fasten, fix, attach, affix mean to make something stay firmly in place. **Fasten** implies an action such as tying, buttoning, nailing, locking, or otherwise securing ⟨*fastened* the horse to a post). **Fix** usu. implies a driving in, implanting, or embedding ⟨*fix* the stake so that it remains upright⟩. **Attach** suggests a connecting or uniting by a bond, link, or tie in order to keep things together ⟨*attach* the W-2 form here⟩. **Affix** implies an imposing of one thing on another by gluing, impressing, or nailing ⟨*affix* your address label here⟩.

fastidious see NICE

fatal see DEADLY

fate, destiny, lot, portion, doom mean a predetermined state or end. **Fate** implies an inevitable and usu. an adverse outcome ⟨the *fate* of the mariners remains unknown⟩. **Destiny** implies something foreordained and often suggests a great or noble course or end ⟨our country's *destiny*⟩. **Lot** and **portion** imply a distribution by fate or destiny, *lot* suggesting blind chance ⟨it was her *lot* to die childless⟩, and *portion* implying the apportioning of good and evil ⟨the *portion* that has been meted out to me⟩. **Doom** distinctly implies a grim or calamitous fate ⟨if the rebellion fails, our *doom* is certain⟩.

fateful see OMINOUS

fatigue see TIRE

fatuous see SIMPLE

fault, failing, frailty, foible, vice mean an imperfection or weakness of character. **Fault** implies a failure, not necessarily culpable, to reach some standard of perfection in disposition, action, or habit ⟨a woman of many virtues and few *faults*⟩. **Failing** suggests a minor shortcoming in character ⟨procrastination is one of my *failings*⟩. **Frailty** implies a general or chronic proneness to yield to temptation ⟨a fondness for chocolate is the most human of *frailties*⟩. **Foible** applies to a harmless or endearing weakness or idiosyncrasy ⟨*foibles* that make him all the more lovable⟩.

Vice can be a general term for any imperfection or weakness, but it often suggests violation of a moral code or the giving of offense to the moral sensibilities of others ⟨gambling and drunkenness were the least of his *vices*⟩.

faultfinding see CRITICAL

favorable, auspicious, propitious mean pointing toward a happy outcome. **Favorable** implies that the persons involved are approving or helpful or that the circumstances are advantageous ⟨*favorable* weather conditions for a rocket launch⟩. **Auspicious** applies to something taken as a sign or omen promising success before or at the beginning of an event ⟨an *auspicious* beginning for a great partnership⟩. **Propitious** may also apply to beginnings but often implies a continuing favorable condition ⟨the time was not *propitious* for starting a new business⟩.

fawn, toady, truckle, cringe, cower mean to behave abjectly before a superior. **Fawn** implies seeking favor by servile flattery or exaggerated attention ⟨waiters *fawning* over a celebrity⟩. **Toady** suggests the attempt to ingratiate oneself by an abjectly menial or subservient attitude ⟨never misses an opportunity to *toady* to his boss⟩. **Truckle** implies the subordination of oneself and one's desires or judgment to those of a superior ⟨the rich are used to seeing others *truckle*⟩. **Cringe** suggests a bowing or shrinking in fear or servility ⟨*cringing* before every supposed superior⟩. **Cower** suggests a display of abject fear in the company of threatening or domineering people ⟨as an adult he still *cowered* before his father⟩.

fealty see FIDELITY

fear, dread, fright, alarm, panic, terror, trepidation mean painful agitation in the presence or anticipation of danger. **Fear** is the most general term and implies anxiety and usu. loss of courage ⟨*fear* of the unknown⟩. **Dread** usu. adds the idea of intense reluctance to face or meet a person or situation and suggests aversion as well as anxiety ⟨the *dread* of having to face her mother⟩. **Fright** implies the shock of sudden, startling fear ⟨imagine our *fright* at being awakened by screams⟩. **Alarm** suggests a sudden and intense awareness of immediate danger ⟨view the situation with *alarm*⟩. **Panic** implies unreasoning and overmastering fear causing hysterical activity ⟨news of the invasion caused great *panic*⟩. **Terror** implies the most extreme degree of fear ⟨immobilized with *terror*⟩. **Trepidation** adds to *dread* the implications of timidity, trembling, and hesitation ⟨raised the subject of marriage with some *trepidation*⟩.

fearful, apprehensive, afraid mean disturbed by fear. **Fearful** implies often a timorous or worrying temperament ⟨the child is *fearful* of loud noises⟩. **Apprehensive** suggests a state of mind and implies a premonition of evil or danger ⟨*apprehensive* that war would break out⟩. **Afraid** often suggests weakness or cowardice and regularly implies inhibition of action or utterance ⟨*afraid* to speak the truth⟩.

feasible see POSSIBLE

feat, exploit, achievement mean a remarkable deed. **Feat** implies strength or dexterity or daring ⟨the *feat* of crossing the Atlantic in a balloon⟩. **Exploit** suggests an adventurous or heroic act ⟨his celebrated *exploits* as a spy⟩. **Achievement** implies hard-won success in the face of difficulty or opposition ⟨honored for her *achievements* as a chemist⟩.

fecund see FERTILE

federation see ALLIANCE

feeble see WEAK

feeling, emotion, affection, sentiment, passion mean a subjective response to a person, thing, or situation. **Feeling** denotes any partly mental, partly physical response marked by pleasure, pain, attraction, or repulsion; it may suggest the mere existence of a response but imply nothing about the nature or intensity of it ⟨whatever *feelings* I had for her are gone⟩. **Emotion** carries a strong implication of excitement or agitation but, like *feeling*, encompasses both positive and negative responses ⟨a play in which the *emotions* are real⟩. **Affection** applies to feelings that are also inclinations or likings ⟨memoirs filled with *affection* and understanding⟩. **Sentiment** implies an emotion inspired by an idea ⟨her feminist *sentiments* are well known⟩. **Passion** suggests a powerful or controlling emotion ⟨revenge became his ruling passion⟩. See in addition ATMOSPHERE.

feign see ASSUME

feint see TRICK

felicitous see FIT

feral see BRUTAL

ferocious see FIERCE

fertile, fecund, fruitful, prolific mean producing or capable of producing offspring or fruit. **Fertile** implies the power to reproduce in kind or to assist in reproduction and growth ⟨*fertile* soil⟩; applied figuratively, it suggests readiness of invention and development ⟨a most *fertile* imagination⟩. **Fecund** emphasizes abundance or rapidity in bearing fruit or offspring ⟨came from a remarkably *fecund* family⟩. **Fruitful** adds to *fertile* and *fecund* the implication of desirable or useful results ⟨undertook *fruitful* research in virology⟩. **Prolific** stresses rapidity of spreading or multiplying by or as if by natural reproduction ⟨one of the most *prolific* writers of science fiction⟩.

fervent see IMPASSIONED

fervid see IMPASSIONED

fervor see PASSION

fetid see MALODOROUS

fetter see HAMPER

fib see LIE

fickle see INCONSTANT

fictitious, fabulous, legendary, mythical, apocryphal mean having the nature of something imagined or invented. **Fictitious** implies fabrication and suggests artificiality or contrivance more than deliberate falsification or deception ⟨all names used in the broadcast are *fictitious*⟩. **Fabulous** stresses the marvelous or incredible character of something without necessarily implying impossibility or actual nonexistence ⟨a land of *fabulous* riches⟩. **Legendary** suggests the elaboration of invented details and distortion of historical facts produced by popular tradition ⟨the *legendary* courtship of Miles Standish⟩. **Mythical** implies a purely fanciful explanation of facts or the creation of beings and events out of the imagination ⟨*mythical* creatures such as centaurs⟩. **Apocryphal** implies an unknown or dubious source or origin or may imply that the thing itself is dubious or inaccurate ⟨a book that repeats many *apocryphal* stories⟩.

fidelity, allegiance, fealty, loyalty, devotion, piety mean faithfulness to something to which one is bound by pledge or duty. **Fidelity** implies strict and continuing faithfulness to an obligation, trust, or duty ⟨*fidelity* in the performance of one's duties⟩. **Allegiance** suggests an adherence like that of a citizen to his country ⟨a politician who owes *allegiance* to no special interest⟩. **Fealty** implies a fidelity acknowledged by the individual and as compelling as a sworn vow ⟨a critic's only *fealty* is to truth⟩. **Loyalty** implies a faithfulness that is steadfast in the face of any temptation to renounce, desert, or betray ⟨valued the *loyalty* of his friends⟩. **Devotion** stresses zeal and service amounting to self-dedication ⟨a painter's *devotion* to her artistic vision⟩. **Piety** stresses fidelity to obligations regarded as natural and fundamental ⟨filial *piety* demands that I visit my parents⟩.

fierce, ferocious, barbarous, savage, cruel mean showing fury or malignity in looks or actions. **Fierce** applies to humans and animals that inspire terror because of their wild and menacing aspect or fury in attack ⟨*fierce* tribes still inhabit the rain forest⟩. **Ferocious** implies extreme fierceness and unrestrained violence and brutality ⟨signs warned of a *ferocious* dog⟩. **Barbarous** implies a ferocity or mercilessness regarded as unworthy of civilized people ⟨the *barbarous* treatment of prisoners⟩. **Savage** implies the absence of inhibitions restraining civilized people filled with rage, lust, or other violent passion ⟨*savage* reviews of the new play⟩. **Cruel** implies indifference to suffering and even positive pleasure in inflicting it ⟨the *cruel* jokes of schoolboys⟩.

figure see FORM

filch see STEAL

filthy see DIRTY

final see LAST

financial, monetary, pecuniary, fiscal mean of or relating to money. **Financial** implies money matters conducted on a large scale or involving some degree of complexity ⟨a business deal secured through a complex *financial* arrangement⟩. **Monetary** refers to money as coined, distributed, or circulating ⟨the country's basic *monetary* unit is the peso⟩. **Pecuniary** implies reference to money matters affecting the individual ⟨a struggling single mother constantly in *pecuniary* difficulties⟩. **Fiscal** refers to money as providing revenue for the state or to the financial affairs of an institution or corporation ⟨the *fiscal* year of the United States ends on June 30⟩.

finicky see NICE

finish see CLOSE

firm, hard, solid mean having a texture or consistency that resists deformation. **Firm** implies such compactness and coherence and often elasticity of substance as to resist pulling, distorting, or pressing ⟨a *firm* mattress with good back support⟩. **Hard** implies impenetrability and nearly complete but inelastic resistance to pressure or tension ⟨a diamond is one of the *hardest* substances known⟩. **Solid** implies a texture of uniform density so as to be not only firm but heavy ⟨*solid* furniture that will last⟩.

fiscal see FINANCIAL

fit, suitable, meet, proper, appropriate, fitting, apt, happy, felicitous mean right with respect to some end, need, use, or circumstance. **Fit** stresses adaptability and sometimes special readiness for use or action ⟨the vessel is now *fit* for service⟩. **Suitable** implies an answering to requirements or demands ⟨shopped for clothes *suitable* for camping⟩. **Meet** suggests a just proportioning ⟨a tip that was *meet* for the services rendered⟩. **Proper** suggests a suitability through essential nature or accordance with custom ⟨the *proper* role of the First Lady⟩. **Appropriate** implies eminent or distinctive fitness ⟨a golf bag is an *appropriate* gift for a golfer⟩. **Fitting** implies harmony of mood or tone ⟨*fitting* subjects for dinner table conversation⟩. **Apt** connotes a fitness marked by nicety and discrimination ⟨a speech laced with some *apt* quotations⟩. **Happy** suggests what is effectively or successfully appropriate ⟨a *happy* choice of words⟩. **Felicitous** suggests an aptness that is opportune, telling, or graceful ⟨a *felicitous* note of apology⟩.

fitful, spasmodic, convulsive mean lacking steadiness or regularity in movement. **Fitful** implies intermittence, a succession of starts and stops or risings and fallings ⟨the *fitful* beginnings of a new enterprise⟩. **Spasmodic** adds to *fitful* the implication of violent activity alternating with inactivity ⟨*spasmodic* trading on the stock exchange⟩. **Convulsive** suggests the breaking of regularity or quiet by uncontrolled movement ⟨the *convulsive* shocks of the earthquake⟩.

fitting see FIT

fix *vb* see FASTEN

fix *n* see PREDICAMENT

flabbergast see SURPRISE

flagrant, glaring, gross, rank mean conspicuously bad or objectionable. **Flagrant** applies usu. to offenses or errors so bad that they can neither escape notice nor be condoned ⟨*flagrant* abuse of the office of president⟩. **Glaring** implies painful or damaging obtrusiveness of something that is conspicuously wrong, faulty, or improper ⟨*glaring* errors in judgment⟩. **Gross** implies the exceeding of reasonable or excusable limits ⟨*gross* carelessness on your part⟩. **Rank** applies to what is openly and extremely objectionable and utterly condemned ⟨it's *rank* heresy to say that⟩.

flash, gleam, glance, glint, sparkle, glitter, glisten, glimmer, shimmer mean to send forth light. **Flash** implies a sudden and transient outburst of bright light ⟨lightning *flashed*⟩. **Gleam** suggests a steady light seen through an obscuring medium or against a dark background ⟨the lights of the town *gleamed* in the valley below⟩. **Glance** suggests a bright darting light relfected from a quickly moving surface ⟨sunlight *glanced* off the hull of the boat⟩. **Glint** implies a cold glancing light ⟨steel bars *glinted* in the moonlight⟩. **Sparkle** suggests innumerable moving points of bright light ⟨the *sparkling* waters of the gulf⟩. **Glitter** connotes a brilliant sparkling or gleaming ⟨*glittering* diamonds⟩. **Glisten** applies to the soft sparkle from a wet or oily surface ⟨rain-drenched sidewalks *glistened* under the street lamps). **Glimmer** suggests a faint or wavering gleam ⟨a lone light *glimmered* in the distance⟩. **Shimmer** implies a soft tremulous gleaming or a blurred reflection ⟨a *shimmering* satin dress⟩.

flashy see GAUDY

flat see INSIPID, LEVEL

flaunt see SHOW

flaw see BLEMISH

fleer see SCOFF

fleet see FAST

fleeting see TRANSIENT

fleshly see CARNAL

flexible see ELASTIC

flightiness see LIGHTNESS

flinch see RECOIL

fling see THROW

flippancy see LIGHTNESS

flirt see TRIFLE

flourish see SWING

flout see SCOFF

flow see SPRING

fluctuate see SWING

fluster see DISCOMPOSE

foible see FAULT

foil see FRUSTRATE

follow, succeed, ensue, supervene mean to come after something or someone. **Follow** may apply to a coming after in time, position, or logical sequence ⟨speeches *followed* the dinner⟩. **Succeed** implies a coming after immediately in a sequence determined by natural order, inheritance, election, or laws of rank ⟨she *succeeded* her father as head of the business⟩. **Ensue** commonly suggests a logical consequence or naturally expected development ⟨after the lecture, a general discussion *ensued*⟩. **Supervene** suggests the following or beginning of something unforeseen or unpredictable ⟨events *supervened* that brought tragedy into his life⟩. See in addition CHASE.

follower, adherent, disciple, partisan mean one who attaches himself to another. **Follower** may apply to a person who attaches himself either to the person or beliefs of another ⟨an evangelist and his *followers*⟩. **Adherent** suggests a close and persistent attachment ⟨*adherents* to Communism⟩. **Disciple** implies a devoted allegiance to the teachings of one chosen as a master ⟨*disciples* of Gandhi⟩. **Partisan** suggests a zealous often prejudiced attachment ⟨*partisans* of the President⟩.

foment see INCITE

foolhardy see ADVENTUROUS

foolish see SIMPLE

forbearing, tolerant, lenient, indulgent mean not inclined to be severe or rigorous. **Forbearing** implies patience under provocation and deliberate abstention from harsh judgment, punishment, or vengeance ⟨the most *forbearing* of music teachers⟩. **Tolerant** implies a freedom from bias or dogmatism and a reluctance to judge others esp. harshly ⟨a very *tolerant* attitude towards drug users⟩. **Lenient** implies softness of temperament and a relaxation of discipline ⟨*lenient* parents pay for it later⟩. **Indulgent** implies compliancy, mercifulness, and a willingness to make concessions ⟨a wife *indulgent* of her husband's shortcomings⟩.

forbid, prohibit, interdict, inhibit mean to debar one from doing something or to order that something not be done. **Forbid** implies that the order is from one in authority and that obedience is expected ⟨smoking is *forbidden* in the building⟩. **Prohibit** suggests the issuing of laws, statutes, or regulations ⟨*prohibited* the manufacture and sale of unapproved drugs⟩. **Interdict** implies prohibition by civil or ecclesiastical authority usu. for a given time or a declared purpose ⟨*interdicted* the administration of the sacraments to proabortionists⟩. **Inhibit** implies the imposition of restraints or restrictions that amount to prohibitions, not only by authority but also by the exigencies of the time or situation ⟨laws that *inhibit* the growth of free trade⟩.

force *vb* Force, compel, coerce, constrain, oblige mean to make someone or something yield. **Force** is the general term and implies the overcoming of resistance by the exertion of strength, power, weight, stress, or duress ⟨*forced* the prisoner to sign the confession⟩. **Compel** typically requires a personal object and suggests the working of an irresistible force ⟨all workers are *compelled* to pay taxes⟩. **Coerce** suggests overcoming resistance or unwillingness by actual or threatened violence or pressure ⟨*coerced* by gangsters into selling his business⟩. **Constrain** suggests the effect of a force or circumstance that limits freedom of action or choice ⟨*constrained* by my conscience to see that justice was done⟩. **Oblige** implies the constraint of necessity, law, or duty ⟨I am *obliged* to inform you of your rights⟩.

force *n* see POWER

foreboding see APPREHENSION

forecast see FORETELL

foregoing see PRECEDING

foreign see EXTRINSIC

foreknow see FORESEE

forerunner, precursor, harbinger, herald mean one who goes before or announces the coming of another. **Forerunner** is applicable to anything that serves as a sign or presage ⟨the international incident was a *forerunner* to war⟩. **Pre-**

cursor applies to a person or thing paving the way for the success or accomplishment of another 〈18th century poets who were *precursors* of the Romantics〉. **Harbinger** and **herald** both apply, chiefly figuratively, to one that proclaims or announces the coming or arrival of a notable event 〈an early victory that was the *harbinger* of a winning season〉 〈the *herald* of a new age in medical science〉.

foresee, foreknow, divine, apprehend, anticipate mean to know beforehand. **Foresee** implies nothing about how the knowledge is derived and may apply to ordinary reasoning and experience 〈no one could *foresee* the economic crisis〉. **Foreknow** usu. implies supernatural assistance, as through revelation 〈if only we could *foreknow* our own destinies〉. **Divine** adds to *foresee* the suggestion of exceptional wisdom or discernment 〈a European traveler who *divined* the course of American destiny〉. **Apprehend** implies foresight mingled with uncertainly, anxiety, or dread 〈*apprehended* that his odd behavior was a sign of a troubled soul〉. **Anticipate** implies taking action about or responding emotionally to something before it happens 〈the servants *anticipated* our every need〉.

forestall see PREVENT

foretaste see PROSPECT

foretell, predict, forecast, prophesy, prognosticate mean to tell beforehand. **Foretell** applies to the telling of the coming of a future event by any procedure or any source of information 〈seers *foretold* of calamitous events〉. **Predict** commonly implies inference from facts or accepted laws of nature 〈astronomers *predicted* the return of the comet〉. **Forecast** adds the implication of anticipating eventualities and differs from *predict* in being usu. concerned with probabilities rather than certainties 〈*forecasted* a snowfall of six inches〉. **Prophesy** connotes inspired or mystic knowledge

of the future esp. as the fulfilling of divine threats or promises ⟨preachers *prophesying* a day of divine retribution⟩.
Prognosticate suggests the learned or skilled interpretation
of signs or symptoms ⟨economists are *prognosticating* a
slow recovery⟩.

forge see MAKE

forget see NEGLECT

forgetful, oblivious, unmindful mean losing one's memory
or knowledge of something. **Forgetful** usu. implies a heedless or negligent habit of failing to keep in mind ⟨I had
been *forgetful* of my duties as host⟩. **Oblivious** suggests a
failure to notice or remember due to external causes or
conditions or to a determination to ignore ⟨lost in thought,
oblivious to the rushing crowd around her⟩. **Unmindful**
may suggest inattention and heedlessness or a deliberate
ignoring ⟨a crusading reformer who was *unmindful* of his
family's needs⟩.

forgive see EXCUSE

forlorn see ALONE

form *n* Form, figure, shape, conformation, configuration
mean outward appearance. **Form** usu. suggests reference to
both internal structure and external outline and often the
principle that gives unity to the whole ⟨an architect who
appreciates the interplay of *forms*⟩. **Figure** applies chiefly
to the form as determined by bounding or enclosing lines
⟨cutting doll *figures* out of paper⟩. **Shape** like *figure,* suggests an outline but carries a stronger implication of the
enclosed body or mass ⟨the *shape* of the monument was
pyramidal⟩. **Conformation** implies structure composed of
related parts ⟨a body *conformation* that is well-propor-
tioned and symmetrical⟩. **Configuration** refers to the disposition and arrangement of component parts ⟨modular
furniture allows for a number of *configurations*⟩.

form *vb* see MAKE
formal see CEREMONIAL
former see PRECEDING
fornication see ADULTERY
forsake see ABANDON
forswear see ABJURE
fortuitous see ACCIDENTAL
fortunate see LUCKY
forward see ADVANCE
foul see DIRTY
foxy see SLY

fragile, frangible, brittle, crisp, friable mean breaking easily. **Fragile** implies extreme delicacy of material or construction and need for careful handling ⟨a *fragile* antique chair⟩. **Frangible** implies susceptibility to being broken without implying weakness or delicacy ⟨*frangible* stone used as paving material⟩. **Brittle** implies hardness together with lack of elasticity or flexibility or toughness ⟨elderly patients with *brittle* bones⟩. **Crisp** implies a firmness and brittleness desirable esp. in some foods ⟨*crisp* lettuce⟩. **Friable** applies to substances that are easily crumbled or pulverized ⟨*friable* soil⟩. See in addition WEAK.

fragment see PART

fragrance, perfume, scent, incense, redolence mean a sweet or pleasant odor. **Fragrance** suggests the odors of flowers or other growing things ⟨household cleansers with the *fragrance* of pine⟩. **Perfume** may suggest a stronger or heavier odor and applies esp. to a prepared or synthetic liquid ⟨the *perfume* of lilacs filled the room⟩. **Scent** is very close to *perfume* but of wider application because more neutral in connotation ⟨furniture polish with a fresh lemon *scent*⟩. **Incense** applies to the smoke from burning spices and gums and suggests an esp. pleasing odor ⟨the odor of *in-*

cense permeated the temple⟩. **Redolence** implies a mixture
of fragrant or pungent odors ⟨the *redolence* of a forest after
a rain⟩.

fragrant see ODOROUS

frail see WEAK

frailty see FAULT

frangible see FRAGILE

frank, candid, open, plain mean showing willingness to tell
what one feels or thinks. **Frank** stresses lack of shyness or
secretiveness or of evasiveness from considerations of tact
or expedience ⟨*frank* discussions on arms control⟩. **Candid**
suggests expression marked by sincerity and honesty esp.
in offering unwelcome criticism or opinion ⟨a *candid* appraisal of her singing ability⟩. **Open** implies frankness but
suggests more indiscretion than *frank* and less earnestness
than *candid* ⟨young children are *open* and artless in saying
what they think⟩. **Plain** suggests outspokenness and freedom from affectation or subtlety in expression ⟨was very
plain about telling them to leave⟩.

fraud see DECEPTION, IMPOSTURE

free *adj* **Free, independent, sovereign, autonomous** mean not
subject to the rule or control of another. **Free** stresses the
complete absence of external rule and the full right to
make all of one's own decisions ⟨you're *free* to do as you
like⟩. **Independent** implies a standing alone; applied to a
state it implies lack of connection with any other having
power to interfere with its citizens, laws, or policies ⟨the
struggle for Ireland to become *independent*⟩. **Sovereign**
stresses the absence of a superior power and implies supremacy within a thing's own domain or sphere ⟨a *sovereign* nation not subject to the laws of another⟩. **Autonomous** stresses independence in matters pertaining to self-

government ⟨a credible investigating committee must be *autonomous*⟩.

free *vb* Free, release, liberate, emancipate, manumit mean to set loose from restraint or constraint. **Free** implies a usu. permanent removal from whatever binds, confines, entangles, or oppresses ⟨*freed* the animals from their cages⟩. **Release** suggests a setting loose from confinement, restraint, or a state of pressure or tension, often without implication of permanent liberation ⟨*released* his anger by exercising⟩. **Liberate** stresses particularly the resulting state of liberty ⟨*liberated* the novel from Victorian inhibitions⟩. **Emancipate** implies the liberation of a person from subjection or domination ⟨labor-saving devices that *emancipated* women from housework⟩. **Manumit** implies emancipation from slavery ⟨the proclamation *manumitted* the slaves⟩.

freedom, liberty, license mean the power or condition of acting without compulsion. **Freedom** has a broad range of application from total absence of restraint to merely a sense of not being unduly hampered or frustrated ⟨*freedom* of the press⟩. **Liberty** suggests release from former restraint or compulsion ⟨the prisoners were willing to fight for their *liberty*⟩. **License** implies freedom specially granted or conceded and may connote an abuse of freedom ⟨the editorial takes considerable *license* with the facts⟩.

fresh see NEW

friable see FRAGILE

friendly see AMICABLE

fright see FEAR

frivolity see LIGHTNESS

frown, scowl, glower, lower mean to put on a dark or threatening face or appearance. **Frown** implies conveying disapproval or displeasure by contracting the brows ⟨the teachers *frowned* on my boyish pranks⟩. **Scowl** suggests a similar facial expression but conveying rather a bad humor, sullenness, or resentful puzzlement ⟨a grumpy old man who *scowled* habitually⟩. **Glower** implies direct staring or glaring as in contempt or defiance ⟨the natives merely *glowered* at the invading tourists⟩. **Lower** suggests a menacing blackness or gloomy anger ⟨*lowered* as he went about his work, never uttering a word⟩.

frugal see SPARING

fruitful see FERTILE

fruitless see FUTILE

frustrate, thwart, foil, baffle, balk, circumvent, outwit mean to check or defeat another's plan or goal. **Frustrate** implies making vain or ineffectual all efforts however vigorous or persistent ⟨*frustrated* all attempts at government reform⟩. **Thwart** suggests frustration or checking by deliberately crossing or opposing ⟨the park department is *thwarted* by public indifference to littering⟩. **Foil** implies checking or defeating so as to discourage further effort ⟨her parents *foiled* my efforts to see her⟩. **Baffle** implies frustration by confusing or puzzling ⟨*baffled* by the maze of rules and regulations⟩. **Balk** suggests the interposing of obstacles or hindrances ⟨legal restrictions *balked* police efforts to control crime⟩. **Circumvent** implies frustration by a particular stratagem ⟨*circumvented* the law by finding loopholes⟩. **Outwit** suggests craft and cunning ⟨the rebels *outwitted* the army repeatedly⟩.

fugitive see TRANSIENT

fulfill see PERFORM

full, complete, plenary, replete mean containing all that is wanted or needed or possible. **Full** implies the presence or inclusion of everything that is wanted or required by something or that can be held, contained, or attained by it ⟨a *full* schedule of appointments⟩. **Complete** applies when all that is needed is present ⟨the report does not give a *complete* picture of the situation⟩. **Plenary** adds to *complete* the implication of fullness without qualification ⟨given *plenary* power as commander in chief⟩. **Replete** implies being filled to the brim or to satiety ⟨a speech *replete* with innuendos and half-truths⟩.

fulsome, oily, unctuous, oleaginous mean too obviously extravagant to be genuine or sincere. **Fulsome** implies that something which is essentially good has been carried to an excessive and tasteless degree ⟨the *fulsome* flattery of a celebrity interviewer⟩. **Oily** implies an offensively ingratiating quality and sometimes suggests a suavity or benevolence that masks a sinister intent ⟨*oily* land developers trying to persuade older residents to sell⟩. **Unctuous** implies the hypocritical adoption of a grave, devout, or spiritual manner ⟨the *unctuous* pleading of the First Amendment by pornographers⟩. **Oleaginous** may be used in place of *oily* to suggest even greater pomposity ⟨an *oleaginous* maître d' fawning over the female diners⟩.

fun, jest, sport, game, play mean action or speech that provides amusement or arouses laughter. **Fun** usu. implies laughter or gaiety but may imply merely a lack of serious or ulterior purpose ⟨played cards just for *fun*⟩. **Jest** implies lack of earnestness in what is said or done and may suggest a hoaxing or teasing ⟨took seriously remarks said only in *jest*⟩. **Sport** applies esp. to the arousing of laughter against someone ⟨teasing begun in *sport* ended in an ugly brawl⟩. **Game** is close to *sport,* and often stresses mischievous or malicious fun ⟨habitually made *game* of their poor relations⟩. **Play** stresses the opposition to *earnest* without implying any element of malice or mischief ⟨pretended to strangle his wife in *play*⟩.

function, office, duty, province mean the acts or operations expected of a person or thing. **Function** implies a definite end or purpose that the one in question serves or a particular kind of work it is intended to perform ⟨the *function* of the stomach is to digest food⟩. **Office** is typically applied to the function or service expected of a person by reason of his trade or profession or his special relationship to others ⟨exercised the *offices* of both attorney and friend⟩. **Duty** applies to a task or responsibility imposed by one's occupation, rank, status, or calling ⟨the lieutenant governor had few official *duties*⟩. **Province** applies to a function, office, or duty that naturally or logically falls to one ⟨it is not the governor's *province* to set foreign policy⟩.

fundamental see ESSENTIAL

furnish, equip, outfit, appoint, accoutre, arm mean to supply one with what is needed. **Furnish** implies the provision of any or all essentials for performing a function ⟨a sparsely *furnished* apartment⟩. **Equip** suggests the provision of something making for efficiency in action or use ⟨a fully *equipped* kitchen with every modern appliance⟩. **Outfit** implies provision of a complete list or set of articles as for a journey, an expedition, or a special occupation ⟨*outfitted* the whole family for a ski trip⟩. **Appoint** implies provision of complete and usu. elegant or elaborate equipment or furnishings ⟨a lavishly *appointed* penthouse apartment⟩. **Accoutre** suggests the supplying of personal dress or equipment for a special activity ⟨the fully *accoutred* members of a polar expedition⟩. **Arm** implies provision for effective action or operation esp. in war ⟨*armed* to the teeth⟩.

further see ADVANCE

furtive see SECRET

fury see ANGER

fuse see MIX

fusty see MALODOROUS

futile, vain, fruitless mean producing no result. **Futile** may connote completeness of failure or unwisdom of undertaking ⟨a *futile* search for survivors of the crash⟩. **Vain** usu. implies simple failure to achieve a desired result ⟨a *vain* attempt to get the car started⟩. **Fruitless** comes close to *vain* but often suggests long and arduous effort or severe disappointment ⟨*fruitless* efforts to obtain a lasting peace⟩.

G

gain see GET
gainsay see DENY
gall see TEMERITY
gallant see CIVIL
gallantry see HEROISM
game see FUN
gamut see RANGE
gape see GAZE
garish see GAUDY
garnish see ADORN
garrulous see TALKATIVE
gastronome see EPICURE
gather, collect, assemble, congregate mean to come or bring together into a group, mass, or unit. **Gather** is the most general term for bringing or coming together from a spread-out or scattered state ⟨a crowd *gathers* whenever there is excitement⟩. **Collect** often implies careful selection or orderly arrangement ⟨*collected* books on gardening⟩. **Assemble** implies an ordered union or organization of persons or things often for a definite purpose ⟨the country's leading experts on aeronautics *assembled* under one roof⟩. **Congregate** implies a spontaneous flocking together into a

crowd or huddle ⟨persons were forbidden to *congregate* under martial law⟩. See in addition INFER.

gauche see AWKWARD

gaudy, tawdry, garish, flashy, meretricious mean vulgarly or cheaply showy. **Gaudy** implies a tasteless use of overly bright, often clashing colors or excessive ornamentation ⟨circus performers in *gaudy* costumes⟩. **Tawdry** applies to what is at once gaudy and cheap and sleazy ⟨*tawdry* saloons along the waterfront⟩. **Garish** describes what is distressingly or offensively bright ⟨*garish* signs along the commercial strip⟩. **Flashy** implies an effect of brilliance quickly and easily seen to be shallow or vulgar ⟨a *flashy* nightclub act with leggy chorus girls⟩. **Meretricious** stresses falsity and may describe a tawdry show that beckons with a false allure or promise ⟨a *meretricious* wasteland of casinos and bars⟩.

gauge see STANDARD

gaunt see LEAN

gay see LIVELY

gaze, gape, stare, glare, peer mean to look (at) long and attentively. **Gaze** implies fixed and prolonged attention (as in wonder, admiration, or abstractedness) ⟨*gazing* at the waves breaking along the shore⟩. **Gape** suggests an open-mouthed often stupid wonder ⟨a crowd *gaped* at the man threatening to jump⟩. **Stare** implies a direct open-eyed gazing denoting curiosity, disbelief, or insolence ⟨kept *staring* at them as they tried to eat⟩. **Glare** is a fierce or angry staring ⟨silently *glared* back at her accusers⟩. **Peer** suggests a looking narrowly and curiously as if through a small opening ⟨*peered* at the bird through his binoculars⟩.

general see UNIVERSAL

generic see UNIVERSAL

generous see LIBERAL

genial see GRACIOUS
genius see GIFT
gentry see ARISTOCRACY
genuine see AUTHENTIC
germane see RELEVANT
get, obtain, procure, secure, acquire, gain, win, earn mean to
come into possession of. **Get** is a very general term and
may or may not imply effort or initiative ⟨*got* a car for my
birthday⟩. **Obtain** suggests the attainment of something
sought for with some expenditure of time and effort ⟨*obtained* statements from all of the witnesses⟩. **Procure** implies effort in obtaining something for oneself or for another ⟨in charge of *procuring* supplies for the office⟩.
Secure implies difficulty in obtaining and keeping in possession or under one's control ⟨an ad agency that *secured*
many top accounts⟩. **Acquire** often suggests an addition to
what is already possessed ⟨*acquired* a greater appreciation
of music⟩. **Gain** suggests struggle and usu. value in the
thing obtained ⟨gradually *gained* a reputation as a skilled
musician⟩. **Win** suggests favoring qualities or circumstances playing a part in the gaining ⟨*won* the admiration
of his fellow actors⟩. **Earn** implies a correspondence between the effort and what one gets by effort ⟨a compelling
performance that *earned* her many awards⟩.
ghastly, grisly, gruesome, macabre, lurid mean horrifying
and repellent in appearance or aspect. **Ghastly** suggests the
terrifying aspects of corpses and ghosts ⟨a *ghastly* portrait
of life after a nuclear war⟩. **Grisly** and **gruesome** suggest
additionally the results of extreme violence or cruelty ⟨the
case of an unusually *grisly* murder⟩ ⟨the *gruesome* history
of the Nazi death camps⟩. **Macabre** implies a morbid
preoccupation with the physical aspects of death ⟨a *macabre* tale of premature burial⟩. **Lurid** adds to *gruesome*

the suggestion of shuddering fascination with violent death and esp. with murder ⟨the tabloids wallowed in the crime's *lurid* details⟩.

gibe see SCOFF

gift, faculty, aptitude, bent, talent, genius, knack mean a special ability for doing something. **Gift** often implies special favor by God or nature ⟨the *gift* of a beautiful singing voice⟩. **Faculty** applies to an innate or less often acquired ability for a particular accomplishment or function ⟨a rare *faculty* for remembering people's names⟩. **Aptitude** implies a natural liking for some activity and the likelihood of success in it ⟨a boy with a definite mechanical *aptitude*⟩. **Bent** is nearly equal to *aptitude* but it stresses inclination perhaps more than specific ability ⟨a family that has always had an artistic *bent*⟩. **Talent** suggests a marked natural ability that needs to be developed ⟨allowed her dancing *talent* to go to waste⟩. **Genius** suggests impressive inborn creative ability ⟨the *genius* of Mozart⟩. **Knack** implies a comparatively minor but special ability making for ease and dexterity in performance ⟨has the *knack* for making swift, cutting retorts⟩.

gigantic see ENORMOUS

give, present, donate, bestow, confer, afford mean to convey to another as his possession. **Give,** the general term, is applicable to any passing over of anything by any means ⟨*give* alms⟩ ⟨*give* a boy a ride on a pony⟩ ⟨*give* my love to your mother⟩. **Present** carries a note of formality and ceremony ⟨*present* an award⟩ ⟨*presented* him the keys to the city⟩. **Donate** is likely to imply a publicized giving (as to charity) ⟨*donate* a piano to the orphanage⟩. **Bestow** implies the conveying of something as a gift and may suggest condescension on the part of the giver ⟨*bestow* unwanted advice⟩. **Confer** implies a gracious giving (as of a favor or honor) ⟨the Pope *conferred* the rank of cardinal on three bishops⟩. **Afford** implies a giving or bestowing usu. as a natural or legitimate consequence of the character of the giver ⟨the trees *afforded* us a welcome shade⟩ ⟨a development that *affords* us some hope⟩.

glance see FLASH

glare see GAZE

glaring see FLAGRANT

gleam see FLASH

glee see MIRTH

glimmer see FLASH

glint see FLASH

glisten see FLASH

glitter see FLASH

gloom see SADNESS

gloomy see DARK, SULLEN

glorious see SPLENDID

glossy see SLEEK

glower see FROWN

glum see SULLEN

glut see SATIATE

gluttonous see VORACIOUS

goad see MOTIVE

goal see INTENTION

good-natured see AMIABLE

gorge see SATIATE

gorgeous see SPLENDID

gory see BLOODY

gourmet see EPICURE

govern, rule mean to exercise power or authority in controlling others. **Govern** implies the aim of keeping in a straight course or smooth operation for the good of the individual and the whole ⟨the British monarch reigns, but the prime minister *governs*⟩. **Rule** may imply no more than laying down laws or issuing commands that must be obeyed but often suggests the exercise of despotic or arbitrary power ⟨the emperor *ruled* with an iron hand⟩.

grab see TAKE

grace see MERCY

gracious, cordial, affable, genial, sociable mean markedly pleasant and easy in social intercourse. **Gracious** implies courtesy and kindly consideration ⟨her *gracious* acceptance of the award⟩. **Cordial** stresses warmth and heartiness ⟨our *cordial* host greeted us at the door⟩. **Affable** implies easy approachability and readiness to respond pleasantly to conversation or requests or proposals ⟨the dean of students was surprisingly *affable*⟩. **Genial** stresses cheerfulness and even joviality ⟨the emcee must be a *genial* extrovert⟩. **Sociable** suggests a genuine liking for the companionship of others ⟨*sociable* people enjoying an ocean cruise⟩.

grand, magnificent, imposing, stately, majestic, grandiose mean large and impressive. **Grand** adds to greatness of size the implications of handsomeness and dignity ⟨a mansion with a *grand* staircase⟩. **Magnificent** implies an impressive largeness proportionate to scale without sacrifice of dignity or good taste ⟨*magnificent* paintings and tapestries⟩. **Imposing** implies great size and dignity but esp. stresses impressiveness ⟨large, *imposing* buildings line the avenue⟩. **Stately** may suggest poised dignity, erectness of bearing, handsomeness of proportions, ceremonious deliberation of movement ⟨the *stately* procession proceeded into the cathedral⟩. **Majestic** combines the implications of *imposing* and *stately* and usu. adds a suggestion of solemn grandeur ⟨a *majestic* waterfall⟩. **Grandiose** implies a size or scope exceeding ordinary experience but is most commonly applied derogatorily to inflated pretension or absurd exaggeration ⟨*grandiose* schemes of world conquest⟩.

grandiose see GRAND

grant, concede, vouchsafe, accord, award mean to give as a favor or a right. **Grant** implies giving to a claimant or petitioner something that could be withheld ⟨*granted* them another month to finish the work⟩. **Concede** implies yielding something reluctantly in response to a rightful or compelling claim ⟨even her critics *concede* she can be charming⟩. **Vouchsafe** implies granting something as a courtesy or an act of gracious condescension ⟨the star refused to *vouchsafe* an interview⟩. **Accord** implies giving to another what is due or proper ⟨*accorded* all the honors befitting a head of state⟩. **Award** implies giving what is deserved or merited usu. after a careful weighing of pertinent factors ⟨*awarded* the company a huge defense contract⟩.

graphic, vivid, picturesque, pictorial mean giving a clear visual impression in words. **Graphic** stresses the evoking of a clear lifelike picture ⟨a *graphic* account of his combat experiences⟩. **Vivid** suggests an impressing on the mind the vigorous aliveness of something ⟨a *vivid* re-creation of an exciting period in history⟩. **Picturesque** suggests the presentation of a striking or effective picture composed of features notable for their distinctness and charm ⟨Dickens is famous for his *picturesque* characters⟩. **Pictorial** implies representation in the manner of painting with emphasis upon colors, shapes, and spatial relations ⟨a *pictorial* style of poetry marked by precise, developed imagery⟩.

grasp see TAKE

grasping see COVETOUS

gratuitous see SUPEREROGATORY

grave see SERIOUS

greedy see COVETOUS

grief see SORROW

grievance see INJUSTICE

grill see AFFLICT

grind see WORK

grisly see GHASTLY

gross see COARSE, FLAGRANT

grotesque see FANTASTIC

grudge see MALICE

gruesome see GHASTLY

gruff see BLUFF

guard see DEFEND

guess see CONJECTURE

guide, lead, steer, pilot, engineer mean to direct in a course or show the way to be followed. **Guide** implies intimate knowledge of the way and of all its difficulties and dangers ⟨*guided* the other scouts through the darkened cave⟩. **Lead** implies a going ahead to show the way and often to keep those that follow under control and in order ⟨the flagship *led* the fleet⟩. **Steer** implies an ability to keep to a chosen course and stresses the capacity of maneuvering correctly ⟨*steered* the ship through the narrow channel⟩. **Pilot** suggests guidance over a dangerous, intricate, or complicated course ⟨successfully *piloted* the bill through the Senate⟩. **Engineer** implies guidance by one who finds ways to avoid or overcome difficulties in achieving an end or carrying out a plan ⟨*engineered* his son's election to the governorship⟩.

guilty see BLAMEWORTHY

gull see DUPE

gumption see SENSE

H

habit, practice, usage, custom, wont mean a way of acting
fixed through repetition. **Habit** implies a doing unconsciously and often compulsively ⟨the *habit* of constantly
tapping his fingers⟩. **Practice** suggests an act or method followed with regularity and usu. through choice ⟨our *practice* is to honor all major credit cards⟩. **Usage** suggests a
customary action so generally followed that it has become
a social norm ⟨western-style dress is now common *usage*
in international business⟩. **Custom** applies to a practice or
usage so steadily associated with an individual or group as
to have almost the force of unwritten law ⟨the *custom* of
mourners wearing black at funerals⟩. **Wont** usu. applies to
an habitual manner, method, or practice distinguishing an
individual or group ⟨as was her *wont,* she slept until
noon⟩.

habitual see USUAL

hackneyed see TRITE

hale see HEALTHY

hallow see DEVOTE

hamper, trammel, clog, fetter, shackle, manacle mean to
hinder or impede in moving, progressing, or acting. **Hamper** may imply the effect of any impeding or restraining
influence ⟨*hampered* the investigation by refusing to co-
operate⟩. **Trammel** suggests entangling by or confining
within a net ⟨rules that serve only to *trammel* the artist's
creativity⟩. **Clog** usu. implies a slowing by something extraneous or encumbering ⟨feels that free enterprise is
clogged by government regulation⟩. **Fetter** suggests a restraining so severe that freedom to move or progress is al-

most lost ⟨a nation that is *fettered* by an antiquated class system⟩. **Shackle** and **manacle** are stronger than *fetter* and suggest total loss of freedom ⟨a mind *shackled* by stubborn pride and prejudice⟩ ⟨hatred can *manacle* the soul⟩.

handle, manipulate, wield mean to manage dexterously or efficiently. **Handle** implies directing an acquired skill to the accomplishment of immediate ends ⟨*handled* the crisis with cool efficiency⟩. **Manipulate** implies adroit handling and in extended use often suggests the use of craft or of fraud ⟨brutally *manipulates* other people for his own selfish ends⟩. **Wield** implies mastery and vigor in handling a tool or a weapon or in exerting influence, authority, or power ⟨the news media *wield* a tremendous influence on the electorate⟩.

handsome see BEAUTIFUL

hanker see LONG

haphazard see RANDOM

happy see FIT, LUCKY

harass see WORRY

harbinger see FORERUNNER

hard, difficult, arduous mean demanding great exertion or effort. **Hard** implies the opposite of all that is easy ⟨farming is *hard* work⟩. **Difficult** implies the presence of obstacles to be surmounted or puzzles to be resolved and suggests the need of skill, patience, or courage ⟨a *difficult* decision requiring much thought and courage⟩. **Arduous** stresses the need of laborious and persevering exertion ⟨the *arduous* task of rebuilding the town⟩. See in addition FIRM.

hardihood see TEMERITY

harm see INJURE

harmony, accord, concord mean the state resulting when different things come together without clashing or disagreement. **Harmony** implies a beautiful effect achieved by the agreeable blending or arrangement of parts ⟨a resort in splendid *harmony* with its natural setting⟩. **Accord** may imply personal agreement or goodwill or the absence of friction ⟨parents and teachers are in *accord* on this issue⟩. **Concord** adds to *accord* additional implications of peace and amity ⟨a planned utopian community in which all would live in *concord*⟩.

harry see WORRY

harsh see ROUGH

haste, hurry, speed, expedition, dispatch mean quickness in movement or action. **Haste** applies to personal action and implies urgency and precipitancy and often rashness ⟨why this headlong *haste* to get married?⟩. **Hurry** often has a strong suggestion of agitated bustle or confusion ⟨in the *hurry* of departure she forgot her toothbrush⟩. **Speed** suggests swift efficiency in movement or action ⟨exercises to increase your reading *speed*⟩. **Expedition** and **dispatch** both imply speed and efficiency in handling affairs but *expedition* stresses ease or efficiency of performance and *dispatch* carries a stronger suggestion of promptness in bringing matters to a conclusion ⟨with surprising *expedition* the case came to trial⟩ ⟨regularly paid her bills with the greatest possible *dispatch*⟩.

hasty see FAST

hate, detest, abhor, abominate, loathe mean to feel strong aversion or intense dislike for. **Hate** implies an emotional aversion often coupled with enmity or malice ⟨*hated* his former friend with a passion⟩. **Detest** suggests violent antipathy ⟨I *detest* moral cowards⟩. **Abhor** implies a deep often shuddering repugnance ⟨child abuse is a crime *abhorred* by all⟩. **Abominate** suggests strong detestation and often moral condemnation ⟨virtually every society *abominates* incest⟩. **Loathe** implies utter disgust and intolerance ⟨*loathed* self-appointed moral guardians⟩.

hateful, odious, abhorrent, detestable, abominable mean deserving of or arousing intense dislike. **Hateful** applies to something or someone that arouses active hatred and hostility ⟨the *hateful* crime of child abuse⟩. **Odious** applies to that which arouses offense or repugnance ⟨you apparently find the plain truth *odious*⟩. **Abhorrent** characterizes that which outrages a sense of what is right, decent, just, or honorable ⟨the *abhorrent* practice of stereotyping minority groups⟩. **Detestable** suggests something deserving extreme contempt ⟨his *detestable* habit of passing the blame to subordinates⟩. **Abominable** suggests something fiercely condemned as vile or unnatural ⟨the *abominable* living conditions of the plantation slaves⟩.

haughty see PROUD

haul see PULL

have, hold, own, possess mean to keep, control, retain, or experience as one's own. **Have** is a general term carrying no specific implication ⟨they *have* plenty of money⟩. **Hold** suggests stronger control, grasp, or retention ⟨*held* absolute power over the whole country⟩. **Own** implies a natural or legal right to hold as one's property and under one's full control ⟨*own* property in several states⟩. **Possess** is often the preferred term when referring to an intangible (as a characteristic, a power, or a quality) ⟨*possesses* a first-rate intellect⟩.

hazardous see DANGEROUS

headlong see PRECIPITATE

headstrong see UNRULY

heal see CURE

healthful, wholesome, salubrious, salutary mean favorable to the health of mind or body. **Healthful** implies a positive contribution to a healthy condition ⟨a *healthful* diet will provide more energy⟩. **Wholesome** applies to what benefits, builds up, or sustains physically, mentally, or spiritually ⟨*wholesome* foods⟩ ⟨the movie is *wholesome* family entertainment⟩. **Salubrious** applies chiefly to the helpful effects of climate or air ⟨the *salubrious* climate of the American Southwest⟩. **Salutary** describes something corrective or beneficially effective, even though it may in itself be unpleasant ⟨a *salutary* warning that resulted in increased production⟩.

healthy, sound, wholesome, robust, hale, well mean enjoying or indicative of good health. **Healthy** implies full strength and vigor as well as freedom from signs of disease ⟨the doctor pronounced the whole family *healthy*⟩. **Sound** emphasizes the absence of disease, weakness, or malfunction ⟨an examination showed his heart to be *sound*⟩. **Wholesome** implies appearance and behavior indicating soundness and balance ⟨she looks especially *wholesome* in her tennis togs⟩. **Robust** implies the opposite of all that is delicate or sickly ⟨a lively, *robust* little boy⟩. **Hale** applies particularly to robustness in old age ⟨still *hale* at the age of eighty⟩. **Well** implies merely freedom from disease or illness ⟨she has never been a *well* person⟩.

hearten see ENCOURAGE

heartfelt see SINCERE

hearty see SINCERE

heave see LIFT

heavy, weighty, ponderous, cumbrous, cumbersome mean having great weight. **Heavy** implies that something has greater density or thickness than the average of its kind or class ⟨a *heavy* child for his age⟩. **Weighty** suggests having actual and not just relative weight ⟨really *weighty* parcels are shipped by freight⟩. **Ponderous** implies having great weight because of size and massiveness with resulting great inertia ⟨*ponderous* galleons were outmaneuvered by smaller vessels⟩. **Cumbrous** and **cumbersome** imply heaviness and bulkiness that make for difficulty in grasping, moving, carrying, or manipulating ⟨abandoned the *cumbrous* furniture rather than move it⟩ ⟨the old cameras were *cumbersome* and inconvenient⟩.

heckle see BAIT

hector see BAIT

height, altitude, elevation mean vertical distance either between the top and bottom of something or between a base and something above it. **Height** refers to something measured vertically whether high or low ⟨a wall two meters in *height*⟩. **Altitude** and **elevation** apply to height as measured by angular measurement or atmospheric pressure; *altitude* is preferable when referring to vertical distance above the surface of the earth or above sea level; *elevation* is used esp. in reference to vertical height on land ⟨fly at an *altitude* of 10,000 meters⟩ ⟨Denver is a city with a high *elevation*⟩.

heighten see INTENSIFY

heinous see OUTRAGEOUS

help, aid, assist mean to supply what is needed to accomplish an end. **Help** carries a strong implication of advance toward an objective ⟨*helped* to find a cure for the disease⟩. **Aid** suggests the evident need of help or relief and so imputes weakness to the one aided and strength to the one aiding ⟨an army of volunteers *aided* the flood victims⟩. **Assist** suggests a secondary role in the assistant or a subordinate character in the assistance ⟨*assisted* the chief surgeon during the operation⟩.

help see IMPROVE

herald see FORERUNNER

hereditary see INNATE

heroism, valor, prowess, gallantry mean courageous behavior esp. in conflict. **Heroism** implies superlative courage esp. in fulfilling a high purpose against odds ⟨the boy's outstanding act of *heroism* during the fire⟩. **Valor** implies illustrious bravery and audacity in fighting ⟨awarded the army's highest honor for *valor* in battle⟩. **Prowess** stresses skill as well as bravery ⟨demonstrated his manly *prowess* in hunting⟩. **Gallantry** implies dash and spirit as well as courage and gay indifference to danger or hardship ⟨special forces with a proud tradition of *gallantry*⟩.

hesitant see DISINCLINED

hesitate, waver, vacillate, falter mean to show irresolution or uncertainty. **Hesitate** implies a pause before deciding or acting or choosing ⟨*hesitated* before answering the question⟩. **Waver** implies hesitation after seeming to decide and so connotes weakness or a retreat ⟨*wavered* in his support of the rebels⟩. **Vacillate** implies prolonged hesitation from inability to reach a firm decision ⟨*vacillated* until it was too late and events were out of control⟩. **Falter** implies a wavering or stumbling and often nervousness, lack of courage, or outright fear ⟨never once *faltered* during her testimony⟩.

hide, conceal, screen, secrete, bury mean to withhold or withdraw from sight. **Hide** may or may not suggest intent ⟨*hide* in a closet⟩ ⟨a house *hidden* by trees⟩. **Conceal** usu. does imply intent and often specif. implies a refusal to divulge ⟨*concealed* the weapon in his jacket⟩. **Screen** implies an interposing of something that prevents discovery ⟨*screened* her true identity from her colleagues⟩. **Secrete** suggests a depositing in a place unknown to others ⟨*secreted* the cocaine in the hold of the ship⟩. **Bury** implies covering up so as to hide completely ⟨*buried* the note in a pile of papers⟩.

high, tall, lofty mean above the average in height. **High** implies marked extension upward and is applied chiefly to things which rise from a base or foundation or are placed at a conspicuous height above a lower level ⟨a *high* hill⟩ ⟨a *high* ceiling⟩. **Tall** applies to what grows or rises high by comparison with others of its kind and usu. implies relative narrowness ⟨a *tall* thin man⟩. **Lofty** suggests great or imposing altitude ⟨*lofty* mountain peaks⟩.

hilarity see MIRTH

hinder, impede, obstruct, block mean to interfere with the activity or progress of. **Hinder** stresses causing harmful or annoying delay or interference with progress ⟨the rain *hindered* our climbing⟩. **Impede** implies making forward progress difficult by clogging, hampering, or fettering ⟨too-tight clothing *impeded* my movement⟩. **Obstruct** implies interfering with something in motion or in progress by the sometimes intentional placing of obstacles in the way ⟨the view was *obstructed* by billboards⟩. **Block** implies complete obstruction to passage or progress ⟨boulders *blocked* the road⟩.

hint see SUGGEST

hire, let, lease, rent, charter mean to engage or grant for use at a price. **Hire** and **let,** strictly speaking, are complementary terms, *hire* implying the act of engaging or taking for use and *let* the granting of use ⟨we *hired* a car for the summer⟩ ⟨decided to *let* the cottage to a young couple⟩. **Lease** strictly implies a letting under the terms of a contract but is often applied to hiring on a lease ⟨the diplomat *leased* an apartment for a year⟩. **Rent** stresses the payment of money for the full use of property and may imply either hiring or letting ⟨instead of buying a house, they decided to *rent*⟩ ⟨will not *rent* to families with children⟩. **Charter** applies to the hiring or letting of a vehicle usu. for exclusive use ⟨*charter* a bus to go to the game⟩.

histrionic see DRAMATIC

hoax see DUPE

hoist see LIFT

hold see CONTAIN, HAVE

hollow see VAIN

homage see HONOR

honest see UPRIGHT

honesty, honor, integrity, probity mean uprightness of character or action. **Honesty** implies a refusal to lie, steal, or deceive in any way ⟨a politician of scrupulous *honesty*⟩. **Honor** suggests an active or anxious regard for the standards of one's profession, calling, or position ⟨a keen sense of *honor* in business matters⟩. **Integrity** implies trustworthiness and incorruptibility to a degree that one is incapable of being false to a trust, responsibility, or pledge ⟨her unimpeachable *integrity* as a journalist⟩. **Probity** implies tried and proven honesty or integrity ⟨a judge with a reputation for *probity*⟩.

honor, homage, reverence, deference mean respect and esteem shown to another. **Honor** may apply to the recognition of one's right to great respect or to any expression of such recognition ⟨an *honor* just to be nominated⟩. **Homage** adds the implication of accompanying praise ⟨for centuries dramatists have paid *homage* to Shakespeare⟩. **Reverence** implies profound respect mingled with love, devotion, or awe ⟨have the greatest *reverence* for my father⟩. **Deference** implies a yielding or submitting to another's judgment or preference out of respect or reverence ⟨refused to show any *deference* to senior staffers⟩. See in addition HONESTY.

honorable see UPRIGHT
hope see EXPECT
hopeless see DESPONDENT
horde see CROWD
horrify see DISMAY
hostility see ENMITY
hound see BAIT
huff see OFFENSE
huge see ENORMOUS
humble, meek, modest, lowly mean lacking all signs of pride, aggressiveness, or self-assertiveness. **Humble** may suggest a virtuous absence of pride or vanity or it may suggest undue self-depreciation or humiliation ⟨a quiet life as a simple, *humble* parish priest⟩. **Meek** may suggest mildness or gentleness of temper or it may connote undue submissiveness ⟨the refugees were *meek* and grateful for whatever they got⟩. **Modest** implies a lack of boastfulness or conceit, without any implication of abjectness ⟨sincerely *modest* about her singing talents⟩. **Lowly** may stress lack of pretentiousness ⟨a volunteer willing to accept the *lowliest* hospital duties⟩.
humbug see IMPOSTURE
humid see WET
humiliate see ABASE
humor *vb* see INDULGE
humor *n* see WIT
humorous see WITTY
hunger see LONG
hurl see THROW
hurry see HASTE
hurt see INJURE
hypercritical see CRITICAL
hypothesis, theory, law mean a formula derived by infer-

ence from scientific data that explains a principle operating in nature. **Hypothesis** implies insufficient evidence to provide more than a tentative explanation ⟨an *hypothesis* regarding the extinction of the dinosaurs⟩. **Theory** implies a greater range of evidence and greater likelihood of truth ⟨the *theory* of evolution⟩. **Law** implies a statement of order and relation in nature that has been found to be invariable under the same conditions ⟨the *law* of gravitation⟩.

I

idea, concept, conception, thought, notion, impression mean what exists in the mind as a representation (as of something comprehended) or as a formulation (as of a plan). **Idea** may apply to a mental image or formulation of something seen or known or imagined, to a pure abstraction, or to something assumed or vaguely sensed ⟨a mind filled with innovative *ideas*⟩ ⟨my *idea* of paradise⟩. **Concept** may apply to the idea formed by consideration of instances of a species or genus or, more broadly, to any idea of what a thing ought to be ⟨a society with no *concept* of private property⟩. **Conception** is often interchangeable with *concept;* it may stress the process of imagining or formulating rather than the result ⟨our changing *conception* of what constitutes art⟩. **Thought** is likely to suggest the result of reflecting, reasoning, or meditating rather than imagining ⟨commit your *thoughts* to paper⟩. **Notion** suggests an idea not much resolved by analysis or reflection and may suggest the capricious or accidental ⟨the oddest *notions* fly in and out of her head⟩. **Impression** applies to an idea or notion resulting immediately from some stimulation of the senses 〈the first *impression* is of soaring height〉.

ideal see MODEL

identical see SAME

idle see INACTIVE, VAIN

ignoble see MEAN

ignominy see DISGRACE

ignorant, illiterate, unlettered, untutored, unlearned mean not having knowledge. **Ignorant** may imply a general condition or it may apply to lack of knowledge or awareness of a particular thing 〈an *ignorant* fool〉 〈he's *ignorant* of nuclear physics〉. **Illiterate** applies to either an absolute or a relative inability to read and write 〈much of that country's population is still *illiterate*〉. **Unlettered** implies ignorance of the knowledge gained by reading 〈a literary reference that is meaningless to the *unlettered* 〉. **Untutored** may imply lack of schooling in the arts and ways of civilization 〈strange monuments left by an *untutored* people〉. **Unlearned** suggests ignorance of advanced subjects 〈a poet who speaks to the *unlearned,* common man〉.

ignore see NEGLECT

ill see BAD

illiterate see IGNORANT

illusory see APPARENT

illustration see INSTANCE

illustrious see FAMOUS

ill will see MALICE

imaginary, fanciful, visionary, fantastic, chimerical, quixotic mean unreal or unbelievable. **Imaginary** applies to something which is fictitious and purely the product of one's imagination 〈a chronic sufferer of several *imaginary* illnesses〉. **Fanciful** suggests the free play of the imagination 〈the *fanciful* characters created by Lewis Carroll〉. Visionary stresses impracticality or incapability of realization ⟨*visionary* schemes for creating a rural utopia⟩. **Fantastic** implies incredibility or strangeness beyond belief ⟨a *fantastic* world inhabited by prehistoric monsters⟩. **Chimerical** combines the implication of *visionary* and *fantastic* ⟨*chimerical* plans for restoring the British Empire⟩. **Quixotic** implies a devotion to romantic or chivalrous ideals unrestrained by ordinary prudence and common sense ⟨the *quixotic* notion that absolute equality is attainable⟩.

imagine see THINK

imbibe see ABSORB

imbue see INFUSE

imitate see COPY

immense see ENORMOUS

immoderate see EXCESSIVE

impair see INJURE

impartial see FAIR

impassioned, passionate, ardent, fervent, fervid, perfervid mean showing intense feeling. **Impassioned** implies warmth and intensity without violence and suggests fluent verbal expression ⟨an *impassioned* plea for international understanding⟩. **Passionate** implies great vehemence and often violence and wasteful diffusion of emotion ⟨*passionate* denunciations of American arrogance⟩. **Ardent** implies an intense degree of zeal, devotion, or enthusiasm ⟨an *ardent* admirer of the novels of Jane Austen⟩. **Fervent** stresses sincerity and steadiness of emotional warmth or zeal ⟨*fervent* Christians on a pilgrimage⟩. **Fervid** suggests warmly and spontaneously and often feverishly expressed emotion ⟨*fervid* love letters that suggested mental unbalance⟩. **Perfervid** implies the expression of exaggerated or overwrought feelings ⟨wary of such *perfervid* expressions of selfless patriotism⟩.

impassive, stoic, phlegmatic, apathetic, stolid mean unresponsive to something that might normally excite interest or emotion. **Impassive** stresses the absence of any external sign of emotion in action or facial expression ⟨just sat there with an *impassive* look⟩. **Stoic** implies an apparent indifference to pleasure or esp. to pain often as a matter of principle or self-discipline ⟨remained resolutely *stoic* even in the face of adversity⟩. **Phlegmatic** implies a temperament or constitution hard to arouse ⟨a *phlegmatic* man immune to amorous advances⟩. **Apathetic** may imply a puzzling or deplorable indifference or inertness ⟨charitable appeals met an *apathetic* response⟩. **Stolid** implies an habitual absence of interest, responsiveness, or curiosity ⟨a *stolid* woman, wedded to routine⟩.

impeach see ACCUSE

impede see HINDER

impel see MOVE

imperative see MASTERFUL

imperious see MASTERFUL

impertinent, officious, meddlesome, intrusive, obtrusive mean given to thrusting oneself into the affairs of others. **Impertinent** implies exceeding the bounds of propriety in showing interest or curiosity or in offering advice ⟨a little brat asking *impertinent* questions⟩. **Officious** implies the offering of services or attentions that are unwelcome or annoying ⟨an *officious* salesman followed me outside⟩. **Meddlesome** stresses an annoying and usu. prying interference in others' affairs ⟨*meddlesome* old gossips with nothing to do⟩. **Intrusive** implies a tactless or otherwise objectionable thrusting into others' affairs ⟨an *intrusive* waiter interrupted our conversation⟩. **Obtrusive** stresses improper or offensive conspicuousness of interfering actions ⟨*obtrusive* relatives dictated the wedding arrangements⟩.

imperturbable see COOL

impetuous see PRECIPITATE

implant, inculcate, instill, inseminate, infix mean to introduce into the mind. **Implant** implies teaching that makes for permanence of what is taught ⟨*implanted* an enthusiasm for reading in her students⟩. **Inculcate** implies persistent or repeated efforts to impress on the mind ⟨*inculcated* in him high moral standards⟩. **Instill** stresses gradual, gentle imparting of knowledge over a long period of time ⟨*instill* traditional values in your children⟩. **Inseminate** applies to a sowing of ideas in many minds so that they spread through a class or nation ⟨*inseminated* an unquestioning faith in technology⟩. **Infix** stresses firmly inculcating a habit of thought ⟨*infixed* a chronic cynicism⟩.

implement, tool, instrument, appliance, utensil mean a relatively simple device for performing work. **Implement** may apply to anything necessary to perform a task ⟨lawn and gardening *implements*⟩. **Tool** suggests an implement adapted to facilitate a definite kind or stage of work and suggests the need of skill more strongly than *implement* ⟨a carpenter's *tools*⟩. **Instrument** suggests a device capable of delicate or precise work ⟨the surgeon's *instruments*⟩. **Appliance** refers to a tool or instrument utilizing a power source and suggests portability or temporary attachment ⟨modern *appliances* that take the drudgery out of housework⟩. **Utensil** applies to a device used in domestic work or some routine unskilled activity ⟨knives, graters, and other kitchen *utensils*⟩.

implore see BEG

imply see SUGGEST

import see MEANING

importance, consequence, moment, weight, significance mean a quality or aspect having great worth or significance. **Importance** implies a value judgment of the superior worth or influence of something or someone ⟨there are no cities of *importance* in this area⟩. **Consequence** may imply importance in social rank but more generally implies importance because of probable or possible effects ⟨whatever style you choose is of little *consequence*⟩. **Moment** implies conspicuous or self-evident consequence ⟨a decision of very great *moment*⟩. **Weight** implies a judgment of the immediate relative importance of something ⟨idle chitchat of no particular *weight*⟩. **Significance** implies a quality or character that should mark a thing as important but that is not self-evident and may or may not be recognized ⟨time would reveal the *significance* of that casual act⟩.

importune see BEG
impose see DICTATE
imposing see GRAND
imposture, fraud, sham, fake, humbug, counterfeit mean a thing made to seem other than it is. **Imposture** applies to any situation in which a spurious object or performance is passed off as genuine ⟨the movie's claim of social concern is an *imposture*⟩. **Fraud** usu. implies a deliberate perversion of the truth ⟨a diary that was exposed as a *fraud*⟩. **Sham** applies to fraudulent imitation of a real thing or action ⟨condemned the election as a *sham* and a travesty of democracy⟩. **Fake** implies an imitation of or substitution for the genuine but does not necessarily imply dishonesty ⟨these are *fakes,* the real jewels being in the vault⟩. **Humbug** suggests elaborate pretense usu. so flagrant as to be transparent ⟨the diet business is populated with *humbugs*⟩. **Counterfeit** applies esp. to the close imitation of something valuable ⟨20-dollar bills that were *counterfeits*⟩.

impoverish see DEPLETE

impregnate see SOAK
impress see AFFECT
impression see IDEA
impressive see MOVING
impromptu see EXTEMPORANEOUS
improper see INDECOROUS
improve, better, help, ameliorate mean to make more acceptable or bring nearer some standard. **Improve** and **better** are general and interchangeable and apply to what is capable of being made better whether it is good or bad ⟨measures to *improve* the quality of medical care⟩ ⟨immigrants hoping to *better* their lot in life⟩. **Help** implies a bettering that still leaves room for improvement ⟨a coat of paint would *help* that house⟩. **Ameliorate** implies making more tolerable or acceptable conditions that are hard to endure ⟨a cancerous condition that cannot be *ameliorated* by chemotherapy⟩.
improvised see EXTEMPORANEOUS
impulse see MOTIVE
impulsive see SPONTANEOUS
impute see ASCRIBE
inactive, idle, inert, passive, supine mean not engaged in work or activity. **Inactive** applies to anyone or anything not in action or in operation or at work ⟨a playwright who's been *inactive* for several years⟩. **Idle** applies to persons that are not busy or occupied or to their powers or their implements ⟨tractors were *idle* in the fields⟩. **Inert** as applied to things implies powerlessness to move or to affect other things; as applied to persons it suggests an inherent or habitual indisposition to activity ⟨*inert* ingredients in drugs⟩ ⟨an *inert* citizenry uninterested in social change⟩. **Passive** implies immobility or lack of normally expected response to an external force or influence and

often suggests deliberate submissiveness or self-control ⟨*passive* obedience⟩ ⟨a *passive* individual incapable of strong emotion⟩. **Supine** applies only to persons and commonly implies abjectness or indolence ⟨remained *supine* in the face of his wife's verbal abuse⟩.

inane see INSIPID

inaugurate see BEGIN

inborn see INNATE

inbred see INNATE

incense see FRAGRANCE

incentive see MOTIVE

inception see ORIGIN

incessant see CONTINUAL

incest see ADULTERY

incident see OCCURRENCE

incisive, trenchant, clear-cut, cutting, biting, crisp mean having or showing a keen mind. **Incisive** implies a power to impress the mind by directness and decisiveness ⟨an *incisive* command that left no room for doubt⟩. **Trenchant** implies an energetic cutting or probing deeply into a matter so as to reveal distinctions or to reach the center ⟨a *trenchant* critic of political pretensions⟩. **Clear-cut** suggests the absence of any blurring, ambiguity, or uncertainty of statement or analysis ⟨made a *clear-cut* distinction between the two military actions⟩. **Cutting** implies a ruthless accuracy or directness wounding to the feelings ⟨makes the most *cutting* remarks with that quiet voice⟩. **Biting** adds a greater implication of harsh vehemence or ironic force ⟨a *biting* commentary on the election⟩. **Crisp** suggests both incisiveness and vigorous terseness ⟨jurors were impressed by the witness's *crisp* answers⟩.

incite, instigate, abet, foment mean to spur to action. **Incite** stresses a stirring up and urging on, and may or may not imply initiating ⟨charged with *inciting* a riot⟩. **Instigate** definitely implies responsibility for initiating another's action and often connotes underhandedness or evil intention ⟨*instigated* a conspiracy against the commander⟩. **Abet** implies both assisting and encouraging ⟨accused of aiding and *abetting* the enemy⟩. **Foment** implies persistence in goading ⟨years of *fomenting* kept the flame of rebellion burning⟩.

incline, bias, dispose, predispose mean to influence one to have or take an attitude toward something. **Incline** implies a tendency to favor one of two or more actions or conclusions ⟨*inclined* to do nothing for the moment⟩. **Bias** suggests a settled and predictable leaning in one direction and connotes unfair prejudice ⟨*biased* against young urban professionals⟩. **Dispose** suggests an affecting of one's mood or temper so as to incline one toward something ⟨a naive nature *disposes* her to trust others too much⟩. **Predispose** implies the operation of a disposing influence well in advance of the opportunity to manifest itself ⟨fictional violence *predisposes* them to accept violence in real life⟩.

include, comprehend, embrace, involve mean to contain within as part of the whole. **Include** suggests the containment of something as a constituent, component, or subordinate part of a larger whole ⟨the price of dinner *includes* dessert⟩. **Comprehend** implies that something comes within the scope of a statement or definition ⟨his notion of manners *comprehends* more than just table etiquette⟩. **Embrace** implies a gathering of separate items within a whole ⟨her faith *embraces* both Christian and non-Christian beliefs⟩. **Involve** suggests inclusion by virtue of the nature of the whole, whether by being its natural or inevitable consequence ⟨a procedural change that will *involve* more work for everyone⟩.

inconstant, fickle, capricious, mercurial, unstable mean lacking firmness or steadiness (as in purpose or devotion). **Inconstant** implies an incapacity for steadiness and an inherent tendency to change ⟨the supply of materials was too *inconstant* to depend on⟩. **Fickle** suggests unreliability because of perverse changeability and incapacity for steadfastness ⟨performers discover how *fickle* the public can be⟩. **Capricious** suggests motivation by sudden whim or fancy and stresses unpredictability ⟨an utterly *capricious* manner of selecting candidates⟩. **Mercurial** implies a rapid changeability in mood ⟨so *mercurial* in temperament that one never knew what to expect⟩. **Unstable** implies an incapacity for remaining in a fixed position or steady course and applies esp. to a lack of emotional balance ⟨in love she was impulsive and *unstable*⟩.

increase, enlarge, augment, multiply mean to make or become greater. **Increase** used intransitively implies progressive growth in size, amount, intensity; used transitively it may imply simple not necessarily progressive addition ⟨his waistline *increased* with age⟩ ⟨*increased* her land holdings⟩. **Enlarge** implies expansion or extension that makes greater in size or capacity ⟨*enlarged* the restaurant to its present capacity⟩. **Augment** implies addition to what is already well grown or well developed ⟨an inheritance that only *augmented* his fortune⟩. **Multiply** implies increase in number by natural generation or by indefinite repetition of a process ⟨with each tampering the problems *multiplied*⟩.

inculcate see IMPLANT

incurious see INDIFFERENT

indecent see INDECOROUS

indecorous, improper, unseemly, indecent, unbecoming, indelicate mean not conforming to what is accepted as right, fitting, or in good taste. **Indecorous** suggests a violation of accepted standards of good manners ⟨your *indecorous* manners marred the wedding reception⟩. **Improper** applies to a broader range of transgressions of rules not only of social behavior but of ethical practice or logical procedure or prescribed method ⟨the *improper* use of campaign contributions⟩. **Unseemly** adds a suggestion of special inappropriateness to a situation or an offensiveness to good taste ⟨married again with *unseemly* haste⟩. **Indecent** implies great unseemliness or gross offensiveness esp. in referring to sexual matters ⟨a scene judged by the censors as *indecent*⟩. **Unbecoming** suggests behavior or language that does not suit one's character or status ⟨conduct *unbecoming* an officer⟩. **Indelicate** implies a lack of modesty or of tact or of refined perception of feeling ⟨*indelicate* expressions for bodily functions⟩.

indefatigable, tireless, untiring, unwearied, unflagging mean capable of prolonged and strenuous effort. **Indefatigable** implies persistent and unremitting activity or effort ⟨an *indefatigable* champion of women's rights⟩. **Tireless** implies a remarkable energy or stamina ⟨honored as a teacher of *tireless* industry and limitless patience⟩. **Untiring** implies the extraordinary ability to go on continuously and without interruption ⟨*untiring* researchers in the fight against the disease⟩. **Unwearied** stresses the apparent absence of any sign of fatigue ⟨detectives remain *unwearied* in their search for the killer⟩. **Unflagging** stresses the absence of any relaxation in one's efforts ⟨an *unflagging* attention to detail⟩.

indelicate see INDECOROUS
indemnify see PAY
independent see FREE
indict see ACCUSE

indifferent, unconcerned, incurious, aloof, detached, disin-terested mean not showing or feeling interest. **Indifferent** implies neutrality of attitude from lack of inclination, pref-erence, or prejudice ⟨*indifferent* to the dictates of fashion⟩. **Unconcerned** suggests a lack of sensitivity or regard for others' needs or troubles ⟨*unconcerned* about the problems of the homeless⟩. **Incurious** implies an inability to take a normal interest due to dullness of mind or to self-centered-ness ⟨*incurious* about the world beyond their village⟩. **Aloof** suggests a cool reserve arising from a sense of supe-riority or disdain for inferiors or from shyness ⟨remained *aloof* from the other club members⟩. **Detached** implies an objective attitude achieved through absence of prejudice or selfishness ⟨observed family gatherings with *detached* amusement⟩. **Disinterested** implies a circumstantial free-dom from concern for personal or esp. financial advantage that enables one to judge or advise without bias ⟨a panel of *disinterested* observers to act as judges⟩.

indigence see POVERTY

indigenous see NATIVE

indignation see ANGER

individual see CHARACTERISTIC, SPECIAL

indolent see LAZY

inducement see MOTIVE

indulge, pamper, humor, spoil, baby, mollycoddle mean to show undue favor to a person's desires and feelings. **In-dulge** implies excessive compliance and weakness in grat-ifying another's or one's own desires ⟨*indulged* herself with food at the slightest excuse⟩. **Pamper** implies inordinate gratification of desire for luxury and comfort with conse-quent enervating effect ⟨*pampered* by the conveniences of modern living⟩. **Humor** stresses a yielding to a person's moods or whims ⟨*humored* him by letting him tell the story). **Spoil** stresses the injurious effects on character by indulging or pampering ⟨fond but foolish parents *spoil* their children⟩. **Baby** suggests excessive care, attention, or solicitude ⟨*babying* students by not holding them accountable⟩. **Mollycoddle** suggests an excessive degree of care and attention to another's health or welfare ⟨refused to *mollycoddle* her teenaged patients⟩.

indulgent see FORBEARING

industrious see BUSY

industry see BUSINESS

inebriated see DRUNK

inept see AWKWARD

inerrable see INFALLIBLE

inerrant see INFALLIBLE

inert see INACTIVE

inexorable see INFLEXIBLE

infallible, inerrable, inerrant, unerring mean having or showing the inability to make errors. **Infallible** may imply that one's freedom from error is divinely bestowed ⟨fundamentalists believe in an *infallible* Bible⟩. **Inerrable** may be preferable when one wishes to avoid any association with religious or papal infallibility ⟨no reference source should be considered *inerrable*⟩. **Inerrant** stresses the fact that no mistakes were made ⟨an *inerrant* interpretation of the most demanding role in drama⟩. **Unerring** stresses reliability, sureness, exactness, or accuracy ⟨a photographer with an *unerring* eye for beauty⟩.

infamy see DISGRACE

infer, deduce, conclude, judge, gather mean to arrive at a mental conclusion. **Infer** implies arriving at a conclusion by reasoning from evidence; if the evidence is slight, the term comes close to *surmise* ⟨from that remark, I *inferred* that they knew each other⟩. **Deduce** adds to *infer* the special implication of drawing a particular inference from a generalization ⟨from that we can *deduce* that man is a mammal⟩. **Conclude** implies arriving at a logically necessary inference at the end of a chain of reasoning ⟨*concluded* that only he could have committed the crime⟩. **Judge** stresses critical examination of the evidence on which a conclusion is based ⟨*judge* people by their actions, not words⟩. **Gather** suggests a direct or intuitive forming of a conclusion from hints or implications ⟨*gathered* that the couple wanted to be alone⟩.

infirm see WEAK

infix see IMPLANT

inflate see EXPAND

inflexible, inexorable, obdurate, adamant mean unwilling to alter a predetermined course or purpose. **Inflexible** implies rigid adherence or even slavish conformity to principle ⟨*inflexible* in her demands⟩. **Inexorable** implies relentlessness of purpose or, esp. when applied to things, inevitableness ⟨the *inexorable* path of progress⟩. **Obdurate** stresses hardness of heart and insensitivity to appeals for mercy or the influence of divine grace ⟨an *obdurate* governor who refused to grant clemency⟩. **Adamant** implies utter immovability in the face of all temptation or entreaty ⟨was *adamant* that the project be completed on time⟩. See in addition STIFF.

influence *n* Influence, authority, prestige, weight, credit mean power exerted over the minds or behavior of others. **Influence** may apply to a force exercised and received consciously or unconsciously ⟨used all of her *influence* to get the bill passed⟩. **Authority** implies the power of winning devotion or allegiance or of compelling acceptance and belief ⟨a policy that has the *authority* of the school board behind it⟩. **Prestige** implies the ascendancy given by conspicuous excellence or reputation for superiority ⟨the *prestige* of the newspaper⟩. **Weight** implies measurable or decisive influence in determining acts or choices ⟨the wishes of the President obviously had much *weight*⟩. **Credit** suggests influence that arises from proven merit or favorable reputation ⟨the *credit* that he had built up in the town⟩.

influence *vb* see AFFECT

inform, acquaint, apprise, notify mean to make one aware of something. **Inform** implies the imparting of knowledge esp. of facts or occurrences ⟨*informed* the President of the crisis⟩. **Acquaint** lays stress on introducing to or familiarizing with ⟨*acquainted* myself with the basics of the game⟩. **Apprise** implies communicating something of special interest or importance ⟨*apprise* me of any rallies in the stock market⟩. **Notify** implies sending notice of something requiring attention or demanding action ⟨*notified* them that their mortgage payment was due⟩.

infraction see BREACH

infrequent, uncommon, scarce, rare, sporadic mean not common or abundant. **Infrequent** implies occurrence at wide intervals in space or time ⟨family visits that were *infrequent* and brief⟩. **Uncommon** suggests a frequency below normal expectation ⟨smallpox is now *uncommon* in many countries⟩. **Scarce** implies falling short of a standard or required abundance ⟨jobs were *scarce* during the Depression⟩. **Rare** suggests extreme scarcity or infrequency and often implies consequent high value ⟨*rare* first editions of classics fetch high prices⟩. **Sporadic** implies occurrence in scattered instances or isolated outbursts ⟨*sporadic* cases of the genetic disorder⟩.

infringe see TRESPASS

infringement see BREACH

infuse, suffuse, imbue, ingrain, inoculate, leaven mean to introduce one thing into another so as to affect it throughout. **Infuse** implies a pouring in of something that gives new life or significance ⟨new members *infused* enthusiasm into the club⟩. **Suffuse** implies a spreading through of something that gives an unusual color or quality ⟨a room *suffused* with light and cheerfulness⟩. **Imbue** implies the introduction of a quality that fills and permeates the whole being ⟨*imbued* her students with intellectual curiosity⟩. **Ingrain** suggests the indelible stamping or deep implanting of a quality or trait ⟨clung to *ingrained* habits and beliefs⟩. **Inoculate** implies an imbuing or implanting with a germinal idea and often suggests surreptitiousness or subtlety ⟨tried to *inoculate* the child with a taste for opera⟩. **Leaven** implies introducing something that enlivens, tempers, or markedly alters the total quality ⟨a serious play *leavened* with comic moments⟩.

ingenious see CLEVER
ingenuous see NATURAL
ingrain see INFUSE
ingredient see ELEMENT
inhibit see FORBID
iniquitous see VICIOUS
initiate see BEGIN
injure, harm, hurt, damage, impair, mar mean to affect injuriously. **Injure** implies the inflicting of anything detrimental to one's looks, comfort, health, or success ⟨an accident that *injured* him physically and emotionally⟩. **Harm** often stresses the inflicting of pain, suffering, or loss ⟨careful not to *harm* the animals⟩. **Hurt** implies inflicting a wound to the body or to the feelings ⟨*hurt* by her callous remarks⟩. **Damage** suggests injury that lowers value or impairs usefulness ⟨a table that was *damaged* in shipping⟩.

Impair suggests a making less complete or efficient by deterioration or diminution ⟨years of smoking had *impaired* his health⟩. **Mar** applies to injury that spoils perfection (as of a surface) or causes disfigurement ⟨the text is *marred* by numerous typos⟩.

injury see INJUSTICE

injustice, injury, wrong, grievance mean an act that inflicts undeserved hurt. **Injustice** applies to any act that involves unfairness to another or violation of his rights ⟨the *injustices* suffered by the lower classes⟩. **Injury** applies in law specif. to an injustice for which one may sue to recover compensation ⟨a libeled reputation is legally considered an *injury*⟩. **Wrong** applies also in law to any act punishable according to the criminal code; it may apply more generally to any flagrant injustice ⟨a crusading reporter determined to right society's *wrongs*⟩. **Grievance** applies to any circumstance or condition that constitutes an injustice to the sufferer and gives him just ground for complaint ⟨a committee for investigating employee *grievances*⟩.

innate, inborn, inbred, congenital, hereditary mean not acquired after birth. **Innate** applies to qualities or characteristics that are part of one's inner essential nature ⟨a person with an *innate* sense of his own superiority⟩. **Inborn** suggests a quality or tendency either actually present at birth or so marked and deep-seated as to seem so ⟨her *inborn* love of the rugged, outdoorsy life⟩. **Inbred** suggests something acquired from parents either by heredity or early nurture but in any case deeply rooted and ingrained ⟨a person with *inbred* extremist political views⟩. **Congenital** and **hereditary** refer to something acquired before or at birth, *congenital* applying to things acquired during fetal development and *hereditary* applying to things transmitted from one's ancestors ⟨a *congenital* heart condition⟩ ⟨eye color is *hereditary*⟩.

inoculate see INFUSE

inordinate see EXCESSIVE

inquire see ASK

inquisitive see CURIOUS

insane, mad, demented, deranged, lunatic, maniac mean having or showing an unsound mind. **Insane** implies that one is unable to function safely and competently in everyday life and is not responsible for one's actions ⟨adjudged *insane* after a period of observation⟩. **Mad** strongly suggests wildness, rabidness, raving, or complete loss of self-control ⟨drove her husband *mad* with jealousy⟩. **Demented** suggests a clear deterioration into mental unsoundness that manifests itself by an incoherence in thought, speech, or action ⟨years of solitary confinement had left him *demented*⟩. **Deranged** stresses a clear loss of control resulting in erratic behavior ⟨assassinated by a *deranged* anarchist⟩. **Lunatic** may imply no more than extreme folly ⟨invested in one *lunatic* scheme after another⟩. **Maniac** is close to *mad* and often suggests violence, fury, or raving ⟨once behind the wheel, she turns into a *maniac* driver⟩.

inseminate see IMPLANT

insert see INTRODUCE

insight see DISCERNMENT

insinuate see INTRODUCE, SUGGEST

insipid, vapid, flat, jejune, banal, inane mean devoid of qualities that make for spirit and character. **Insipid** implies a lack of sufficient taste or savor to please or interest ⟨*insipid* art and dull prose⟩. **Vapid** suggests a lack of liveliness, force, or spirit ⟨a potentially exciting story given a *vapid* treatment⟩. **Flat** applies to things that have lost their sparkle or zest ⟨although well-regarded in its day, this novel now seems *flat*). **Jejune** suggests a lack of rewarding or satisfying substance ⟨on close reading the poem comes across as *jejune*⟩. **Banal** stresses the complete absence of freshness, novelty, or immediacy ⟨a *banal* tale of unrequited love⟩. **Inane** implies a lack of any significant or convincing quality ⟨an *inane* interpretation of the play⟩.

insolent see PROUD

inspect see SCRUTINIZE

inspirit see ENCOURAGE

instance, case, illustration, example, sample, specimen mean something that exhibits distinguishing characteristics in its category. **Instance** applies to any individual person, act, or thing that may be offered to illustrate or explain ⟨an *instance* of history repeating itself⟩. **Case** is used to direct attention to a real or assumed occurrence or situation that is to be considered, studied, or dealt with ⟨a *case* of mistaken identity⟩. **Illustration** applies to an instance offered as a means of clarifying or illuminating a general statement ⟨an *illustration* of Murphy's law⟩. **Example** applies to a typical, representative, or illustrative instance or case ⟨a typical *example* of bureaucratic waste⟩. **Sample** implies a part or unit taken at random from a larger whole and so presumed to be typical of its qualities ⟨show us a *sample* of your work⟩. **Specimen** applies to any example or sample whether representative or merely existent and available ⟨one of the finest *specimens* of the jeweler's art⟩.

instigate see INCITE

instill see IMPLANT

instinctive see SPONTANEOUS

instruct see COMMAND, TEACH

instrument see IMPLEMENT

insult see OFFEND

insure see ENSURE
insurrection see REBELLION
intact see PERFECT
integrity see HONESTY, UNITY
intelligent, clever, alert, quick-witted mean mentally keen or quick. **Intelligent** stresses success in coping with new situations and solving problems ⟨an *intelligent* person could assemble it in 10 minutes⟩. **Clever** implies native ability or aptness and sometimes suggests a lack of more substantial qualities ⟨a hack writer who was somewhat *clever* with words⟩. **Alert** stresses quickness in perceiving and understanding ⟨*alert* to new developments in technology⟩. **Quick-witted** implies promptness in finding answers in debate or in devising expedients in moments of danger or challenge ⟨no match for her *quick-witted* opponent⟩.
intensify, aggravate, heighten, enhance mean to increase markedly in measure or degree. **Intensify** implies a deepening or strengthening of a thing or of its characteristic quality ⟨police *intensified* their investigation⟩. **Aggravate** implies an increasing in gravity or seriousness, esp. the worsening of something already bad or undesirable ⟨the problem has been *aggravated* by neglect⟩. **Heighten** suggests a lifting above the ordinary or accustomed ⟨special effects *heightened* the sense of terror⟩. **Enhance** implies a raising or strengthening above the normal in desirability, value, or attractiveness ⟨shrubbery *enhanced* the grounds of the estate⟩.
intent see INTENTION
intention, intent, purpose, design, aim, end, object, objective, goal mean what one purposes to accomplish or attain. **Intention** implies little more than what one has in mind to do or bring about ⟨announced his *intention* to marry⟩. **Intent** suggests clearer formulation or greater deliberateness

⟨the clear *intent* of the law⟩. **Purpose** suggests a more set-tled determination ⟨she stopped for a *purpose,* not an idle chat⟩. **Design** implies a more carefully calculated plan ⟨the order of events was by accident, not *design*⟩. **Aim** adds to these implications of effort directed toward attaining or ac-complishing ⟨pursued her *aims* with great courage⟩. **End** stresses the intended effect of action often in distinction or contrast to the action or means as such ⟨will use any means to achieve his *end*⟩. **Object** may equal *end* but more often applies to a more individually determined wish or need ⟨the *object* of the research study⟩. **Objective** implies something tangible and immediately attainable ⟨their *ob-jective* is to seize the oil fields⟩. **Goal** suggests something attained only by prolonged effort and hardship ⟨worked years to achieve her *goal*⟩.

intentional see VOLUNTARY

intercalate see INTRODUCE

intercede see INTERPOSE

interdict see FORBID

interfere see INTERPOSE

interject see INTRODUCE

interlope see INTRUDE

interpolate see INTRODUCE

interpose, interfere, intervene, mediate, intercede mean to come or go between. **Interpose** implies no more than this ⟨a road *interposed* between the house and the beach⟩. **In-terfere** implies a getting in the way or otherwise hindering ⟨noise *interfered* with my concentration⟩. **Intervene** may imply an occurring in space or time between two things or a stepping in to halt or settle a quarrel or conflict ⟨family duties *intervened,* and the work came to a halt⟩. **Mediate** implies intervening between hostile factions ⟨chosen to *mediate* between union and management⟩. **Intercede** im-

plies acting in behalf of an offender in begging mercy or
forgiveness ⟨asked to *intercede* on the daughter's behalf⟩.
See in addition INTRODUCE.

interpret see EXPLAIN

interrogate see ASK

intervene see INTERPOSE

intimate *adj* see FAMILIAR

intimate *vb* see SUGGEST

intimidate, cow, bulldoze, bully, browbeat mean to frighten
into submission. **Intimidate** implies inducing fear or a
sense of inferiority into another ⟨*intimidated* by all the
other bright young freshmen⟩. **Cow** implies reduction to a
state where the spirit is broken or all courage is lost ⟨not
at all *cowed* by the odds against making it in show busi-
ness⟩. **Bulldoze** implies an intimidating or an overcoming
of resistance usu. by urgings, demands, or threats ⟨*bull-
dozed* the city council into approving the plan⟩. **Bully** implies intimidation through swaggering threats or insults
⟨tourists being *bullied* by taxi drivers⟩. **Browbeat** implies
a cowing through arrogant, scornful, contemptuous, or insolent treatment ⟨inmates were routinely *browbeaten* by
the staff⟩.

intoxicated see DRUNK

intractable see UNRULY

intricate see COMPLEX

intrigue see PLOT

**introduce, insert, insinuate, interpolate, intercalate, inter-
pose, interject** mean to put between or among others. **Introduce** is a general term for bringing or placing a thing or
person into a group or body already in existence ⟨*introduced* a new topic into the conversation⟩. **Insert** implies
putting into a fixed or open space between or among ⟨*insert* a clause in the contract⟩. **Insinuate** implies introducing

gradually or by gentle pressure ⟨slyly *insinuated* himself into their confidence⟩. **Interpolate** applies to the inserting of something extraneous or spurious ⟨*interpolated* her own comments into the report⟩. **Intercalate** suggests an intrusive inserting of something in an existing series or sequence ⟨a book in which new material is *intercalated* with the old⟩. **Interpose** suggests inserting an obstruction or cause of delay ⟨rules that *interpose* barriers between children and creativity⟩. **Interject** implies an abrupt or forced introduction ⟨quickly *interjected* a question⟩.

intrude, obtrude, interlope, butt in mean to thrust oneself or something in without invitation or authorization. **Intrude** suggests rudeness or officiousness in invading another's property, time, or privacy ⟨didn't mean to *intrude* upon the family's private gathering⟩. **Obtrude** stresses the impropriety or offensiveness of the intrusion ⟨never hesitant about *obtruding* her opinions even when they were least welcome⟩. **Interlope** implies placing oneself in a position leading to adverse consequences ⟨*interloping* nouveaux riches who didn't belong in the club⟩. **Butt in** implies an abrupt or offensive intrusion lacking in propriety or decent restraint ⟨in-laws who *butt in* and tell newlyweds what to do⟩.

intrusive see IMPERTINENT

invade see TRESPASS

invalidate see NULLIFY

invaluable see COSTLY

invective see ABUSE

inveigle see LURE

invent, create, discover mean to bring something new into existence. **Invent** implies fabricating something useful usu. as a result of ingenious thinking or experiment ⟨*invented* numerous energy-saving devices⟩. **Create** implies an evok-

ing of life out of nothing or producing a thing for the sake
of its existence rather than its function or use ⟨*created* few
lasting works of art⟩. **Discover** presupposes preexistence of
something and implies a finding rather than a making ⟨at-
tempts to *discover* the source of the Nile⟩.

invert see TRANSPOSE

inveterate, confirmed, chronic, deep-seated, deep-rooted
mean firmly established. **Inveterate** applies to a habit, attitude, feeling of such long existence as to be practically
ineradicable or unalterable ⟨an *inveterate* smoker⟩. **Confirmed** implies a growing stronger and firmer with time so
as to resist change or reform ⟨a *confirmed* bachelor⟩.
Chronic suggests what is persistent or endlessly recurrent
and troublesome ⟨sick and tired of his *chronic* complain-
ing⟩. **Deep-seated** and **deep-rooted** apply to qualities or attitudes so deeply embedded as to become part of the core
of character or of lasting endurance ⟨a *deep-seated* fear of
heights⟩ ⟨the causes of the problem are *deep-rooted* and
cannot be eliminated overnight⟩.

invidious see REPUGNANT

invite, solicit, court mean to request or encourage to respond
or act. **Invite** commonly implies a formal or courteous requesting of one's presence or participation, but may also
apply to a tacit or unintended attracting or tempting ⟨a
movie remake that *invites* comparison with the original⟩.
Solicit suggests urgency rather than courtesy in encouraging or asking ⟨continually *solicited* our advice⟩. **Court** suggests an endeavoring to win favor or gain love by suitable
acts or words ⟨a candidate *courting* the votes of young
urban professionals⟩.

involve see INCLUDE

involved see COMPLEX

irascible, choleric, splenetic, testy, touchy, cranky, cross

mean easily angered. **Irascible** implies a tendency to be angered on slight provocation ⟨teenagers got a rise out of the *irascible* old man⟩. **Choleric** may suggest impatient excitability and unreasonableness in addition to hot temper ⟨a *choleric* invalid who sorely tried the nurses' patience⟩. **Splenetic** suggests moroseness, and bad rather than hot temper ⟨the *splenetic* type that habored a grudge⟩. **Testy** suggests irascibility over small annoyances ⟨everyone grew *testy* under the emotional strain⟩. **Touchy** implies undue sensitiveness as from jealousy or bad conscience ⟨*touchy* about references to her weight⟩. **Cranky** suggests an habitual fretful irritability ⟨*cranky* neighbors much given to complaining⟩. **Cross** suggests a snappishness or grumpy irritability as from disappointment or discomfort ⟨a squabble that left her feeling *cross* all day⟩.

ire see ANGER

irk see ANNOY

ironic see SARCASTIC

irony see WIT

irregular, anomalous, unnatural mean not conforming to rule, law, or custom. **Irregular** implies not conforming to a law or regulation imposed for the sake of uniformity in methods, practice, or conduct ⟨concerned about her *irregular* behavior⟩. **Anomalous** implies not conforming to what might be expected because of the class or type to which it belongs or the laws that govern its existence ⟨an *anomalous* position of favoring better schools but not wanting to pay for them⟩. **Unnatural** suggests what is contrary to nature or to principles or standards felt to be essential to the well-being of civilized society ⟨treated their prisoners of war with *unnatural* cruelty⟩.

irritate, exasperate, nettle, provoke, rile, peeve mean to excite a feeling of anger or annoyance. **Irritate** implies an often gradual arousing of angry feelings that may range from impatience to rage ⟨her constant nagging *irritated* him to no end⟩. **Exasperate** suggests galling annoyance or vexation and the arousing of extreme impatience ⟨his *exasperating* habit of putting off every decision⟩. **Nettle** suggests a light stinging or piquing ⟨your high-handed attitude *nettled* several people⟩. **Provoke** implies an arousing of strong annoyance or vexation that may excite to action ⟨remarks that were made solely to *provoke* him⟩. **Rile** implies inducing an angry or resentful agitation ⟨the new rules *riled* up the employees⟩. **Peeve** suggests arousing fretful often petty or querulous irritation ⟨she is easily *peeved* after a sleepless night⟩.

isolation see SOLITUDE

issue *n* see EFFECT

issue *vb* see SPRING

item, detail, particular mean one of the distinct parts of a whole. **Item** applies to each thing specified separately in a list or in a group of things that might be listed or enumerated ⟨ordered every *item* on the list⟩. **Detail** applies to one of the small component parts of a larger whole such as a task, building, painting, narration, or process ⟨leave the petty *details* to others⟩. **Particular** stresses the smallness, singleness, and esp. the concreteness of a detail or item ⟨a verbal attack that included few *particulars*⟩.

J

jade see TIRE
jam see PREDICAMENT
jargon see DIALECT
jeer see SCOFF
jejune see INSIPID
jest, joke, quip, witticism, wisecrack mean something said
for the purpose of evoking laughter. **Jest** is chiefly literary
and applies to any utterance not seriously intended
whether sarcastic, ironic, witty, or merely playful ⟨literary
jests that were lost on her unsophisticated friends⟩. **Joke**
may apply to an act as well as an utterance and suggests
no intent to hurt feelings ⟨he's very good at taking a *joke*⟩.
Quip implies lightness and neatness of phrase more definitely than *jest* ⟨whatever the topic, she's ready with a
quick *quip*⟩. **Witticism** and **wisecrack** both stress cleverness of phrasing and both may suggest flippancy or un-
feelingness ⟨many felt the sting of his *witticisms*⟩ ⟨a comic
known for abrasive *wisecracks*⟩. See in addition FUN.
job see TASK
jocose see WITTY
jocular see WITTY
jocund see MERRY
join, combine, unite, connect, link, associate, relate mean to
bring or come together into some manner of union. **Join**
implies a bringing into contact or conjunction of any degree of closeness ⟨*joined* forces in an effort to win⟩. **Combine** implies some merging or mingling with corresponding
loss of identity of each unit ⟨*combine* the ingredients for a
cake⟩. **Unite** implies somewhat greater loss of separate

identity ⟨the colonies *united* to form a republic⟩. **Connect**
suggests a loose or external attachment with little or no
loss of identity ⟨a bridge *connects* the island to the main-
land⟩. **Link** may imply strong connection or inseparability
of elements still retaining identity ⟨a name forever *linked*
with liberty⟩. **Associate** stresses the mere fact of frequent
occurrence or existence together in space or in logical relation ⟨opera is popularly *associated* with high society⟩.
Relate suggests the existence of a real or presumed logical
connection ⟨the two events were not *related*⟩.

joke see JEST
jollity see MIRTH
jolly see MERRY
jovial see MERRY
judge see INFER
judgment see SENSE
judicious see WISE
**juncture, pass, exigency, emergency, contingency, pinch,
straits, crisis** mean a critical or crucial time or state of affairs. **Juncture** stresses the significant concurrence or con-
vergence of events ⟨at an important *juncture* in our country's history⟩. **Pass** implies a bad or distressing state or
situation brought about by a combination of causes
⟨things have come to a sorry *pass* when it's not safe to be
on the streets⟩. **Exigency** stresses the pressure of restrictions or urgency of demands created by a special situation
⟨made no effort to provide for *exigencies*⟩. **Emergency** applies to a sudden unforeseen situation requiring prompt
action to avoid disaster ⟨the presence of mind needed to
deal with *emergencies*⟩. **Contingency** implies an emergency or exigency that is regarded as possible but uncertain
of occurrence ⟨*contingency* plans prepared by the Penta-
gon⟩. **Pinch** implies urgency or pressure for action to a less

intense degree than *exigency* or *emergency* ⟨this will do in a *pinch*⟩. **Straits** applies to a troublesome situation from which escape is extremely difficult ⟨in dire *straits* since the death of her husband⟩. **Crisis** applies to a juncture whose outcome will make a decisive difference ⟨the fever broke and the *crisis* passed⟩.

junk see DISCARD
jurisdiction see POWER
just see FAIR, UPRIGHT
justify see MAINTAIN
juxtaposed see ADJACENT

K

keen see EAGER, SHARP
keep *vb* **Keep, observe, celebrate, commemorate** mean to notice or honor a day, occasion, or deed. **Keep** stresses the idea of not neglecting or violating ⟨*keep* the Sabbath⟩. **Observe** suggests marking the occasion by ceremonious performance ⟨not all holidays are *observed* nationally⟩. **Celebrate** suggests acknowledging an occasion by festivity ⟨traditionally *celebrates* Thanksgiving with a huge dinner⟩. **Commemorate** suggests that an occasion is marked by observances that remind one of the origin and significance of the day ⟨*commemorate* Memorial Day with the laying of wreaths⟩.

keep *vb* **Keep, retain, detain, withhold, reserve** mean to hold in one's possession or under one's control. **Keep** may suggest a holding securely in one's possession, custody, or control ⟨*keep* this while I'm gone⟩. **Retain** implies continued keeping, esp. against threatened seizure or forced loss ⟨managed to *retain* their dignity even in poverty⟩. **Detain**

suggests a delay in letting go ⟨*detained* them for questioning⟩. **Withhold** implies restraint in letting go or a refusal to let go ⟨*withheld* information from the authorities⟩. **Reserve** suggests a keeping in store for future use ⟨*reserve* some of your energy for the last mile⟩.

kick see OBJECT

kill, slay, murder, assassinate, dispatch, execute mean to deprive of life. **Kill** merely states the fact of death caused by an agency in any manner ⟨routinely *killed* little bugs⟩ ⟨frost *killed* the plants⟩. **Slay** is a chiefly literary term implying deliberateness and violence but not necessarily motive ⟨*slew* thousands of the Philistines⟩. **Murder** specif. implies stealth and motive and premeditation and therefore full moral responsibility ⟨convicted of *murdering* his parents⟩. **Assassinate** applies to deliberate killing openly or secretly often for political motives ⟨terrorists *assassinated* the Senator⟩. **Dispatch** stresses quickness and directness in putting to death ⟨*dispatched* the sentry with a single stab⟩. **Execute** stresses putting to death as a legal penalty ⟨to be *executed* by firing squad at dawn⟩.

kind *adj* **Kind, benign, benignant** mean showing a gentle, considerate nature. **Kind** stresses a disposition to be helpful ⟨a *kind* heart beneath a gruff exterior⟩. **Kindly** stresses more the expression of a sympathetic nature or impulse ⟨take a *kindly* interest in the poor of the community⟩. **Benign** and **benignant** stress mildness and mercifulness and apply more often to gracious or patronizing acts or utterances of a superior rather than an equal ⟨the belief that a *benign* supreme being controls destiny⟩ ⟨cultural exchange programs have a *benignant* influence in world affairs⟩.

kind *n* see TYPE

kindly see KIND

knack see GIFT

knotty see COMPLEX

knowledge, learning, erudition, scholarship mean what is or can be known by an individual or by mankind. **Knowledge** applies to facts or ideas acquired by study, investigation, observation, or experience ⟨rich in the *knowledge* gained from life⟩. **Learning** applies to knowledge acquired esp. through formal, often advanced, schooling ⟨a book that is evidence of the author's vast *learning*⟩. **Erudition** strongly implies the acquiring of profound, recondite, or bookish learning ⟨an *erudition* unusual even for a classicist⟩. **Scholarship** implies the possession of learning characteristic of the advanced scholar in a specialized field of study or investigation ⟨a work of first-rate literary *scholarship*⟩.

L

labor see WORK

laconic see CONCISE

lag see DELAY

lament see DEPLORE

languor see LETHARGY

lank see LEAN

lanky see LEAN

lapse see ERROR

lassitude see LETHARGY

last *adj* **Last, final, terminal, eventual, ultimate** mean following all others (as in time, order, or importance). **Last** applies to something that comes at the end of a series but does not always imply that the series is completed or stopped ⟨the *last* page of a book⟩ ⟨the *last* news we had of him⟩. **Final** applies to that which definitely closes a series, process, or progress ⟨the *final* day of school⟩. **Terminal**

may indicate a limit of extension, growth, or development ⟨the *terminal* phase of a disease⟩. **Eventual** applies to something that is bound to follow sooner or later as the final effect of causes already operating ⟨the *eventual* defeat of the enemy⟩. **Ultimate** implies the last degree or stage of a long process beyond which further progress or change is impossible ⟨the *ultimate* collapse of civilization⟩.

last *vb* see CONTINUE

lasting, permanent, durable, stable mean enduring for so long as to seem fixed or established. **Lasting** implies a capacity to continue indefinitely ⟨a book that left a *lasting* impression on me⟩. **Permanent** adds usu. the implication of being designed or planned to stand or continue indefinitely ⟨a *permanent* living arrangement⟩. **Durable** implies power to resist destructive agencies ⟨*durable* fabrics⟩. **Stable** implies lastingness because of resistance to being overturned or displaced ⟨a *stable* government⟩.

late see DEAD

latent, dormant, quiescent, potential, abeyant mean not now showing signs of activity or existence. **Latent** applies to a power or quality that has not yet come forth but may emerge and develop ⟨a *latent* sadism that emerged during the war⟩. **Dormant** suggests the inactivity of something (as a feeling or power) as though sleeping ⟨a *dormant* passion existed between them⟩. **Quiescent** suggests a usu. temporary cessation of activity ⟨racial tensions were *quiescent* for the moment⟩. **Potential** applies to what does not yet have existence or effect but is likely soon to have ⟨a toxic waste dump that is a *potential* disaster⟩. **Abeyant** applies to what is for the time being held off or suppressed ⟨an *abeyant* distrust of the neighbors⟩.

laughable, ludicrous, ridiculous, comic, comical mean provoking laughter or mirth. **Laughable** applies to anything occasioning laughter intentionally or unintentionally ⟨her attempts at roller-skating were *laughable*⟩. **Ludicrous** suggests absurdity or preposterousness that excites both laughter and scorn or sometimes pity ⟨a spy thriller with a *ludicrous* plot⟩. **Ridiculous** suggests extreme absurdity, foolishness, or contemptibility ⟨a *ridiculous* portrayal of wartime combat⟩. **Comic** applies esp. to that which arouses thoughtful amusement ⟨Falstaff is one of Shakespeare's great *comic* characters⟩. **Comical** applies to that which arouses unrestrained spontaneous hilarity ⟨his *comical* appearance would have tested a saint⟩.

lavish see PROFUSE

law, rule, regulation, precept, statute, ordinance, canon mean a principle governing action or procedure. **Law** implies imposition by a sovereign authority and the obligation of obedience on the part of all subject to that authority ⟨obey the *law*⟩. **Rule** applies to more restricted or specific situations ⟨the *rules* of a game⟩. **Regulation** implies prescription by authority in order to control an organization or system ⟨*regulations* affecting nuclear power plants⟩. **Precept** commonly suggests something advisory and not obligatory communicated typically through teaching ⟨the *precepts* of effective writing⟩. **Statute** implies a law enacted by a legislative body ⟨a *statute* requiring the use of seat belts⟩. **Ordinance** applies to an order governing some detail of procedure or conduct enforced by a limited authority such as a municipality ⟨a city *ordinance*⟩. **Canon** suggests in nonreligious use a principle or rule of behavior or procedure commonly accepted as a valid guide ⟨a house that violates all the *canons* of good taste⟩. See in addition HYPOTHESIS.

lawful, legal, legitimate, licit mean being in accordance with law. **Lawful** may apply to conformity with law of any sort (as natural, divine, common, or canon) ⟨the *lawful* sovereign⟩. **Legal** applies to what is sanctioned by law or in conformity with the law, esp. as it is written or administered by the courts ⟨*legal* residents of the state⟩. **Legitimate** may apply to a legal right or status but also, in extended use, to a right or status supported by tradition, custom, or accepted standards ⟨a perfectly *legitimate* question about finances⟩. **Licit** applies to a strict conformity to the provisions of the law and applies esp. to what is regulated by law ⟨the *licit* use of the drug by hospitals⟩.

lax see NEGLIGENT

lazy, indolent, slothful mean not easily aroused to activity. **Lazy** suggests a disinclination to work or to take trouble ⟨his habitually *lazy* son⟩. **Indolent** suggests a love of ease and a settled dislike of movement or activity ⟨the summer's heat made us all *indolent*⟩. **Slothful** implies a temperamental inability to act promptly or speedily when action or speed is called for ⟨the agency is usually *slothful* about fulfilling requests⟩.

lead see GUIDE

league see ALLIANCE

lean, spare, lank, lanky, gaunt, rawboned, scrawny, skinny mean thin because of an absence of excess flesh. **Lean** stresses lack of fat and of curving contours ⟨a *lean* racehorse⟩. **Spare** suggests leanness from abstemious living or constant exercise ⟨the *spare* form of a long-distance runner⟩. **Lank** implies tallness as well as leanness ⟨the pale, *lank* limbs of a prisoner of war⟩. **Lanky** suggests awkwardness and loose-jointedness as well as thinness ⟨a *lanky* youth, all arms and legs⟩. **Gaunt** implies marked thinness or emaciation as from overwork or suffering ⟨her *gaunt* face showed the strain of poverty⟩. **Rawboned** suggests a large ungainly build without implying undernourishment

⟨*rawboned* lumberjacks squeezed into the booth⟩.
Scrawny and **skinny** imply an extreme leanness that suggests deficient strength and vitality ⟨*scrawny* village children⟩ ⟨*skinny* fashion models⟩.

leaning, propensity, proclivity, penchant mean a strong instinct or liking for something. **Leaning** suggests a liking or attraction not strong enough to be decisive or uncontrollable ⟨accused of having socialist *leanings*⟩. **Propensity** implies a deeply ingrained and usu. irresistible longing ⟨the natural *propensity* of in-laws to offer advice⟩. **Proclivity** suggests a strong natural proneness usu. to something objectionable or evil ⟨movies that reinforce viewers' *proclivities* for violence⟩. **Penchant** implies a strongly marked taste in the person or an irresistible attraction in the object ⟨has a *penchant* for overdramatizing his troubles⟩.

learn see DISCOVER

learning see KNOWLEDGE

lease see HIRE

leaven see INFUSE

leech see PARASITE

legal see LAWFUL

legendary see FICTITIOUS

legitimate see LAWFUL

lengthen see EXTEND

lenient see FORBEARING

lenity see MERCY

lessen see DECREASE

let, allow, permit mean not to forbid or prevent. **Let** may imply a positive giving of permission but more often implies failure to prevent either through inadvertence and negligence or through lack of power or effective authority ⟨the goalie *let* the puck get by him⟩. **Allow** implies little more than a forbearing to prohibit ⟨a teacher who *allows* her pupils to do as they like). **Permit** implies willingness or acquiescence ⟨the park *permits* powerboats on the lake⟩. See in addition HIRE.

lethal see DEADLY

lethargy, languor, lassitude, stupor, torpor mean physical or mental inertness. **Lethargy** implies such drowsiness or aversion to activity as is induced by disease, injury, drugs ⟨months of *lethargy* followed my skiing accident⟩. **Languor** suggests inertia induced by an enervating climate or illness or love ⟨*languor* induced by a tropical vacation⟩. **Lassitude** stresses listlessness or indifference resulting from fatigue or poor health ⟨a deepening depression marked by *lassitude*⟩. **Stupor** implies a deadening of the mind and senses by shock, narcotics, or intoxicants ⟨lapsed into a *stupor* following a night of drinking⟩. **Torpor** implies a state of suspended animation as of hibernating animals but may suggest merely extreme sluggishness ⟨a once-alert mind now in a state of *torpor*⟩.

level, flat, plane, even, smooth mean having a surface without bends, curves, or irregularities. **Level** applies to a horizontal surface that lies on a line parallel with the horizon ⟨the vast prairies are nearly *level*⟩. **Flat** applies to a surface devoid of noticeable curvatures, prominences, or depressions ⟨the work surface must be totally *flat*⟩. **Plane** applies to any real or imaginary flat surface in which a straight line between any two points on it lies wholly within that surface ⟨the *plane* sides of a crystal⟩. **Even** applies to a surface that is noticeably flat or level or to a line that is observably straight ⟨trim the hedge so that it is *even*⟩. **Smooth** applies esp. to a polished surface free of irregularities ⟨a *smooth* dance floor⟩.

levity see LIGHTNESS

liable, open, exposed, subject, prone, susceptible, sensitive

mean being by nature or through circumstances likely to experience something adverse. **Liable** implies a possibility or probability of incurring something because of position, nature, or particular situation ⟨unless you're careful, you're *liable* to fall⟩. **Open** stresses a lack of barriers preventing incurrence ⟨a claim that is *open* to question⟩. **Exposed** suggests lack of protection or powers of resistance against something actually present or threatening ⟨the town's *exposed* position makes it impossible to defend⟩. **Subject** implies an openness for any reason to something that must be suffered or undergone ⟨all reports are *subject* to editorial revision⟩. **Prone** stresses natural tendency or propensity to incur something ⟨a person who is *prone* to procrastination⟩. **Susceptible** implies conditions existing in one's nature or individual constitution that make incurrence probable ⟨young children are *susceptible* to colds⟩. **Sensitive** implies a readiness to respond to or be influenced by forces or stimuli ⟨her eyes are *sensitive* to light⟩. See in addition RESPONSIBLE.

liberal, generous, bountiful, munificent mean giving freely and unstintingly. **Liberal** suggests openhandedness in the giver and largeness in the thing or amount given ⟨a teacher *liberal* in bestowing praise⟩. **Generous** stresses warmhearted readiness to give more than size or importance of the gift ⟨a friend's *generous* offer of assistance⟩. **Bountiful** suggests lavish, unremitting giving or providing ⟨*bountiful* grandparents spoiling the children⟩. **Munificent** suggests a scale of giving appropriate to lords or princes ⟨the Queen was especially *munificent* to her favorite⟩.

liberate see FREE
liberty see FREEDOM
license see FREEDOM
licit see LAWFUL

lie, prevaricate, equivocate, palter, fib mean to tell an untruth. **Lie** is the blunt term, imputing dishonesty ⟨to *lie* under oath is a serious crime⟩. **Prevaricate** softens the bluntness of *lie* by implying quibbling or confusing the issue ⟨during the hearings the witness did his best to *prevaricate*⟩. **Equivocate** implies using words having more than one sense so as to seem to say one thing but intend another ⟨*equivocated*, dodged questions, and generally misled her inquisitors⟩. **Palter** implies making unreliable statements of fact or intention or insincere promises ⟨a cad *paltering* with a naive, young girl⟩. **Fib** applies to a telling of a trivial untruth ⟨*fibbed* about the price of the suit⟩.

lift, raise, rear, elevate, hoist, heave, boost mean to move from a lower to a higher place or position. **Lift** usu. implies exerting effort to overcome resistance of weight ⟨*lift* the chair while I vacuum⟩. **Raise** carries a stronger implication of bringing up to the vertical or to a high position ⟨soldiers *raising* a flagpole⟩. **Rear** may add an element of suddenness to *raise* ⟨suddenly a flag of truce was *reared*⟩. **Elevate** may replace *lift* or *raise* esp. when exalting or enhancing is implied ⟨*elevated* the musical tastes of the public⟩. **Hoist** implies lifting something heavy esp. by mechanical means ⟨*hoisted* the cargo on board⟩. **Heave** implies lifting with great effort or strain ⟨struggled to *heave* the heavy crate⟩. **Boost** suggests assisting to climb or advance by a push ⟨*boosted* his brother over the fence⟩.

light see EASY

lighten see RELIEVE

lightness, levity, frivolity, flippancy, volatility, flightiness mean gaiety or indifference when seriousness is expected. **Lightness** implies a lack of weight and seriousness in character, mood, or conduct ⟨the only bit of *lightness* in a dreary, ponderous drama⟩. **Levity** suggests trifling or unseasonable gaiety ⟨injected a moment of *levity* in the solemn proceedings⟩. **Frivolity** suggests irresponsible indulgence in gaieties or in idle speech or conduct ⟨a playgirl living a life of uninterrupted *frivolity*⟩. **Flippancy** implies an unbecoming levity esp. in speaking of grave or sacred matters ⟨spoke of the bombing with annoying *flippancy*⟩. **Volatility** implies such fickleness of disposition as prevents long attention to any one thing ⟨the *volatility* of the public interest in foreign aid⟩. **Flightiness** implies extreme volatility that may approach loss of mental balance ⟨the *flightiness* of my grandmother in her old age⟩.

likeness, similarity, resemblance, similitude, analogy, affinity mean agreement or correspondence in details. **Likeness** implies a closer correspondence than **similarity** which often implies that things are merely somewhat alike ⟨a remarkable *likeness* to his late father⟩ ⟨some *similarity* between the two cases⟩. **Resemblance** implies similarity chiefly in appearance or external qualities ⟨statements that bear no *resemblance* to the truth⟩. **Similitude** applies chiefly to correspondence between abstractions ⟨the *similitude* of environments was rigidly maintained⟩. **Analogy** implies likeness or parallelism in relations rather than in appearance or qualities ⟨pointed out the *analogies* to past wars⟩. **Affinity** suggests a cause such as kinship or experiences or influences in common which is accountable for the similarity ⟨a writer with a striking *affinity* for American Indian culture⟩.

limit, restrict, circumscribe, confine mean to set bounds for. **Limit** implies setting a point or line (as in time, space, speed, or degree) beyond which something cannot or is not permitted to go ⟨visits are *limited* to 30 minutes⟩. **Restrict** suggests a narrowing or tightening or restraining within or as if within an encircling boundary ⟨laws intended to *re-*

strict the freedom of the press⟩. **Circumscribe** stresses a restriction on all sides and by clearly defined boundaries ⟨the work of the investigating committee was carefully *circumscribed*⟩. **Confine** suggests severe restraint and a resulting cramping, fettering, or hampering ⟨our freedom of choice was *confined* by finances⟩.

limpid see CLEAR

lingo see DIALECT

link see JOIN

little see SMALL

lively, animated, vivacious, sprightly, gay mean keenly alive and spirited. **Lively** suggests briskness, alertness, or energy ⟨a *lively* hour of news and information⟩. **Animated** applies to what is spirited, active, and sparkling ⟨an *animated* discussion of current events⟩. **Vivacious** suggests an activeness of gesture and wit, often playful or alluring ⟨a *vivacious* party hostess⟩. **Sprightly** suggests lightness and spirited vigor of manner or of wit ⟨a tuneful, *sprightly* musical revue⟩. **Gay** stresses complete freedom from care and overflowing spirits ⟨the *gay* spirit of Paris in the 1920s⟩.

living, alive, animate, animated, vital mean having or showing life. **Living** and **alive** apply to organic bodies having life as opposed to those from which life has gone ⟨*living* artists⟩ ⟨toss the lobster into the pot while it's still *alive*⟩. **Animate** is used chiefly in direct opposition to *inanimate* to denote things capable of life ⟨a child seemingly afraid of every *animate* object⟩. **Animated** is applied to that which comes alive and active or is given motion simulating life ⟨an *animated* cartoon⟩. **Vital** often suggests the opposite of *mechanical* in implying the energy and esp. the power to grow and reproduce characteristic of life ⟨all of his *vital* functions seemed normal⟩.

loath see DISINCLINED

loathe see HATE
lofty see HIGH
loiter see DELAY
lone see ALONE
lonely see ALONE
lonesome see ALONE
long, yearn, hanker, pine, hunger, thirst mean to have a strong desire for something. **Long** implies a wishing with one's whole heart and often a striving to attain ⟨*longed* for some peace and quiet⟩. **Yearn** suggests an eager, restless, or painful longing ⟨*yearned* for a career on the stage⟩. **Hanker** suggests the uneasy promptings of unsatisfied appetite or desire ⟨always *hankering* for more money⟩. **Pine** implies a languishing or a fruitless longing for what is impossible ⟨*pined* for long-lost love⟩. **Hunger** and **thirst** imply an insistent or impatient craving or a compelling need ⟨*hungered* for a business of his own⟩ ⟨*thirsted* for absolute power⟩.

look see EXPECT
loot see SPOIL
loquacious see TALKATIVE
lordly see PROUD
lot see FATE
loud, stentorian, earsplitting, raucous, strident mean marked by intensity or volume of sound. **Loud** applies to any volume above normal and may suggest undue vehemence or obtrusiveness ⟨a *loud* obnoxious person⟩. **Stentorian** implies great power and range ⟨an actor with a *stentorian* voice⟩. **Earsplitting** implies loudness that is physically discomforting ⟨the *earsplitting* sound of a siren⟩. **Raucous** implies a loud harsh grating tone, esp. of voice, and may suggest rowdiness ⟨a barroom filled with the *raucous* shouts of drunken revelers⟩. **Strident** implies a rasping dis-

cordant but insistent quality, esp. of voice 〈the *strident* voices of hecklers〉.

loutish see BOORISH

lovely see BEAUTIFUL

low see BASE

lower see FROWN

lowly see HUMBLE

loyal see FAITHFUL

loyalty see FIDELITY

lucid see CLEAR

lucky, fortunate, happy, providential mean meeting with unforeseen success. **Lucky** stresses the agency of chance in bringing about a favorable result 〈the *lucky* day I met my future wife〉. **Fortunate** suggests being rewarded beyond one's deserts 〈have been *fortunate* in my business investments〉. **Happy** combines the implications of *lucky* and *fortunate* with stress on being blessed 〈a life that has been a series of *happy* accidents〉. **Providential** more definitely implies the help or intervention of a higher power 〈it was *providential* that rescuers arrived in the nick of time〉.

ludicrous see LAUGHABLE

luminous see BRIGHT

lunatic see INSANE

lure, entice, inveigle, decoy, tempt, seduce mean to lead astray from one's true course. **Lure** implies a drawing into danger, evil, or difficulty through attracting and deceiving 〈*lured* naive investors with get-rich-quick schemes〉. **Entice** suggests drawing by artful or adroit means 〈advertising designed to *entice* new customers〉. **Inveigle** implies enticing by cajoling or flattering 〈*inveigled* her suitor into proposing marriage〉. **Decoy** implies a luring away or into entrapment by artifice 〈the female bird attempted to *decoy* us away from her nest〉. **Tempt** implies the presenting of an attraction so strong that it overcomes the restraints of conscience or better judgment ⟨*tempted* her to leave her husband and children⟩. **Seduce** implies a leading astray by persuasion or false promises ⟨*seduced* young runaways into the criminal life⟩.

lurid see GHASTLY

lurk, skulk, slink, sneak mean to behave so as to escape attention. **Lurk** implies a lying in wait in a place of concealment and often suggests an evil intent ⟨suspicious men *lurking* in alleyways⟩. **Skulk** suggests more strongly cowardice or fear or sinister intent ⟨spied something *skulking* in the shadows⟩. **Slink** implies moving stealthily often merely to escape attention ⟨during the festivities, I *slunk* away⟩. **Sneak** may add an implication of entering or leaving a place or evading a difficulty by furtive, indirect, or underhanded methods ⟨he *sneaked* out after the others had fallen asleep⟩.

lush see PROFUSE

lustrous see BRIGHT

lusty see VIGOROUS

luxuriant see PROFUSE

luxurious, sumptuous, opulent mean ostentatiously rich or magnificent. **Luxurious** applies to what is choice and costly and suggests gratification of the senses and desire for comfort ⟨a millionaire's *luxurious* penthouse apartment⟩. **Sumptuous** applies to what is extravagantly rich, splendid, or luxurious ⟨an old-fashioned grand hotel with a *sumptuous* lobby⟩. **Opulent** suggests a flaunting of luxuriousness, luxuriance, or costliness ⟨an *opulent* wedding intended to impress the guests⟩. See in addition SENSUOUS.

lying see DISHONEST

M

macabre see GHASTLY
machination see PLOT
mad see INSANE
magisterial see DICTATORIAL
magnificent see GRAND

maim, cripple, mutilate, batter, mangle mean to injure so severely as to cause lasting damage. **Maim** implies the loss or injury of a bodily member through violence ⟨a swimmer *maimed* by a shark⟩. **Cripple** implies the loss or serious impairment of an arm or leg ⟨the fall *crippled* her for life⟩. **Mutilate** implies the cutting off or removal of an essential part of a person or thing thereby impairing its completeness, beauty, or function ⟨a poignant drama *mutilated* by inept acting⟩. **Batter** implies a series of blows that bruise deeply, deform, or mutilate ⟨a ship *battered* by fierce storms at sea⟩. **Mangle** implies a tearing or crushing that leaves deep extensive wounds ⟨thousands are *mangled* every year by auto accidents⟩.

maintain, assert, defend, vindicate, justify mean to uphold as true, right, just, or reasonable. **Maintain** stresses firmness of conviction ⟨steadfastly *maintained* his client's innocence⟩. **Assert** suggests determination to make others accept one's claim ⟨fiercely *asserted* that credit for the discovery belonged to her⟩. **Defend** implies maintaining in the face of attack or criticism ⟨I need not *defend* my wartime record⟩. **Vindicate** implies successfully defending ⟨his success *vindicated* our faith in him⟩. **Justify** implies showing to be true, just, or valid by appeal to a standard or to precedent ⟨threats to public safety *justified* such drastic steps⟩.

majestic see GRAND

make, form, shape, fashion, fabricate, manufacture, forge mean to cause to come into being. **Make** applies to producing or creating whether by an intelligent agency or blind forces and to either material or immaterial existence ⟨*make* a wish⟩ ⟨the factory *makes* furniture⟩. **Form** implies a definite outline, structure, or design in the thing produced ⟨*form* a plan⟩ ⟨*form* a line outside the door⟩. **Shape** suggests impressing a form upon some material ⟨*shaped* shrubbery into animal figures⟩. **Fashion** suggests the use of inventive power or ingenuity ⟨*fashioned* a bicycle out of spare parts⟩. **Fabricate** suggests a uniting of many parts into a whole and often implies an ingenious inventing of something false ⟨*fabricated* an exotic background for her studio biography⟩. **Manufacture** implies making repeatedly by a fixed process and usu. by machinery ⟨*manufacture* shoes⟩. **Forge** implies a making or effecting by great physical or mental effort ⟨*forged* an agreement after months of negotiating⟩.

makeshift see RESOURCE

maladroit see AWKWARD

malevolence see MALICE

malice, malevolence, ill will, spite, malignity, spleen, grudge mean the desire to see another experience pain, injury, or distress. **Malice** implies a deep-seated often unexplainable desire to see another suffer ⟨felt no *malice* for their former enemies⟩. **Malevolence** suggests a bitter persistent hatred that is likely to be expressed in malicious conduct ⟨deep *malevolence* governed his every act⟩. **Ill will** implies a feeling of antipathy of limited duration ⟨a directive that provoked *ill will* among the employees⟩. **Spite** implies petty feelings of envy and resentment that are often expressed in small harassments ⟨petty insults inspired only by *spite*⟩. **Malignity** implies deep passion and relentlessness ⟨never viewed her daughter-in-law with anything but *malignity*⟩. **Spleen** suggests the wrathful release of latent spite or persistent malice ⟨quick to vent his *spleen* at incompetent subordinates⟩. **Grudge** implies a harbored feeling of resentment or ill will that seeks satisfaction ⟨never one to harbor a *grudge*⟩.

malign *vb* Malign, traduce, asperse, vilify, calumniate, defame, slander mean to injure by speaking ill of. **Malign** suggests specific and often subtle misrepresentation but may not always imply deliberate lying ⟨the most *maligned* monarch in British history⟩. **Traduce** stresses the resulting ignominy and distress to the victim ⟨so *traduced* the governor that he was driven from office⟩. **Asperse** implies continued attack on a reputation often by indirect or insinuated detraction ⟨both candidates *aspersed* the other's motives⟩. **Vilify** implies attempting to destroy a reputation by open and direct abuse ⟨no President was more *vilified* in the press⟩. **Calumniate** imputes malice to the speaker and falsity to his assertion ⟨threatened with a lawsuit for publicly *calumniating* the company⟩. **Defame** stresses the actual loss of or injury to one's good name ⟨forced to pay a substantial sum for *defaming* her reputation⟩. **Slander** stresses the suffering of the victim ⟨town gossips carelessly *slandered* their good name⟩.

malign *adj* see SINISTER

malignity see MALICE

malleable see PLASTIC

malodorous, stinking, fetid, noisome, putrid, rank, fusty, musty mean bad-smelling. **Malodorous** may range from the unpleasant to the strongly offensive ⟨*malodorous* un-

identifiable substances in the refrigerator). **Stinking** and
fetid suggest the foul or disgusting ⟨prisoners were held in
stinking cells⟩ ⟨skunk cabbage is a *fetid* weed⟩. **Noisome**
adds a suggestion of being harmful or unwholesome as
well as offensive ⟨a *noisome* toxic waste dump⟩. **Putrid**
implies particularly the sickening odor of decaying organic
matter ⟨the typically *putrid* smell of a fish pier⟩. **Rank** suggests a strong unpleasant smell ⟨rooms filled with the
smoke of *rank* cigars⟩. **Fusty** and **musty** suggest lack of
fresh air and sunlight, *fusty* also implying prolonged un-
cleanliness, *musty* stressing the effects of dampness, mildew, or age ⟨the *fusty* rooms of a boarded-up mansion⟩
⟨the *musty* odor of a damp cellar⟩.

mammoth see ENORMOUS
manacle see HAMPER
manage see CONDUCT
maneuver see TRICK
mangle see MAIM
maniac see INSANE
manifest *adj* see EVIDENT
manifest *vb* see SHOW
manipulate see HANDLE
manner see BEARING, METHOD
mannerism see POSE
manufacture see MAKE
manumit see FREE
mar see INJURE
margin see BORDER
marital see MATRIMONIAL
mark see SIGN
marshal see ORDER
mask see DISGUISE
mass see BULK

masterful, domineering, imperious, peremptory, imperative mean tending to impose one's will on others. **Masterful** implies a strong personality and ability to act authoritatively ⟨her *masterful* personality soon dominated the movement⟩. **Domineering** suggests an overbearing or arbitrary manner and an obstinate determination to enforce one's will ⟨*domineering* mothers refusing to let their sons go⟩. **Imperious** implies a commanding nature or manner and often suggests arrogant assurance ⟨an *imperious* executive used to getting his own way⟩. **Peremptory** implies an abrupt dictatorial manner coupled with an unwillingness to brook disobedience or dissent ⟨his *peremptory* style does not allow for consultation or compromise⟩. **Imperative** implies peremptoriness arising more from the urgency of the situation than from an inherent will to dominate ⟨an *imperative* appeal for assistance⟩.

material, physical, corporeal, phenomenal, sensible, objective mean of or belonging to actuality. **Material** implies formation out of tangible matter; used in contrast with *spiritual* or *ideal* it may connote the mundane, crass, or grasping ⟨*material* possessions⟩. **Physical** applies to what is perceived directly by the senses and may contrast with *mental, spiritual,* or *imaginary* ⟨the *physical* benefits of exercise⟩. **Corporeal** implies having the tangible qualities of a body such as shape, size, or resistance to force ⟨artists have portrayed angels as *corporeal* beings⟩. **Phenomenal** applies to what is known or perceived through the senses rather than by intuition or rational deduction ⟨scientists concerned only with the *phenomenal* world⟩. **Sensible** stresses the capability of readily or forcibly impressing the senses ⟨the earth's rotation is not *sensible* to us⟩. **Objective** may stress material or independent existence apart from a subject perceiving it ⟨tears are the *objective* manifestation of grief⟩. See in addition RELEVANT.

matrimonial, marital, conjugal, connubial, nuptial mean of, relating to, or characteristic of marriage. **Matrimonial** and **marital** apply to whatever has to do with marriage and the married state ⟨enjoyed 40 years of *matrimonial* bliss⟩ ⟨a *marital* relationship built upon mutual trust and understanding⟩. **Conjugal** specif. applies to married persons and their rights ⟨inmates of the prison now have *conjugal* rights⟩. **Connubial** may refer to the married state itself ⟨a *connubial* contract of no legal standing⟩. **Nuptial** usu. refers to the marriage ceremony ⟨busy all week with the *nuptial* preparations⟩.

meager, scanty, scant, skimpy, spare, sparse mean falling short of what is normal, necessary, or desirable. **Meager** implies the absence of elements, qualities, or numbers necessary to a thing's richness, substance, or potency ⟨a *meager* portion of meat⟩. **Scanty** stresses insufficiency in amount, quantity, or extent ⟨supplies too *scanty* to last the winter⟩. **Scant** suggests a falling short of what is desired or desirable rather than of what is essential ⟨in January the daylight hours are *scant*⟩. **Skimpy** usu. suggests niggardliness or penury as the cause of the deficiency ⟨tacky housing developments on *skimpy* lots⟩. **Spare** may suggest a slight falling short of adequacy or merely an absence of superfluity ⟨a *spare*, concise style of writing⟩. **Sparse** implies a thin scattering of units ⟨a *sparse* population⟩.

mean *adj* **Mean, ignoble, abject, sordid** mean below the normal standards of human decency and dignity. **Mean** suggests having repellent characteristics (as small-mindedness, ill temper, or cupidity) ⟨*mean* and petty characterizations of former colleagues⟩. **Ignoble** suggests a loss or lack of some essential high quality of mind or spirit

⟨*ignoble* collectors who view artworks merely as investments⟩. **Abject** may imply degradation, debasement, or servility ⟨the *abject* poverty of her youth⟩. **Sordid** is stronger than all of these in stressing physical or spiritual degradation and abjectness ⟨a *sordid* story of murder and revenge⟩.

mean *n* see AVERAGE

meander see WANDER

meaning, sense, acceptation, signification, significance, import denote the idea conveyed to the mind. **Meaning** is the general term used of anything (as a word, sign, poem, or action) requiring or allowing of interpretation ⟨the poem's *meaning* has been fiercely debated⟩. **Sense** denotes the meaning or more often a particular meaning of a word or phrase ⟨used "nighthawk" in its figurative *sense*⟩. **Acceptation** is used of a sense of a word or phrase as regularly understood by a large number of speakers and writers ⟨the writer isn't using "sane" in its common *acceptation*⟩. **Signification** denotes the established meaning of a term, symbol, or character ⟨any Christian would immediately know the *signification* of "INRI"⟩. **Significance** applies specif. to a covert as distinguished from the ostensible meaning of an utterance, act, or work of art ⟨an agreement that seemed to have little *significance* at the time⟩. **Import** suggests the meaning a speaker tries to convey esp. through language ⟨failed at first to appreciate the *import* of the news⟩.

mechanical see SPONTANEOUS

meddlesome see IMPERTINENT

median see AVERAGE

mediate see INTERPOSE

meditate see PONDER

meek see HUMBLE

meet see FIT

melancholia see SADNESS

melancholy see SADNESS

melodramatic see DRAMATIC

member see PART

memory, remembrance, recollection, reminiscence mean the capacity for or the act of remembering, or the thing remembered. **Memory** applies both to the power of remembering and to what is remembered ⟨gifted with a remarkable *memory*⟩ ⟨no *memory* of that incident⟩. **Remembrance** applies to the act of remembering or the fact of being remembered ⟨any *remembrance* of his deceased wife was painful⟩. **Recollection** adds an implication of consciously bringing back to mind often with some effort ⟨after a moment's *recollection* he produced the name⟩. **Reminiscence** suggests the recalling of incidents, experience, or feelings from a remote past ⟨recorded my grandmother's *reminiscences* of her Iowa girlhood⟩.

mend, repair, patch, rebuild mean to put into good order something that has been injured, damaged, or defective. **Mend** implies making whole or sound something broken, torn, or injured ⟨the wound *mended* slowly⟩. **Repair** applies to the mending of more extensive damage or dilapidation ⟨the car needs to be *repaired* by a mechanic⟩. **Patch** implies an often temporary mending of a rent or breach with new material ⟨*patch* potholes with asphalt⟩. **Rebuild** suggests making like new without completely replacing ⟨a *rebuilt* telephone is cheaper than a brand-new one⟩.

mendacious see DISHONEST

mercurial see INCONSTANT

mercy, charity, clemency, grace, lenity mean a disposition to show kindness or compassion. **Mercy** implies compassion that forbears punishing even when justice demands it

⟨admitted his guilt and then begged for *mercy*⟩. **Charity** stresses benevolence and goodwill shown in broad understanding and tolerance of others ⟨show a little *charity* for the weak-willed⟩. **Clemency** implies a mild or merciful disposition in one having the power or duty of punishing ⟨a judge little inclined to show *clemency*⟩. **Grace** implies a benign attitude and a willingness to grant favors or make concessions ⟨the victor's *grace* in treating the vanquished⟩. **Lenity** implies lack of severity in punishing ⟨criticized the courts for excessive *lenity*⟩.

meretricious see GAUDY

merge see MIX

merry, blithe, jocund, jovial, jolly mean showing high spirits or lightheartedness. **Merry** suggests cheerful, joyous, uninhibited enjoyment of frolic or festivity ⟨a *merry* group of holiday revelers⟩. **Blithe** suggests carefree, innocent, or even heedless gaiety ⟨arrived late in her usual *blithe* way⟩. **Jocund** stresses elation and exhilaration of spirits ⟨good news had left him in a *jocund* mood⟩. **Jovial** suggests the stimulation of conviviality and good fellowship ⟨grew increasingly *jovial* with every drink⟩. **Jolly** suggests high spirits expressed in laughing, bantering, and jesting ⟨our *jolly* host enlivened the party⟩.

metamorphose see TRANSFORM

method, mode, manner, way, fashion, system mean the means taken or procedure followed in achieving an end. **Method** implies an orderly logical effective arrangement usu. in steps ⟨effective *methods* of birth control⟩. **Mode** implies an order or course followed by custom, tradition, or personal preference ⟨the preferred *mode* of transportation⟩. **Manner** is close to *mode* but may imply a procedure or method that is individual or distinctive ⟨a highly distinctive *manner* of conducting⟩. **Way** is very general and may be used for any of the preceding words ⟨her usual slapdash *way* of doing things⟩. **Fashion** may suggest a peculiar or characteristic way of doing something ⟨rushing about, in typical New Yorker *fashion*⟩. **System** suggests a fully developed or carefully formulated method often emphasizing the idea of rational orderliness ⟨follows no *system* in playing the horses⟩.

methodize see ORDER

meticulous see CAREFUL

métier see WORK

mettle see COURAGE

mien see BEARING

might see POWER

milieu see BACKGROUND

militant see AGGRESSIVE

mimic see COPY

mingle see MIX

miniature see SMALL

minimize see DECRY

minute see CIRCUMSTANTIAL, SMALL

mirth, glee, jollity, hilarity mean a feeling of high spirits that is expressed in laughter, play, or merrymaking. **Mirth** implies generally lightness of heart and love of gaiety ⟨family gatherings that were the occasions of much *mirth*⟩. **Glee** stresses exultation shown in laughter, cries of joy, or sometimes malicious delight ⟨cackled with *glee* at their misfortune⟩. **Jollity** suggests exuberance or lack of restraint in mirth or glee ⟨his endless flow of jokes added to the *jollity*⟩. **Hilarity** suggests loud or irrepressible laughter or high-spirited boisterousness ⟨a dull comedy not likely to inspire much *hilarity*⟩.

misanthropic see CYNICAL

mischance see MISFORTUNE

mise-en-scène see BACKGROUND

miserly see STINGY

misery see DISTRESS

misfortune, mischance, adversity, mishap mean adverse
fortune or an instance of this. **Misfortune** may apply to
either the incident or conjunction of events that is the
cause of an unhappy change of fortune or to the ensuing
state of distress ⟨never lost hope even in the depths of *misfortune*⟩. **Mischance** applies esp. to a situation involving
no more than slight inconvenience or minor annoyance
⟨took the wrong road by *mischance*⟩. **Adversity** applies to
a state of grave or persistent misfortune ⟨had never experienced much *adversity* in life⟩. **Mishap** applies to a trivial
instance of bad luck ⟨the usual *mishaps* that are part of a
family vacation⟩.

misgiving see APPREHENSION

mishap see MISFORTUNE

mislead see DECEIVE

misogynistic see CYNICAL

mistake see ERROR

mistrust see UNCERTAINTY

mitigate see RELIEVE

**mix, mingle, commingle, blend, merge, coalesce, amalga-
mate, fuse** mean to combine into a more or less uniform
whole. **Mix** may or may not imply loss of each element's
identity ⟨*mix* the salad greens⟩. **Mingle** usu. suggests that
the elements are still somewhat distinguishable or separately active ⟨fear *mingled* with anticipation in my mind⟩.
Commingle implies a closer or more thorough mingling ⟨a
sense of duty *commingled* with a fierce pride⟩. **Blend** implies that the elements as such disappear in the resulting
mixture ⟨*blended* several teas to create a balanced brew⟩.
Merge suggests a combining in which one or more ele-

ments are lost in the whole ⟨in her mind reality and fantasy *merged*⟩. **Coalesce** implies an affinity in the merging elements and usu. a resulting organic unity ⟨telling details that *coalesce* into a striking portrait⟩. **Amalgamate** implies the forming of a close union without complete loss of individual identities ⟨immigrants that were readily *amalgamated* into the population⟩. **Fuse** stresses oneness and indissolubility of the resulting product ⟨a building in which modernism and classicism are *fused*⟩.

mob see CROWD

mock see COPY, RIDICULE

mode see FASHION, METHOD

model, example, pattern, exemplar, ideal mean someone or something set before one for guidance or imitation. **Model** applies to something taken or proposed as worthy of imitation ⟨a performance that is a *model* of charm and intelligence⟩. **Example** applies to a person to be imitated or in some contexts on no account to be imitated but to be regarded as a warning ⟨for better or worse, children follow the *example* of their parents⟩. **Pattern** suggests a clear and detailed archetype or prototype ⟨American industry set a *pattern* for others to follow⟩. **Exemplar** suggests either a faultless example to be emulated or a perfect typification ⟨cited Hitler as the *exemplar* of power-mad egomania⟩. **Ideal** implies the best possible exemplification either in reality or in conception ⟨never found a suitor who matched her *ideal*⟩.

modern see NEW

modest see CHASTE, HUMBLE, SHY

modify see CHANGE

moist see WET

mollify see PACIFY

mollycoddle see INDULGE

moment see IMPORTANCE
momentary see TRANSIENT
monetary see FINANCIAL
monstrous, prodigious, tremendous, stupendous mean extremely impressive. **Monstrous** implies a departure from the normal (as in size, form, or character) and often carries suggestions of deformity, ugliness, or fabulousness ⟨the *monstrous* waste of the project⟩. **Prodigious** suggests a marvelousness exceeding belief, usu. in something felt as going far beyond a previous maximum (as of goodness, greatness, intensity, or size) ⟨made a *prodigious* effort and rolled the stone aside⟩. **Tremendous** may imply a power to terrify or inspire awe ⟨the *tremendous* roar of the cataract⟩, but in more general and much weakened use it means little more than very large or great or intense ⟨success gave him *tremendous* satisfaction⟩. **Stupendous** implies a power to stun or astound, usu. because of size, numbers, complexity, or greatness beyond one's power to describe ⟨a *stupendous* volcanic eruption that destroyed the city⟩. See in addition OUTRAGEOUS.
moral, ethical, virtuous, righteous, noble mean conforming to a standard of what is right and good. **Moral** implies conformity to established sanctioned codes or accepted notions of right and wrong ⟨the basic *moral* values of a community⟩. **Ethical** may suggest the involvement of more difficult or subtle questions of rightness, fairness, or equity ⟨his strict *ethical* code would not tolerate it⟩. **Virtuous** implies the possession or manifestation of moral excellence in character ⟨a person not conventionally religious, but *virtuous* in all other respects⟩. **Righteous** stresses guiltlessness or blamelessness and often suggests the sanctimonious ⟨responded to the charge with *righteous* indignation⟩. **Noble** implies moral eminence and freedom from any-

thing petty, mean, or dubious in conduct and character ⟨had only the *noblest* of reasons for pursuing the case⟩.

mordant see CAUSTIC

morose see SULLEN

mortal see DEADLY

motive, impulse, incentive, inducement, spur, goad mean a stimulus to action. **Motive** implies an emotion or desire operating on the will and causing it to act ⟨a crime without apparent *motive*⟩. **Impulse** suggests a driving power arising from personal temperament or constitution ⟨my first *impulse* was to hit him⟩. **Incentive** applies to an external influence (as an expected reward) inciting to action ⟨a bonus was offered as an *incentive* for meeting the deadline⟩. **Inducement** suggests a motive prompted by the deliberate enticements or allurements of another ⟨offered a watch as an *inducement* to subscribe⟩. **Spur** applies to a motive that stimulates the faculties or increases energy or ardor ⟨fear was the *spur* that kept me going⟩. **Goad** suggests a motive that keeps one going against one's will or desire ⟨the need to earn a living is the daily *goad*⟩.

move, actuate, drive, impel mean to set or keep in motion. **Move** is very general and implies no more than the fact of changing position ⟨the force that *moves* the moon around the earth⟩. **Actuate** stresses transmission of power so as to work or set in motion ⟨turbines are *actuated* by the force of a current of water⟩. **Drive** implies imparting forward and continuous motion and often stresses the effect rather than the impetus ⟨a ship *driven* aground by hurricane winds⟩. **Impel** suggests a greater impetus producing more headlong action ⟨burning ambition *impelled* her to the seat of power⟩.

moving, impressive, poignant, affecting, touching, pathetic mean having the power to produce deep emotion. **Moving**

may apply to any strong emotional effect including thrilling, agitating, saddening, or calling forth pity or sympathy ⟨a *moving* appeal for charitable contributions⟩. **Impressive** implies compelling attention, admiration, wonder, or conviction ⟨an *impressive* list of achievements⟩. **Poignant** applies to what keenly or sharply affects one's sensitivities ⟨a *poignant* documentary on the plight of the homeless⟩. **Affecting** is close to *moving* but most often suggests pathos ⟨an *affecting* reunion of a mother and her child⟩. **Touching** implies arousing tenderness or compassion ⟨the *touching* innocence in a child's eyes⟩. **Pathetic** implies moving to pity or sometimes contempt ⟨*pathetic* attempts to justify gross negligence⟩.

mulish see OBSTINATE
multiply see INCREASE
mundane see EARTHLY
munificent see LIBERAL
murder see KILL
murky see DARK
muse see PONDER
muster see SUMMON
musty see MALODOROUS
mutilate see MAIM
mutiny see REBELLION
mutual see RECIPROCAL
mystery, problem, enigma, riddle, puzzle, conundrum mean something which baffles or perplexes. **Mystery** applies to what cannot be fully understood by human reason or less strictly to whatever resists or defies explanation ⟨the *mystery* of the stone monoliths on Easter Island⟩. **Problem** applies to any question or difficulty calling for a solution or causing concern ⟨the *problems* created by high technology⟩. **Enigma** applies to utterance or behavior that is very

difficult to interpret ⟨his suicide was an *enigma* his family never solved⟩. **Riddle** suggests an enigma or problem involving paradox or apparent contradiction ⟨the *riddle* of the reclusive billionaire⟩. **Puzzle** applies to an enigma or problem that challenges ingenuity for its solution ⟨the mechanisms of heredity were long a *puzzle* for scientists⟩. **Conundrum** applies to a question whose answer involves a pun or less often to a problem whose solution can only be speculative ⟨posed *conundrums* to which there are no practical solutions⟩.

mythical see FICTITIOUS

N

naive see NATURAL
naked see BARE
nasty see DIRTY
national see CITIZEN
native, indigenous, endemic, aboriginal mean belonging to a locality. **Native** implies birth or origin in a place or region and may suggest compatibility with it ⟨*native* tribal customs⟩ ⟨a *native* New Yorker⟩. **Indigenous** applies to species or races and adds to *native* the implication of not having been introduced from elsewhere ⟨maize is *indigenous* to America⟩. **Endemic** implies being peculiar to a region ⟨edelweiss is *endemic* in the Alps⟩. **Aboriginal** implies having no known race preceding in occupancy of the region ⟨the *aboriginal* peoples of Australia⟩.

natural, ingenuous, naive, unsophisticated, artless mean free from pretension or calculation. **Natural** implies lacking artificiality and self-consciousness and having a spontaneousness suggesting the natural rather than the man-made world ⟨her unaffected, *natural* quality comes across on film⟩. **Ingenuous** implies inability to disguise or conceal one's feelings or intentions ⟨the *ingenuous,* spontaneous utterances of children⟩. **Naive** suggests lack of worldly wisdom often connoting credulousness and unchecked innocence ⟨in money matters she was distressingly *naive*⟩. **Unsophisticated** implies a lack of experience and training necessary for social ease and adroitness ⟨the store intimidates *unsophisticated* customers⟩. **Artless** suggests a naturalness resulting from unawareness of the effect one is producing on others ⟨gave an *artless* impromptu speech at the dinner⟩. See in addition REGULAR.

nature see TYPE

naughty see BAD

nefarious see VICIOUS

negate see NULLIFY

neglect, omit, disregard, ignore, overlook, slight, forget mean to pass over without giving due attention. **Neglect** implies giving insufficient attention to something that has a claim to one's attention ⟨habitually *neglected* his studies⟩. **Omit** implies absence of all attention ⟨*omitted* to remove the telltale fingerprints⟩. **Disregard** suggests voluntary inattention ⟨*disregarded* the wishes of the other members⟩. **Ignore** implies a failure to regard something obvious ⟨*ignored* the snide remarks of passersby⟩. **Overlook** suggests disregarding or ignoring through haste or lack of care ⟨in my rush I *overlooked* some relevant examples⟩. **Slight** implies contemptuous or disdainful disregarding or omitting ⟨*slighted* several worthy authors in her survey⟩. **Forget** may suggest either a willful ignoring or a failure to impress something on one's mind ⟨*forget* what others say and listen to your conscience⟩.

neglectful see NEGLIGENT

negligent, neglectful, lax, slack, remiss mean culpably care-less or indicative of such carelessness. **Negligent** implies inattention to one's duty or business ⟨I had been *negligent* in my letter-writing⟩. **Neglectful** adds a more disapproving implication of laziness or deliberate inattention ⟨a society callously *neglectful* of the poor⟩. **Lax** implies a blame-worthy lack of strictness, severity, or precision ⟨a reporter who is *lax* about getting the facts straight⟩. **Slack** implies want of due or necessary diligence or care ⟨the *slack* work-manship and slipshod construction⟩. **Remiss** implies blameworthy carelessness shown in slackness, forgetful-ness, or neglect ⟨had been *remiss* in her domestic duties⟩.

neighborly see AMICABLE

nerve see TEMERITY

nervous see VIGOROUS

nettle see IRRITATE

new, novel, modern, original, fresh mean having recently come into existence or use. **New** may apply to what is freshly made and unused ⟨*new* brick⟩ or has not been known before ⟨*new* designs⟩ or not experienced before ⟨starts his *new* job⟩. **Novel** applies to what is not only new but strange or unprecedented ⟨a *novel* approach to the problem⟩. **Modern** applies to what belongs to or is char-acteristic of the present time or the present era ⟨the life-style of the *modern* woman⟩. **Original** applies to what is the first of its kind to exist ⟨a man without one *original* idea⟩. **Fresh** applies to what has not lost its qualities of newness such as liveliness, energy, brightness ⟨*fresh* tow-els⟩ ⟨a *fresh* start⟩.

nice, dainty, fastidious, finicky, particular, squeamish mean having or showing exacting standards. **Nice** implies fine discrimination in perception and evaluation ⟨makes a *nice* distinction between an artist and a craftsman⟩. **Dainty** suggests a tendency to reject what does not satisfy one's delicate taste or sensibility ⟨when camping, one cannot afford to be *dainty* about food⟩. **Fastidious** implies having very high and often capricious ethical, artistic, or social standards ⟨a woman too *fastidious* to tolerate messy little boys⟩. **Finicky** implies an affected often exasperating fastidiousness ⟨small children are usually *finicky* eaters⟩. **Particular** implies an insistence that one's exacting standards be met ⟨a customer who is very *particular* about his fried eggs⟩. **Squeamish** suggests an oversensitive or prudish readiness to be nauseated, disgusted, or offended ⟨*squeamish* about erotic art⟩. See in addition CORRECT.

niggardly see STINGY
nimble see AGILE
nobility see ARISTOCRACY
noble see MORAL
noisome see MALODOROUS
nonchalant see COOL
nonplus see PUZZLE
norm see AVERAGE
normal see REGULAR
note see SIGN
noted see FAMOUS
noticeable, remarkable, prominent, outstanding, conspicuous, salient, striking mean attracting notice or attention.
Noticeable applies to something unlikely to escape observation ⟨a piano recital with no *noticeable* errors⟩. **Remarkable** applies to something so extraordinary or exceptional as to invite comment ⟨a film of *remarkable* intelligence and wit⟩. **Prominent** applies to something commanding notice by standing out from its surroundings or background ⟨a doctor who occupies a *prominent* position in the town⟩. **Outstanding** applies to something that rises above

and excels others of the same kind ⟨honored for her *outstanding* contributions to science⟩. **Conspicuous** applies to something that is obvious and unavoidable to the sight or mind ⟨the *conspicuous* waste of the corrupt regime⟩. **Salient** applies to something of significance that merits the attention given it ⟨list the *salient* points of the speech⟩. **Striking** applies to something that impresses itself powerfully and deeply upon the observer's mind or vision ⟨the backwardness of the area is *striking* to even casual observers⟩.

notify see INFORM

notion see IDEA

notorious see FAMOUS

novel see NEW

noxious see PERNICIOUS

nude see BARE

nugatory see VAIN

nullify, negate, annul, abrogate, invalidate mean to deprive of effective or continued existence. **Nullify** implies counteracting completely the force, effectiveness, or value of something ⟨his critical insights are *nullified* by tiresome puns⟩. **Negate** implies the destruction or canceling out of each of two things by the other ⟨a relationship *negated* by petty jealousies⟩. **Annul** suggests making ineffective or nonexistent often by legal or official action ⟨the treaty *annuls* all previous agreements⟩. **Abrogate** is like *annul* but more definitely implies a legal or official purposeful act ⟨a law that would *abrogate* certain diplomatic privileges⟩. **Invalidate** implies making something powerless or unacceptable by declaration of its logical or moral or legal unsoundness ⟨the absence of witnesses *invalidates* the will⟩.

nuptial see MATRIMONIAL

O

obdurate see INFLEXIBLE

obedient, docile, tractable, amenable mean submissive to the will of another. **Obedient** implies compliance with the demands or requests of one in authority ⟨cadets must be *obedient* to the honor code⟩. **Docile** implies a predisposition to submit readily to control or guidance ⟨a *docile* child who never caused trouble⟩. **Tractable** suggests having a character that permits easy handling or managing ⟨Indian elephants are more *tractable* than their African cousins⟩. **Amenable** suggests a willingness to yield or to cooperate either because of a desire to be agreeable or because of a natural open-mindedness ⟨he's usually *amenable* to suggestions and new ideas⟩.

object *vb* **Object, protest, remonstrate, expostulate, kick** mean to oppose by arguing against. **Object** stresses dislike or aversions⟨*objected* to his sweeping generalizations⟩. **Protest** suggests an orderly presentation of objections in speech or writing ⟨an open letter *protesting* the government's foreign policy⟩. **Remonstrate** implies an attempt to convince by warning or reproving ⟨*remonstrated* on his son's free-spending ways at college⟩. **Expostulate** suggests an earnest explanation of one's objection and firm insistence on change ⟨mother *expostulated,* but my room remained a mess⟩. **Kick** suggests more informally a strenuous protesting or complaining ⟨everybody *kicks* when taxes are raised⟩.

object *n* see INTENTION

objective *adj* see FAIR, MATERIAL

objective *n* see INTENTION

oblige see FORCE

obliging see AMIABLE

obliterate see ERASE

oblivious see FORGETFUL

obloquy see ABUSE

obnoxious see REPUGNANT

obscene see COARSE

obscure, dark, vague, enigmatic, cryptic, ambiguous, equivocal mean not clearly understandable. **Obscure** implies a hiding or veiling of meaning through some inadequacy of expression or withholding of full knowledge ⟨the poem is *obscure* to those unlearned in the classics⟩. **Dark** implies an imperfect or clouded revelation often with ominous or sinister suggestion ⟨muttered *dark* hints of revenge⟩. **Vague** implies a lack of clear formulation due to inadequate conception or consideration ⟨*vague* promises of reimbursement were made⟩. **Enigmatic** stresses a puzzling, mystifying quality ⟨left behind *enigmatic* works on alchemy⟩. **Cryptic** implies a purposely concealed meaning ⟨a *cryptic* message only a spy could decode⟩. **Ambiguous** applies to a difficulty of understanding arising from the use of a word or words of multiple meanings ⟨an *ambiguous* directive that could be taken either way⟩. **Equivocal** applies to the deliberate use of language open to differing interpretations with the intention of deceiving or evading ⟨the prisoner would give only *equivocal* answers⟩.

obsequious see SUBSERVIENT

observe see KEEP

obsolete see OLD

obstinate, dogged, stubborn, pertinacious, mulish mean fixed and unyielding in course or purpose. **Obstinate** implies usu. a perverse or unreasonable persistence ⟨a President who was resolute but never *obstinate*⟩. **Dogged** suggests a tenacious unwavering persistence 〈pursued the story with *dogged* perseverance〉. **Stubborn** implies sturdiness in resisting attempts to change or abandon a course or opinion 〈swallow your *stubborn* pride and admit that you are wrong〉. **Pertinacious** suggests an annoying or irksome persistence 〈a *pertinacious* salesman who wouldn't take no for an answer〉. **Mulish** implies a thoroughly unreasonable obstinacy 〈a *mulish* determination to stick with a lost cause〉.

obstreperous see VOCIFEROUS

obstruct see HINDER

obtain see GET

obtrude see INTRUDE

obtrusive see IMPERTINENT

obtuse see DULL

obviate see PREVENT

obvious see EVIDENT

occasion see CAUSE

occupation see WORK

occurrence, event, incident, episode, circumstance mean something that happens or takes place. **Occurrence** may apply to a happening without intent, volition, or plan 〈a meeting that was a chance *occurrence*〉. **Event** usu. implies an occurrence of some importance and frequently one having antecedent cause 〈the sequence of *events* following the assassination〉. **Incident** suggests an occurrence of brief duration or secondary importance 〈one of the minor *incidents* of the war〉. **Episode** stresses the distinctiveness or apartness of an incident 〈recounted some amusing *episodes* from his youth〉. **Circumstance** implies a specific detail attending an action or event as part of its setting or background 〈couldn't remember the exact *circumstances*〉.

odd see STRANGE

odious see HATEFUL

odor see SMELL

odorous, fragrant, redolent, aromatic mean emitting and diffusing scent. **Odorous** applies to whatever has a strong distinctive smell whether pleasant or unpleasant ⟨*odorous* cheeses should be tightly wrapped⟩. **Fragrant** applies to things (as flowers or spices) with sweet or agreeable odors ⟨roses that were especially *fragrant*⟩. **Redolent** applies usu. to a place or thing impregnated with odors ⟨the kitchen was often *redolent* of garlic and tomatoes⟩. **Aromatic** applies to things emitting pungent often fresh odors ⟨an *aromatic* blend of rare tobaccos⟩.

offend, outrage, affront, insult mean to cause hurt feelings or deep resentment. **Offend** need not imply an intentional hurting but it may indicate merely a violation of the victim's sense of what is proper or fitting ⟨hoped that my remarks had not *offended* her⟩. **Outrage** implies offending beyond endurance and calling forth extreme feelings ⟨corruption that *outrages* every citizen⟩. **Affront** implies treating with deliberate rudeness or contemptuous indifference to courtesy ⟨a movie that *affronts* your intelligence⟩. **Insult** suggests deliberately causing humiliation, hurt pride, or shame ⟨managed to *insult* every guest at the party⟩.

offense *n* Offense, resentment, umbrage, pique, dudgeon, huff mean an emotional response to a slight or indignity. **Offense** implies hurt displeasure ⟨takes deep *offense* at racial slurs⟩. **Resentment** suggests a longer lasting indignation or smoldering ill will ⟨harbored a life-long *resentment* of his brother⟩. **Umbrage** implies a feeling of being snubbed or ignored ⟨took *umbrage* at a lecturer who debunked American legends⟩. **Pique** applies to a transient feeling of wounded vanity ⟨in a *pique* she foolishly declined the invitation⟩. **Dudgeon** suggests an angry fit of indignation ⟨walked out of the meeting in high *dudgeon*⟩. **Huff** implies a peevish short-lived spell of anger usu. at a petty cause ⟨in a *huff* she threw the ring in his face⟩.

offense *n* Offense, sin, vice, crime, scandal mean a transgression of law. **Offense** applies to the infraction of any law, rule, or code ⟨at that school no *offense* went unpunished⟩. **Sin** implies an offense against the moral law ⟨the *sin* of blasphemy⟩. **Vice** applies to a habit or practice that degrades or corrupts ⟨gambling was traditionally the gentleman's *vice*⟩. **Crime** implies a serious offense punishable by the law of the state ⟨the *crime* of murder⟩. **Scandal** applies to an offense that outrages the public conscience ⟨the woman's affairs were a public *scandal*⟩.

offhand see EXTEMPORANEOUS

office see FUNCTION

officious see IMPERTINENT

offset see COMPENSATE

oily see FULSOME

old, ancient, venerable, antique, antiquated, archaic, obsolete mean having come into existence or use in the more or less distant past. **Old** may apply to either actual or merely relative length of existence ⟨*old* houses⟩ ⟨an *old* sweater of mine⟩. **Ancient** applies to occurrence, existence, or use in or survival from the distant past ⟨*ancient* accounts of dragons⟩. **Venerable** stresses the impressiveness and dignity of great age ⟨the family's *venerable* patriarch⟩. **Antique** applies to what has come down from a former or ancient time ⟨collected *antique* Chippendale furniture⟩. **Antiquated** implies being discredited or outmoded or otherwise inappropriate to the present time ⟨*antiquated* teaching methods⟩. **Archaic** implies having the character or characteristics of a much earlier time ⟨the play used *archaic* language to convey a sense of period⟩. **Obsolete** implies having gone out of currency or habitual practice ⟨this nuclear missile will make all others *obsolete*⟩.

oleaginous see FULSOME

ominous, portentous, fateful mean having a menacing or threatening aspect. **Ominous** implies a menacing, alarming character foreshadowing evil or disaster ⟨*ominous* rumblings from a dormant volcano⟩. **Portentous** suggests being frighteningly big or impressive but now seldom definitely connotes forwarning of calamity ⟨the *portentous* voice of the host of a televised mystery series⟩. **Fateful** suggests being of momentous or decisive importance ⟨the *fateful* conference that led to war⟩.

omit see NEGLECT

omnipresent, ubiquitous mean present or existent everywhere. **Omnipresent** in its strict sense is a divine attribute equivalent to *immanent;* more commonly it implies never being absent ⟨residents of the ghetto have an *omnipresent* sense of fear⟩. **Ubiquitous** implies being so active or so numerous as to seem to be found everywhere ⟨*ubiquitous* tourists toting their *omnipresent* cameras⟩.

onerous, burdensome, oppressive, exacting mean imposing hardship. **Onerous** stresses being laborious and heavy esp. because distasteful ⟨the *onerous* task of informing the family of his death⟩. **Burdensome** suggests causing mental as well as physical strain ⟨*burdensome* government regulations⟩. **Oppressive** implies extreme harshness or severity in what is imposed ⟨found the pressure to conform socially *oppressive*⟩. **Exacting** implies rigor or sternness rather than tyranny or injustice in the demands made or in the one demanding ⟨an *exacting* employer⟩.

open see FRANK, LIABLE

opinion, view, belief, conviction, persuasion, sentiment mean a judgment one holds as true. **Opinion** implies a conclusion thought out yet open to dispute ⟨each expert seemed to be of a different *opinion*⟩. **View** suggests a subjective opinion ⟨very assertive in stating his *views*⟩. **Belief** implies often deliberate acceptance and intellectual assent ⟨a firm *belief* in a supreme being⟩. **Conviction** applies to a firmly and seriously held belief ⟨a *conviction* that animal life is as sacred as human⟩. **Persuasion** suggests a belief grounded on assurance (as by evidence) of its truth ⟨was of the *persuasion* that Republicans were better for business⟩. **Sentiment** suggests a settled opinion reflective of one's feelings ⟨her feminist *sentiments* were well-known⟩.

opponent, antagonist, adversary mean one that takes an opposite position. **Opponent** implies little more than position on the other side as in a debate, election, contest, or conflict ⟨*opponents* of the project cite cost as a factor⟩. **Antagonist** implies sharper opposition in a struggle for supremacy ⟨a formidable *antagonist* in the struggle for corporate control⟩. **Adversary** may carry an additional implication of active hostility ⟨two peoples that have been bitter *adversaries* for centuries⟩.

oppose, combat, resist, withstand, antagonize mean to set oneself against someone or something. **Oppose** can apply to any conflict, from mere objection to bitter hostility or warfare ⟨*opposed* the plan to build a nuclear power plant⟩. **Combat** stresses the forceful or urgent countering of something ⟨*combat* the disease by educating the public⟩. **Resist** implies an overt recognition of a hostile or threatening force and a positive effort to counteract or repel it ⟨struggled valiantly to *resist* the temptation⟩. **Withstand** suggests a more passive resistance ⟨unable to *withstand* peer pressure⟩. **Antagonize** implies an arousing of resistance or hostility in another ⟨statements that *antagonized* even his own supporters⟩.

opposite, contradictory, contrary, antithetical mean being so far apart as to be or seem irreconcilable. **Opposite** applies to things in sharp contrast or in conflict ⟨they held *opposite* views on foreign aid⟩. **Contradictory** applies to two things that completely negate each other so that if one is true or valid the other must be untrue or invalid ⟨made *contradictory* predictions about the stock market⟩. **Contrary** implies extreme divergence or diametrical opposition ⟨*contrary* accounts of the late president's character⟩. **Antithetical** stresses clear and unequivocal diametrical opposition ⟨a law that is *antithetical* to the basic idea of democracy⟩.

oppress see WRONG

oppressive see ONEROUS

option see CHOICE

opulent see LUXURIOUS, RICH

oracular see DICTATORIAL

orbit see RANGE

ordain see DICTATE

order, arrange, marshal, organize, systematize, methodize mean to put persons or things into their proper places in relation to each other. **Order** suggests a straightening out so as to eliminate confusion ⟨*ordered* her business affairs before going on extended leave⟩. **Arrange** implies a setting in sequence, relationship, or adjustment ⟨a bouquet of elaborately *arranged* flowers⟩. **Marshal** suggests gathering and arranging in preparation for a particular operation or effective use ⟨an argument won by carefully *marshalled* facts⟩. **Organize** implies arranging so that the whole aggregate works as a unit with each element having a proper function ⟨*organized* the volunteers into teams⟩. **Systematize** implies arranging according to a predetermined scheme ⟨billing procedures that have yet to be *systema-*

tized⟩. **Methodize** suggests imposing an orderly procedure rather than a fixed scheme ⟨*methodizes* every aspect of her daily living⟩. See in addition COMMAND.

ordinance see LAW

ordinary see COMMON

organize see ORDER

origin, source, inception, root mean the point at which something begins its course or existence. **Origin** applies to the things or persons from which something is ultimately derived and often to the causes operating before the thing itself comes into being ⟨an investigation into the *origins* of baseball⟩. **Source** applies more often to the point where something springs into being ⟨the *source* of the Nile⟩ ⟨the *source* of recurrent trouble⟩. **Inception** stresses the beginning of something without implying causes ⟨the business has been a success since its *inception*⟩. **Root** suggests a first, ultimate, or fundamental source often not easily discerned ⟨a need to find the real *root* of the violence⟩.

original see NEW

originate see SPRING

ornament see ADORN

oscillate see SWING

ostensible see APPARENT

ostentatious see SHOWY

otiose see VAIN

oust see EJECT

outcome see EFFECT

outdo see EXCEED

outfit see FURNISH

outlandish see STRANGE

outline, contour, profile, silhouette mean the line that bounds and gives form to something. **Outline** applies to a line marking the outer limits or edges of a body or mass

⟨chalk *outlines* of the bodies on the sidewalk⟩. **Contour** stresses the quality of an outline or a bounding surface as being smooth, jagged, curving, or sharply angled ⟨a car with smoothly flowing *contours*⟩. **Profile** suggests a varied and sharply defined outline against a lighter background ⟨her face in *profile* accentuates her patrician beauty⟩. **Silhouette** suggests a shape esp. of a head or figure with all detail blacked out in shadow leaving only the outline clearly defined ⟨a photograph of two figures in *silhouette* on a mountain ridge⟩.

outlook see PROSPECT

outrage see OFFEND

outrageous, monstrous, heinous, atrocious mean enormously bad or horrible. **Outrageous** implies exceeding the limits of what is bearable or endurable ⟨*outrageous* terrorist acts against civilians⟩. **Monstrous** applies to what is abnormally or fantastically wrong, absurd, or horrible ⟨a *monstrous* waste of the taxpayers' money⟩. **Heinous** implies being so flagrantly evil as to excite hatred or horror ⟨*heinous* crimes that exceeded normal wartime actions⟩. **Atrocious** implies merciless cruelty, savagery, or contempt of ordinary values ⟨decent people cannot condone such *atrocious* treatment of prisoners⟩.

outstanding see NOTICEABLE

outstrip see EXCEED

outwit see FRUSTRATE

overbearing see PROUD

overcome see CONQUER

overlook see NEGLECT

overthrow see CONQUER

own see ACKNOWLEDGE, HAVE

P

pacify, appease, placate, mollify, propitiate, conciliate mean
to ease the anger or disturbance of. **Pacify** suggests a
smoothing or calming ⟨a sincere apology seemed to *pacify*
him⟩. **Appease** implies quieting insistent demands by
making concessions ⟨nothing seemed to *appease* their appetite for territorial expansion⟩. **Placate** suggests changing
resentment or bitterness to goodwill ⟨bought flowers to
placate his irate wife⟩. **Mollify** implies soothing hurt feelings or rising anger ⟨a promise of a hearing *mollified* the
demonstrators⟩. **Propitiate** implies averting anger or malevolence esp. of a superior being ⟨*propitiated* his mother-
in-law by getting the clean-cut look⟩. **Conciliate** suggests
ending an estrangement by persuasion, concession, or settling of differences ⟨America's role in *conciliating* the nations of the Middle East⟩.

pains see EFFORT

palatable, appetizing, savory, tasty, toothsome mean agreeable or pleasant esp. to the sense of taste. **Palatable** often
applies to something that is unexpectedly found to be
agreeable ⟨surprised to find Indian food quite *palatable*⟩.
Appetizing suggests a whetting of the appetite and applies
to aroma and appearance as well as taste ⟨select from a
cart filled with *appetizing* desserts⟩. **Savory** applies to both
taste and aroma and suggests piquancy and often spiciness
⟨egg rolls variously filled with *savory* fillings⟩. **Tasty** implies a pronounced taste ⟨stale shrimp that were far from
tasty⟩. **Toothsome** stresses the notion of agreeableness and
sometimes implies tenderness or daintiness ⟨a dazzling
array of *toothsome* hors d'oeuvres⟩.

pall see SATIATE
palpable see PERCEPTIBLE
palter see LIE
pamper see INDULGE
panegyric see ENCOMIUM
panic see FEAR
parade see SHOW
parallel see SIMILAR
paramount see DOMINANT

parasite, sycophant, toady, leech, sponge mean an obsequious flatterer or self-seeker. **Parasite** applies to one who clings to a person of wealth, power, or influence or is useless to society ⟨a jet-setter with the usual entourage of *parasites*⟩. **Sycophant** adds to this a strong suggestion of fawning, flattery, or adulation ⟨a religious cult leader surrounded by *sycophants*⟩. **Toady** emphasizes the servility and snobbery of the self-seeker ⟨the president's own *toady* made others grovel⟩. **Leech** stresses persistence in clinging to or bleeding another for one's own advantage ⟨*leeches* who abandoned her when the money ran out⟩. **Sponge** stresses the parasitic laziness, dependence, and opportunism of the cadger ⟨her brother, a shiftless *sponge*, often came by for a free meal⟩.

pardon see EXCUSE
parley see CONFER
parody see CARICATURE
parsimonious see STINGY

part *n* Part, portion, piece, member, division, section, segment, fragment** mean something less than the whole. **Part** is a general term appropriate when indefiniteness is required ⟨they ran only *part* of the way⟩. **Portion** implies an assigned or allotted part ⟨cut the pie into six *portions*⟩. **Piece** applies to a separate or detached part of a whole ⟨a puzzle with 500 *pieces*). **Member** suggests one of the functional units composing a body 〈an arm is a bodily *member*〉. **Division** applies to a large or diversified part 〈the manufacturing *division* of the company〉. **Section** applies to a relatively small or uniform part 〈the entertainment *section* of the newspaper〉. **Segment** applies to a part separated or marked out by or as if by natural lines of cleavage 〈the retired *segment* of the population〉. **Fragment** applies to a part produced by or as if by breaking off or shattering 〈only a *fragment* of the play still exists〉.

part *vb* see SEPARATE
partake see SHARE
participate see SHARE
particular *adj* see CIRCUMSTANTIAL, NICE, SINGLE, SPECIAL
particular *n* see ITEM
partisan see FOLLOWER
partner see CONFEDERATE
pass see JUNCTURE
passion, fervor, ardor, enthusiasm, zeal mean intense emotion compelling action. **Passion** applies to an emotion that is deeply stirring or ungovernable 〈developed a *passion* for reading〉. **Fervor** implies a warm and steady emotion 〈read the poem aloud with great *fervor*〉. **Ardor** suggests warm and excited feeling likely to be fitful or short-lived 〈the *ardor* of their honeymoon soon faded〉. **Enthusiasm** applies to lively or eager interest in or admiration for a proposal or cause or activity 〈never showed much *enthusiasm* for sports〉. **Zeal** implies energetic and unflagging pursuit of an aim or devotion to a cause 〈preaches with the *zeal* of the converted〉. See in addition FEELING.

passionate see IMPASSIONED
passive see INACTIVE
pastoral see RURAL

patch see MEND
patent see EVIDENT
pathetic see MOVING
pattern see MODEL
pay, compensate, remunerate, satisfy, reimburse, indemnify, repay, recompense mean to give money or its equivalent in return for something. **Pay** implies the discharge of an obligation incurred ⟨we *pay* taxes in exchange for government services⟩. **Compensate** implies a making up for services rendered or help given ⟨an attorney well *compensated* for her services⟩. **Remunerate** more clearly suggests paying for services rendered and may extend to payment that is generous or not contracted for ⟨promised to *remunerate* the searchers handsomely⟩. **Satisfy** implies paying a person what is demanded or required by law ⟨all creditors will be *satisfied* in full⟩. **Reimburse** implies a return of money that has been expended for another's benefit ⟨the company will *reimburse* employees for expenses incurred⟩. **Indemnify** implies making good a loss suffered through accident, disaster, warfare ⟨the government cannot *indemnify* the families of military casualties⟩. **Repay** stresses paying back an equivalent in kind or amount ⟨*repay* a loan⟩. **Recompense** suggests due return in amends, friendly repayment, or reward ⟨the hotel *recompensed* us with a free bottle of champagne⟩.

peaceful see CALM
peak see SUMMIT
peculiar see CHARACTERISTIC, STRANGE
pecuniary see FINANCIAL
peer see GAZE
peeve see IRRITATE
pejorative see DEROGATORY
penchant see LEANING

penetrate see ENTER

penetration see DISCERNMENT

penitence, repentance, contrition, compunction, remorse
mean regret for sin or wrongdoing. **Penitence** implies sad
and humble realization of and regret for one's misdeeds
⟨absolution is dependent upon sincere *penitence*⟩. **Repentance** adds the implication of a resolve to change ⟨a complete change of character accompanied his *repentance*⟩.
Contrition stresses the sorrowful regret that constitutes
true penitence ⟨the beatings were usually followed by tearful expressions of *contrition*⟩. **Compunction** implies a painful sting of conscience esp. for contemplated wrongdoing
⟨have no *compunctions* about taking back what is mine⟩.
Remorse suggests prolonged and insistent self-reproach
and mental anguish for past wrongs and esp. for those
whose consequences cannot be remedied ⟨swindlers are
not usually plagued by feelings of *remorse*⟩.

penurious see STINGY

penury see POVERTY

perceptible, sensible, palpable, tangible, appreciable, ponderable mean apprehensible as real or existent. **Perceptible**
applies to what can be discerned by the senses often to a
minimal extent ⟨a *perceptible* difference in sound⟩. **Sensible** applies to whatever is clearly apprehended through the
senses or impresses itself strongly on the mind ⟨a *sensible*
change in the weather⟩. **Palpable** applies either to what has
physical substance or to what is obvious and unmistakable
⟨the tension in the air was almost *palpable*⟩. **Tangible** suggests what is capable of being handled or grasped both
physically and mentally ⟨submitted the gun as *tangible* evidence⟩. **Appreciable** applies to what is distinctly discernible by the senses or definitely measurable ⟨an *appreciable*
increase in temperature⟩. **Ponderable** suggests having def-

initely measurable weight or importance esp. as distinguished from eluding such determination ⟨exerted a *ponderable* influence on world events⟩.

perception see DISCERNMENT

peremptory see MASTERFUL

perennial see CONTINUAL

perfect, whole, entire, intact mean not lacking or faulty in any particular. **Perfect** implies the soundness and the excellence of every part, element, or quality of a thing frequently as an unattainable or theoretical state ⟨a *perfect* set of teeth⟩ ⟨the *perfect* woman⟩. **Whole** suggests a completeness or perfection that can be sought, gained, or regained ⟨an experience that made him feel a *whole* man again⟩. **Entire** implies perfection deriving from integrity, soundness, or completeness of a thing ⟨recorded the *entire* Beethoven corpus⟩. **Intact** implies retention of perfection of a thing in its natural or original state ⟨somehow the building survived the storm *intact*⟩.

perfervid see IMPASSIONED

perfidious see FAITHLESS

perform, execute, discharge, accomplish, achieve, effect, fulfill mean to carry out or into effect. **Perform** implies action that follows established patterns or procedures or fulfills agreed-upon requirements and often connotes special skill ⟨*performed* gymnastics on the parallel bars⟩. **Execute** stresses the carrying out of what exists in plan or in intent ⟨*executed* the heist exactly as planned⟩. **Discharge** implies execution and completion of appointed duties or tasks ⟨*discharged* his duties promptly and effectively⟩. **Accomplish** stresses the successful completion of a process rather than the means of carrying it out ⟨*accomplished* in a year what had taken others a lifetime⟩. **Achieve** adds to *accomplish* the implication of conquered difficulties ⟨a nation struggling to *achieve* greatness). **Effect** adds to *achieve* an emphasis on the inherent force in the agent capable of surmounting obstacles ⟨a dynamic personality who *effected* sweeping reforms⟩. **Fulfill** implies a complete realization of ends or possibilities⟨the rare epic that *fulfills* its ambitions⟩.

perfume see FRAGRANCE

perilous see DANGEROUS

period, epoch, era, age mean a division of time. **Period** may designate an extent of time of any length ⟨*periods* of economic prosperity⟩. **Epoch** applies to a period begun or set off by some significant or striking quality, change, or series of events ⟨the steam engine marked a new *epoch* in industry⟩. **Era** suggests a period of history marked by a new or distinct order of things ⟨the *era* of global communications⟩. **Age** is used frequently of a fairly definite period dominated by a prominent figure or feature ⟨the *age* of Samuel Johnson⟩.

permanent see LASTING

permit see LET

pernicious, baneful, noxious, deleterious, detrimental mean exceedingly harmful. **Pernicious** implies irreparable harm done through evil or insidious corrupting or undermining ⟨the claim that pornography has a *pernicious* effect on society⟩. **Baneful** implies injury through poisoning or destroying ⟨the *baneful* notion that discipline destroys creativity⟩. **Noxious** applies to what is both offensive and injurious to the health of a body or mind ⟨*noxious* fumes emanating from a chemical plant⟩. **Deleterious** applies to what has an often unsuspected harmful effect ⟨megadoses of vitamins can have *deleterious* effects⟩. **Detrimental** implies obvious harmfulness to something specified ⟨the *detrimental* effects of prolonged fasting⟩.

perpendicular see VERTICAL
perpetual see CONTINUAL
perplex see PUZZLE
persecute see WRONG
persist see CONTINUE
personality see DISPOSITION
perspicacious see SHREWD
perspicuous see CLEAR
persuasion see OPINION
pertinacious see OBSTINATE
pertinent see RELEVANT
perturb see DISCOMPOSE
perverse see CONTRARY
pervert see DEBASE
pessimistic see CYNICAL
pester see WORRY
phase, aspect, side, facet, angle mean one of the possible
  ways of viewing or being presented to view. **Phase** implies
  a change in appearance often without clear reference to an
  observer ⟨the second *phase* of the investigation⟩. **Aspect**
  may stress the point of view of an observer and its limi-
  tation of what is seen or considered ⟨an article that considers the financial *aspect* of divorce⟩. **Side** stresses one of
  several aspects from which something may be viewed ⟨a
  broadcast that told only one *side* of the story⟩. **Facet** implies one of a multiplicity of sides each of which manifests
  the central quality of the whole ⟨explores the many *facets*
  of life in New York City⟩. **Angle** suggests an aspect seen
  from a very restricted or specific point of view ⟨find a fresh
  angle for covering the political convention⟩.
phenomenal see MATERIAL
phlegm see EQUANIMITY
phlegmatic see IMPASSIVE

physical see BODILY, MATERIAL
physiognomy see FACE
pickle see PREDICAMENT
pictorial see GRAPHIC
picturesque see GRAPHIC
piece see PART
pierce see ENTER
pietistic see DEVOUT
piety see FIDELITY
pilfer see STEAL
pillage *vb* see RAVAGE
pillage *n* see SPOIL
pilot see GUIDE
pinch see JUNCTURE
pine see LONG
pinnacle see SUMMIT
pious see DEVOUT
piquant see PUNGENT
pique *n* see OFFENSE
pique *vb* see PROVOKE
pitch see THROW
pithy see CONCISE
pitiable see CONTEMPTIBLE

pity, compassion, commiseration, ruth, condolence, sympathy mean the act or capacity for sharing the interests of another. **Pity** implies tender or sometimes slightly contemptuous sorrow for one in misery or distress ⟨no *pity* was shown to the captives⟩. **Compassion** implies pity coupled with an urgent desire to aid or to spare ⟨treats alcoholics with great *compassion*⟩. **Commiseration** suggests pity expressed outwardly in exclamations, tears, words of comfort ⟨murmurs of *commiseration* filled the loser's headquarters⟩. **Ruth** implies pity coming from a change of heart or a relenting ⟨not a trace of *ruth* in the judge's sentencing⟩. **Condolence** applies chiefly to formal expression of grief to one who has suffered loss ⟨expressed their *condolences* to the widow⟩. **Sympathy** implies a power to enter into another's emotional experience of any sort ⟨my *sympathies* are with the rebels' cause⟩.

placate see PACIFY

placid see CALM

plague see WORRY

plain see COMMON, EVIDENT, FRANK

plan, design, plot, scheme, project mean a method devised for making or doing something or achieving an end. **Plan** always implies mental formulation and sometimes graphic representation ⟨studied the *plans* for the proposed industrial park⟩. **Design** often suggests a particular pattern and some degree of achieved order or harmony ⟨*designs* for three new gowns⟩. **Plot** implies a laying out in clearly distinguished sections with attention to their relations and proportions ⟨outlined the *plot* of the new play⟩. **Scheme** stresses calculation of the end in view and may apply to a plan motivated by craftiness and self-interest ⟨a *scheme* to swindle senior citizens of their savings⟩. **Project** often stresses imaginative scope and vision ⟨a *project* to develop the waterfront⟩.

plane see LEVEL

plastic, pliable, pliant, ductile, malleable, adaptable mean susceptible of being modified in form or nature. **Plastic** applies to substances soft enough to be molded yet capable of hardening into the desired fixed form ⟨*plastic* materials allow the sculptor greater freedom⟩. **Pliable** suggests something easily bent, folded, twisted, or manipulated ⟨headphones that are *pliable* and can be bent to fit⟩. **Pliant** may stress flexibility and sometimes connote springiness ⟨select an athletic shoe with a *pliant* sole⟩. **Ductile** applies to what can be drawn out or extended with ease ⟨copper is one of the most *ductile* of metals⟩. **Malleable** applies to what may be pressed or beaten into shape ⟨the *malleable* properties of gold enhance its value⟩. **Adaptable** implies the capability of being easily modified to suit other conditions, needs, or uses ⟨computer hardware that is *adaptable*⟩.

play see FUN

plea see APOLOGY

plenary see FULL

plentiful, ample, abundant, copious mean more than sufficient without being excessive. **Plentiful** implies a great or rich supply ⟨peaches are *plentiful* this summer⟩. **Ample** implies a generous sufficiency to satisfy a particular requirement ⟨an *ample* amount of food to last the winter⟩. **Abundant** suggests an even greater or richer supply than does *plentiful* ⟨has surprisingly *abundant* energy for a woman her age⟩. **Copious** stresses largeness of supply rather than fullness or richness ⟨*copious* examples of bureaucratic waste⟩.

pliable see PLASTIC

pliant see PLASTIC

plight see PREDICAMENT

plot, intrigue, machination, conspiracy, cabal mean a plan secretly devised to accomplish an evil or treacherous end. **Plot** implies careful foresight in planning a complex scheme ⟨foiled an assassination *plot*⟩. **Intrigue** suggests secret underhanded maneuvering in an atmosphere of duplicity ⟨finagled the nomination by means of back-room *intrigues*⟩. **Machination** implies a contriving of annoyances, injuries, or evils by indirect means ⟨through *machinations* she pieced together a publishing empire⟩. **Conspiracy** implies a secret agreement among several people usu. involving treason or great treachery ⟨a *conspiracy* of oil companies to set prices⟩. **Cabal** typically applies to political intrigue involving persons of some eminence ⟨the infamous *cabal* against General Washington⟩. See in addition PLAN.

plumb see VERTICAL

plunder see SPOIL

poignant see MOVING, PUNGENT

poise see TACT

polite see CIVIL

politic see EXPEDIENT, SUAVE

pollute see CONTAMINATE

ponder, meditate, muse, ruminate mean to consider or examine attentively or deliberately. **Ponder** implies a careful weighing of a problem or, often, prolonged inconclusive thinking about a matter ⟨*pondered* at length the various recourses open to him⟩. **Meditate** implies a definite focusing of one's thoughts on something so as to understand it deeply ⟨the sight of ruins prompted her to *meditate* upon human vanity⟩. **Muse** suggests a more or less focused daydreaming as in remembrance ⟨*mused* upon the adventures had by heroines of gothic novels⟩. **Ruminate** implies going over the same matter in one's thoughts again and again but suggests little of either purposive thinking or rapt absorption ⟨the product of fifty years of *ruminating* on the meaning of life⟩.

ponderable see PERCEPTIBLE

ponderous see HEAVY

popular see COMMON

portentous see OMINOUS

portion see FATE, PART

pose, air, airs, affectation, mannerism mean an adopted way of speaking or behaving. **Pose** implies an attitude deliberately assumed in order to impress others ⟨her shyness was just a *pose*⟩. **Air** may suggest natural acquirement through environment or way of life ⟨years of living in Europe had given him a sophisticated *air*⟩. **Airs** always implies artificiality and pretentiousness ⟨a snobby couple much given to putting on *airs*⟩. **Affectation** applies to a trick of speech or behavior that strikes the observer as insincere ⟨his foreign accent is an *affectation*⟩. **Mannerism** applies to an acquired eccentricity that has become a habit ⟨gesturing with a cigarette was her most noticeable *mannerism*⟩.

positive see SURE

possess see HAVE

possible, practicable, feasible mean capable of being realized. **Possible** implies that a thing may certainly exist or occur given the proper conditions ⟨contends that life on other planets is *possible*⟩. **Practicable** implies that something may be easily or readily effected by available means or under current conditions ⟨when television became *practicable*⟩. **Feasible** applies to what is likely to work or be useful in attaining the end desired ⟨commercially *feasible* for mass production⟩.

postpone see DEFER

potential see LATENT

poverty, indigence, penury, want, destitution mean the state of one with insufficient resources. **Poverty** may cover a range from extreme want of necessities to an absence of material comforts ⟨the extreme *poverty* of Third World countries⟩. **Indigence** implies seriously straitened circumstances ⟨the *indigence* of her years as a graduate student⟩. **Penury** suggests a cramping or oppressive lack of money ⟨given the *penury* of their lifestyle, few suspected their wealth⟩. **Want** and **destitution** imply extreme poverty that threatens life itself through starvation or exposure ⟨lived in a perpetual state of *want*⟩ ⟨the widespread *destitution* in countries beset by famine⟩.

power *n* Power, authority, jurisdiction, control, command, sway, dominion mean the right to govern or rule or determine. **Power** implies possession of ability to wield force, permissive authority, or substantial influence ⟨the *power* of the President to mold public opinion⟩. **Authority** implies the granting of power for a specific purpose within specified limits ⟨gave her attorney the *authority* to manage her estate⟩. **Jurisdiction** applies to official power exercised within prescribed limits ⟨the bureau that has *jurisdiction* over Indian affairs⟩. **Control** stresses the power to direct and restrain ⟨you are responsible for students under your *control*⟩. **Command** implies the power to make arbitrary decisions and compel obedience ⟨the respect of the men under his *command*⟩. **Sway** suggests the extent or scope of exercised power or influence ⟨an empire that extended its *sway* over the known world⟩. **Dominion** stresses sovereign power or supreme authority ⟨a world government that would have *dominion* over all nations⟩.

power *n* Power, force, energy, strength, might mean the ability to exert effort. **Power** may imply latent or exerted physical, mental, or spiritual ability to act or be acted upon ⟨the incredible *power* of flowing water⟩. **Force** implies the actual effective exercise of power ⟨used enough *force* to push the door open⟩. **Energy** applies to power expended or capable of being transformed into work ⟨a social reformer of untiring *energy*⟩. **Strength** applies to the quality or property of a person or thing that makes possible the exertion of force or the withstanding of strain, pressure, or attack ⟨use weight training to build your *strength*⟩. **Might** implies great or overwhelming power or strength ⟨all of his *might* was needed to budge the boulder⟩.

practicable, practical mean capable of being put to use or put into practice. **Practicable** applies to what has been proposed and seems feasible but has not been actually tested in use ⟨the question of whether colonies in space are *practicable*⟩. **Practical** applies to things and to persons and implies proven success in meeting the demands made by actual living or use ⟨the copier is the most *practical* machine in the office⟩. See in addition POSSIBLE.

practical see PRACTICABLE

practice see HABIT

precarious see DANGEROUS

preceding, antecedent, foregoing, previous, prior, former, anterior mean being before. **Preceding** usu. implies being immediately before in time or in place ⟨the last sentence of the *preceding* paragraph⟩. **Antecedent** applies to order in time and may suggest a causal relation ⟨study the revolution and its *antecedent* economic conditions⟩. **Foregoing** applies chiefly to statements ⟨a restatement of the *foregoing* paragraph⟩. **Previous** and **prior** imply existing or occurring earlier, but *prior* often adds an implication of greater importance ⟨her life in a *previous* marriage⟩ ⟨the prices in this catalogue supersede all *prior* prices⟩. **Former** implies always a definite comparison or contrast with something that is latter ⟨the *former* name of the company⟩. **Anterior** applies to position before or ahead of usu. in space, sometimes in time or order ⟨the *anterior* lobe of the brain⟩.

precept see LAW

precious see COSTLY

precipitate, headlong, abrupt, impetuous, sudden mean showing undue haste or unexpectedness. **Precipitate** stresses lack of due deliberation and implies prematureness of action ⟨the army's *precipitate* withdrawal⟩. **Head-**

long stresses rashness and lack of forethought ⟨a *headlong* flight from arrest⟩. **Abrupt** stresses curtness and a lack of warning or ceremony ⟨an *abrupt* refusal⟩. **Impetuous** stresses extreme impatience or impulsiveness ⟨it's a bit *impetuous* to propose on the third date⟩. **Sudden** stresses unexpectedness and sharpness or violence of action ⟨flew into a *sudden* rage⟩.

precipitous see STEEP

précis see COMPENDIUM

precise see CORRECT

preclude see PREVENT

precursor see FORERUNNER

predicament, dilemma, quandary, plight, fix, jam, pickle mean a situation from which escape is difficult. **Predicament** suggests a difficult situation usu. offering no satisfactory solution ⟨the *predicament* posed by increasing automation⟩. **Dilemma** implies a predicament presenting a choice between equally bad alternatives ⟨faced with the *dilemma* of putting him in a nursing home or caring for him ourselves⟩. **Quandary** stresses puzzlement and perplexity ⟨in a *quandary* about how to repair it⟩. **Plight** suggests an unfortunate or trying situation ⟨a study on the *plight* of AIDS victims⟩. **Fix** and **jam** are informal equivalents of *plight* but are more likely to suggest involvement through some fault or wrongdoing ⟨constantly getting their son out of some *fix*⟩ ⟨in a real financial *jam* now that she's lost her job⟩. **Pickle** implies a distressing or embarrassing situation ⟨conflicting commitments that left me in a sorry *pickle*⟩.

predict see FORETELL

predilection, prepossession, prejudice, bias mean an attitude of mind that predisposes one to favor something. **Predilection** implies a strong liking deriving from one's temperament or experience ⟨teenagers with a *predilection* for gory horror movies). **Prepossession** suggests a fixed conception likely to preclude objective judgment of anything counter to it ⟨a slave to his *prepossessions*⟩. **Prejudice** usu. implies an unfavorable prepossession and connotes a feeling rooted in suspicion, fear, or intolerance ⟨strong *prejudices* that are based upon neither reason nor experience⟩. **Bias** implies an unreasoned and unfair distortion of judgment in favor of or against a person or thing ⟨employers show a *bias* against overweight people⟩.

predispose see INCLINE

predominant see DOMINANT

preempt see APPROPRIATE

preference see CHOICE

prejudice see PREDILECTION

preponderant see DOMINANT

prepossession see PREDILECTION

prescribe see DICTATE

present see GIVE

presentiment see APPREHENSION

prestige see INFLUENCE

pretend see ASSUME

pretension see AMBITION

pretentious see SHOWY

pretext see APOLOGY

pretty see BEAUTIFUL

prevailing, prevalent, rife, current mean generally circulated, accepted, or used in a certain time or place. **Prevailing** stresses predominance ⟨the *prevailing* medical opinion regarding smoking⟩. **Prevalent** implies only frequency ⟨dairy farms were once *prevalent* in the area⟩. **Rife** implies a growing prevalence or rapid spread ⟨during the epidemic rumors were *rife*⟩. **Current** applies to what is subject to change and stresses prevalence at the present time ⟨the *current* migration towards the Sunbelt⟩.

prevalent see PREVAILING

prevaricate see LIE

prevent *vb* Prevent, anticipate, forestall mean to deal with beforehand. **Prevent** implies taking advance measures against something possible or probable ⟨measures taken to *prevent* an epidemic⟩. **Anticipate** may imply merely getting ahead of another by being a precursor or forerunner or it may imply checking another's intention by acting first ⟨*anticipated* the firing so she decided to quit first⟩. **Forestall** implies a getting ahead so as to stop or interrupt something in its course ⟨a government order that effectively *forestalled* a free election⟩.

prevent *vb* Prevent, preclude, obviate, avert, ward off mean to stop something from coming or occurring. **Prevent** implies the existence of or the placing of an insurmountable obstacle ⟨the blizzard *prevented* us from going⟩. **Preclude** implies the shutting out of every possibility of a thing's happening or taking effect ⟨an accident that *precluded* a career in football⟩. **Obviate** suggests the use of forethought to avoid the necessity for unwelcome or disagreeable actions or measures ⟨her quitting *obviated* the task of firing her⟩. **Avert** and **ward off** imply taking immediate and effective measures to avoid, repel, or counteract threatening evil ⟨deftly *averted* a hostile corporate takeover⟩ ⟨a hot drink to *ward off* a chill⟩.

previous see PRECEDING

priceless see COSTLY

prior see PRECEDING

prize *vb* see APPRECIATE

prize *n* see SPOIL

probe see ENTER

probity see HONESTY
problem see MYSTERY
problematic see DOUBTFUL
proceed see SPRING
proclaim see DECLARE
proclivity see LEANING
procrastinate see DELAY
procure see GET
prodigal see PROFUSE
prodigious see MONSTROUS
proficient, adept, skilled, skillful, expert mean having great
knowledge and experience in a trade or profession. **Profi-**
cient implies a thorough competence derived from training
and practice ⟨a translator thoroughly *proficient* in Rus-
sian⟩. **Adept** implies special aptitude as well as proficiency
⟨*adept* at handling large numbers in his head⟩. **Skilled**
stresses mastery of technique ⟨a delicate operation requiring a *skilled* surgeon⟩. **Skillful** implies individual dexterity
in execution or performance ⟨a shrewd and *skillful* manipulation of public opinion⟩. **Expert** implies extraordinary
proficiency and often connotes knowledge as well as technical skill ⟨*expert* in the identification and evaluation of
wines⟩.
profile see OUTLINE
profitable see BENEFICIAL
profuse, lavish, prodigal, luxuriant, lush, exuberant mean
giving or given out in great abundance. **Profuse** implies
pouring forth without restraint ⟨uttered *profuse* apolo-
gies⟩. **Lavish** suggests an unstinted or unmeasured profusion ⟨a *lavish* wedding reception of obvious expense⟩.
Prodigal implies reckless or wasteful lavishness threatening to lead to early exhaustion of resources ⟨*prodigal*
spending exhausted the fortune⟩. **Luxuriant** suggests a rich

and splendid abundance ⟨the *luxuriant* vegetation of a tropical rain forest⟩. **Lush** suggests rich, soft luxuriance ⟨nude portraits that have a *lush,* sensual quality⟩. **Exuberant** implies marked vitality or vigor in what produces abundantly ⟨a fantasy writer with an *exuberant* imagination⟩.

prognosticate see FORETELL

prohibit see FORBID

project see PLAN

projection, protrusion, protuberance, bulge mean an extension beyond the normal line or surface. **Projection** implies a jutting out esp. at a sharp angle ⟨those *projections* along the wall are safety hazards⟩. **Protrusion** suggests a thrusting out so that the extension seems a deformity ⟨the bizarre *protrusions* of a coral reef⟩. **Protuberance** implies a growing or swelling out in rounded form ⟨a skin disease marked by warty *protuberances*⟩. **Bulge** suggests an expansion caused by internal pressure ⟨*bulges* soon appeared in the tile floor⟩.

prolific see FERTILE

prolix see WORDY

prolong see EXTEND

prominent see NOTICEABLE

promote see ADVANCE

prompt see QUICK

promulgate see DECLARE

prone, supine, prostrate, recumbent mean lying down. **Prone** implies a position with the front of the body turned toward the supporting surface ⟨push-ups require the body to be in a *prone* position⟩. **Supine** implies lying on one's back and suggests inertness or abjectness ⟨lying *supine* upon a couch⟩. **Prostrate** implies lying full-length as in submission, defeat, or physical collapse ⟨a runner fell *prostrate* at

the finish line). **Recumbent** implies the posture of one
sleeping or resting ⟨he was *recumbent* and relaxed in his
hospital bed⟩. See in addition LIABLE.

propel see PUSH

propensity see LEANING

proper see FIT

property see QUALITY

prophesy see FORETELL

propitiate see PACIFY

propitious see FAVORABLE

proportional, proportionate, commensurate, commensurable mean duly proportioned to something else. **Proportional** may apply to several closely related things that change without altering their relations ⟨medical fees are *proportional* to one's income⟩. **Proportionate** applies to one thing that bears a reciprocal relationship to another ⟨a punishment not at all *proportionate* to the offense⟩. **Commensurate** stresses an equality between things different from but in some way dependent on each other ⟨the salary will be *commensurate* with experience⟩. **Commensurable** more strongly implies a common scale by which two quite different things can be shown to be significantly equal or proportionate ⟨equal pay for jobs that are *commensurable* in worth⟩.

proportionate see PROPORTIONAL

propriety see DECORUM

prospect, outlook, anticipation, foretaste mean an advance realization of something to come. **Prospect** implies expectation of a particular event, condition, or development of definite interest or concern ⟨the appealing *prospect* of a quiet weekend⟩. **Outlook** suggests a forecasting of the future ⟨a favorable *outlook* for the state's economy⟩. **Anticipation** implies a prospect or outlook that involves advance suffering or enjoyment of what is foreseen ⟨the *anticipation* of the meeting was the worst of it⟩. **Foretaste** implies an actual though brief or partial experience of something forthcoming ⟨the frost was a *foretaste* of winter⟩.

prostrate see PRONE

protect see DEFEND

protest see ASSERT, OBJECT

protract see EXTEND

protrusion see PROJECTION

protuberance see PROJECTION

proud, arrogant, haughty, lordly, insolent, overbearing, supercilious, disdainful mean showing scorn for inferiors. **Proud** may suggest an assumed superiority or loftiness ⟨a *proud* man, unwilling to admit failure⟩. **Arrogant** implies a claiming for oneself of more consideration or importance than is warranted ⟨an *arrogant* business executive used to being kowtowed to⟩. **Haughty** suggests a consciousness of superior birth or position ⟨a *haughty* manner that barely concealed his scorn⟩. **Lordly** implies pomposity or an arrogant display of power ⟨a *lordly* indifference to the consequences of their carelessness⟩. **Insolent** implies contemptuous haughtiness ⟨suffered the stares of *insolent* waiters⟩. **Overbearing** suggests a tyrannical manner or an intolerable insolence ⟨an *overbearing* society hostess⟩. **Supercilious** implies a cool, patronizing haughtiness ⟨*supercilious* parvenus asserting their position⟩. **Disdainful** suggests a more active and openly scornful superciliousness ⟨*disdainful* of their social inferiors⟩.

providential see LUCKY

province see FUNCTION

provoke, excite, stimulate, pique, quicken mean to arouse as if by pricking. **Provoke** directs attention to the response called forth ⟨my stories usually *provoke* laughter⟩. **Excite** implies a stirring up or moving profoundly ⟨news that *excited* anger and frustration⟩. **Stimulate** suggests a rousing out of lethargy, quiescence, or indifference ⟨*stimulating* conversation⟩. **Pique** suggests stimulating by mild irritation or challenge ⟨that remark *piqued* my interest⟩. **Quicken** implies beneficially stimulating and making active or lively ⟨the high salary *quickened* her desire to have the job⟩. See in addition IRRITATE.

prowess see HEROISM
prudent see WISE
prying see CURIOUS
publish see DECLARE
pugnacious see BELLIGERENT
pull, draw, drag, haul, tug mean to cause to move in the direction determined by an applied force. **Pull** is the general term but may emphasize the force exerted rather than resulting motion ⟨to open the drawer, *pull* hard⟩. **Draw** implies a smoother, steadier motion and generally a lighter force than *pull* ⟨a child *drawing* his sled across the snow⟩. **Drag** suggests great effort overcoming resistance or friction ⟨*dragged* the dead body across the room⟩. **Haul** implies sustained pulling or dragging of heavy or bulky objects ⟨a team of horses *hauling* supplies⟩. **Tug** applies to strenuous often spasmodic efforts to move ⟨the little girl *tugged* at her mother's hand⟩.
punctilious see CAREFUL
pungent, piquant, poignant, racy mean sharp and stimulating to the mind or the senses. **Pungent** implies a sharp, stinging, or biting quality esp. of odors ⟨a cheese with a *pungent* odor⟩. **Piquant** suggests a power to whet the appetite or interest through tartness or mild pungency ⟨grapefruit juice gave the punch its *piquant* taste⟩. **Poi-**

gnant suggests something is sharply or piercingly effective in stirring one's consciousness or emotions 〈upon her departure he felt a *poignant* sense of loss〉. **Racy** implies having a strongly characteristic natural quality fresh and unimpaired 〈the spontaneous, *racy* prose of the untutored writer〉.

punish, chastise, castigate, chasten, discipline, correct mean to inflict a penalty on in requital for wrongdoing. **Punish** implies subjecting to a penalty for wrongdoing 〈*punished* for stealing〉. **Chastise** may apply to either the infliction of corporal punishment or to verbal censure or denunciation 〈*chastised* his son for neglecting his studies〉. **Castigate** usu. implies a severe, typically public censure 〈an editorial *castigating* the entire city council〉. **Chasten** suggests any affliction or trial that leaves one humbled or subdued 〈a stunning election defeat that left him *chastened*〉. **Discipline** implies a punishing or chastening in order to bring under control 〈the duty of parents to *discipline* their children〉. **Correct** implies punishing aimed at reforming an offender 〈the function of prison is to *correct* the wrongdoer〉.

pure see CHASTE

purloin see STEAL

purpose see INTENTION

pursue see CHASE

pursuit see WORK

push, shove, thrust, propel mean to cause to move ahead or aside by force. **Push** implies application of force by a body already in contact with the body to be moved 〈*push* the door open〉. **Shove** implies a fast or rough pushing of something usu. along a surface 〈*shoved* the man out of my way〉. **Thrust** suggests less steadiness and greater violence than *push* 〈*thrust* the money in my hand and ran away〉.

Propel suggests rapidly driving forward or onward by force
applied in any manner ⟨ships *propelled* by steam⟩.
pushing see AGGRESSIVE
pusillanimous see COWARDLY
putrefy see DECAY
putrid see MALODOROUS
puzzle *vb* Puzzle, perplex, bewilder, distract, nonplus, confound, dumbfound mean to baffle and disturb mentally.
   Puzzle implies existence of a problem difficult to solve ⟨a
   persistent fever which *puzzled* the doctor⟩. **Perplex** adds a
   suggestion of worry and uncertainty esp. about making a
   necessary decision ⟨an odd change of personality that *perplexed* her friends⟩. **Bewilder** stresses a confusion of mind
   that hampers clear and decisive thinking ⟨the number of
   videotapes available *bewilders* consumers⟩. **Distract** implies agitation or uncertainty induced by conflicting preoc-
   cupations or interests ⟨a political scandal that *distracted*
   the country for two years⟩. **Nonplus** implies a bafflement
   that makes orderly planning or deciding impossible ⟨she
   was utterly *nonplussed* by the abrupt change in plans⟩.
   Confound implies temporary mental paralysis caused by
   astonishment or profound abasement ⟨tragic news that
   confounded us all⟩. **Dumbfound** suggests intense but momentary confounding; often the idea of astonishment is so
   stressed that it becomes a near synonym of *astound*
   ⟨*dumbfounded* by her rejection of his marriage proposal⟩.
puzzle *n* see MYSTERY

Q

quail see RECOIL
quaint see STRANGE
qualified see ABLE
quality, property, character, attribute mean an intelligible feature by which a thing may be identified. **Quality** is a general term applicable to any trait or characteristic whether individual or generic ⟨a star whose acting had a persistently amateurish *quality*⟩. **Property** implies a characteristic that belongs to a thing's essential nature and may be used to describe a type or species ⟨name the basic *properties* of mammals⟩. **Character** applies to a peculiar and distinctive quality of a thing or a class ⟨each of the island's villages has a distinctive *character*⟩. **Attribute** implies a quality ascribed to a thing or a being ⟨a man with none of the traditional *attributes* of a popular hero⟩.
qualm, scruple, compunction, demur mean a misgiving about what one is doing or going to do. **Qualm** implies an uneasy fear that one is not following one's conscience or better judgment ⟨no *qualms* about traveling in the Middle East⟩. **Scruple** implies doubt of the rightness of an act on grounds of principle ⟨a lawyer totally devoid of *scruples*⟩. **Compunction** implies a spontaneous feeling of responsibility or compassion for a potential victim ⟨not likely to have *compunctions* about knocking out his opponent⟩. **Demur** implies hesitation caused by objection to an outside suggestion or influence ⟨accepted her resignation without *demur*⟩.
quandary see PREDICAMENT
quarrel, wrangle, altercation, squabble, spat, tiff mean an

angry dispute. **Quarrel** implies a verbal clash followed by strained or severed relations ⟨a bitter *quarrel* that ended their friendship⟩. **Wrangle** suggests a noisy, insistent dispute ⟨an ongoing *wrangle* over the town's finances⟩. **Altercation** suggests determined verbal quarreling often with blows ⟨a violent *altercation* between pro- and anti-abortion groups⟩. **Squabble** implies childish and unseemly wrangling ⟨the children constantly *squabble* over toys⟩. **Spat** implies a lively but brief dispute over a trifle ⟨the couple averages a *spat* a week⟩. **Tiff** suggests a trivial dispute without serious consequence ⟨a *tiff* that was forgotten by dinnertime⟩.

quarrelsome see BELLIGERENT

quash see CRUSH

queer see STRANGE

quell see CRUSH

query see ASK

question see ASK

questionable see DOUBTFUL

quick, prompt, ready, apt mean able to respond without delay or hesitation or indicative of such ability. **Quick** stresses instancy of response and is likely to connote native rather than acquired power ⟨very *quick* in his reflexes⟩ ⟨a keen *quick* mind⟩. **Prompt** is more likely to connote training and discipline that fits one for instant response ⟨the *prompt* response of emergency medical technicians⟩. **Ready** suggests facility or fluency in response ⟨backed by a pair of *ready* assistants⟩. **Apt** stresses the possession of qualities (as intelligence, a particular talent, or a strong bent) that makes quick effective response possible ⟨an *apt* student⟩ ⟨her answer was *apt* and to the point⟩. See in addition FAST.

quicken, animate, enliven, vivify mean to make alive or

lively. **Quicken** stresses a sudden renewal of life or activity esp. in something inert ⟨the arrival of spring *quickens* the earth⟩. **Animate** emphasizes the imparting of motion or vitality to what is mechanical or artificial ⟨telling details that *animate* the familiar story⟩. **Enliven** suggests a stimulus that arouses from dullness or torpidity ⟨*enlivened* his lecture with humorous anecdotes⟩. **Vivify** implies a freshening or energizing through renewal of vitality ⟨her appearance *vivifies* a dreary drawing-room drama⟩. See in addition PROVOKE.

quick-witted see INTELLIGENT
quiescent see LATENT
quip see JEST
quit see STOP
quixotic see IMAGINARY

R

rack see AFFLICT
racy see PUNGENT
radiant see BRIGHT
rage see ANGER, FASHION
rail see SCOLD
raise see LIFT
ramble see WANDER
rancor see ENMITY
random, haphazard, casual, desultory mean determined by accident rather than design. **Random** stresses lack of definite aim, fixed goal, or regular procedure ⟨a *random* sampling of public opinion⟩. **Haphazard** applies to what is done without regard for regularity or fitness or ultimate consequence ⟨his selection of college courses was entirely

haphazard). **Casual** suggests working or acting without deliberation, intention, or purpose ⟨a *casual* tour of the sights⟩. **Desultory** implies a jumping or skipping from one thing to another without method or system ⟨a *desultory* discussion of current events⟩.

range, gamut, compass, sweep, scope, orbit mean the extent that lies within the powers of something (as to cover or control). **Range** is a general term indicating the extent of one's perception or the extent of powers, capacities, or possibilities ⟨the entire *range* of human experience⟩. **Gamut** suggests a graduated series running from one possible extreme to another ⟨a performance that included a *gamut* of emotions⟩. **Compass** implies a sometimes limited extent of perception, knowledge, or activity ⟨your concerns lie beyond the narrow *compass* of this study⟩. **Sweep** suggests extent, often circular or arc-shaped, of motion or activity ⟨the book covers the entire *sweep* of criminal activity⟩. **Scope** is applicable to an area of activity, predetermined and limited, but somewhat flexible ⟨as time went on, the *scope* of the investigation widened⟩. **Orbit** suggests an often circumscribed range of activity or influence within which forces work toward accommodation ⟨within that restricted *orbit* they tried to effect social change⟩.

rank see FLAGRANT, MALODOROUS

ransom see RESCUE

rapacious see VORACIOUS

rapid see FAST

rapture see ECSTASY

rare see CHOICE, INFREQUENT

rash see ADVENTUROUS

rate see ESTIMATE

rattle see EMBARRASS

raucous see LOUD

ravage, devastate, waste, sack, pillage, despoil mean to lay waste by plundering or destroying. **Ravage** implies violent often cumulative depredation and destruction ⟨a hurricane that *ravaged* the Gulf Coast⟩. **Devastate** implies the complete ruin and desolation of a wide area ⟨the atomic bomb that *devastated* Hiroshima⟩. **Waste** may imply producing the same result by a slow process rather than sudden and violent action ⟨years of drought had *wasted* the area⟩. **Sack** implies carrying off all valuable possessions from a place ⟨barbarians *sacked* ancient Rome⟩. **Pillage** implies ruthless plundering at will but without the completeness suggested by *sack* ⟨settlements *pillaged* by Vikings⟩. **Despoil** applies to looting or robbing of a place or person without suggesting accompanying destruction ⟨the Nazis *despoiled* the art museums of Europe⟩.

ravenous see VORACIOUS

raw see RUDE

rawboned see LEAN

ready see QUICK

realize see THINK

rear see LIFT

reason *n* see CAUSE

reason *vb* see THINK

rebellion, revolution, uprising, revolt, insurrection, mutiny mean an armed outbreak against authority. **Rebellion** implies an open formidable resistance that is often unsuccessful ⟨the *rebellion* failed for lack of popular support⟩. **Revolution** applies to a successful rebellion resulting in a major change (as in government) ⟨the American *Revolution*⟩. **Uprising** implies a brief, limited and often immediately ineffective rebellion ⟨quickly put down the *uprising*⟩. **Revolt** and **insurrection** imply an armed uprising that quickly fails or succeeds ⟨a *revolt* by the young Turks that surprised party leaders⟩ ⟨Nat Turner's unsuccessful slave *insurrection*⟩. **Mutiny** applies to group insubordination or insurrection esp. against naval authority ⟨the famous *mutiny* aboard the Bounty⟩.

rebuild see MEND

rebuke see REPROVE

rebut see DISPROVE

recalcitrant see UNRULY

recall see REMEMBER

recant see ABJURE

recede, retreat, retrograde, retract, back mean to move backward. **Recede** implies a gradual withdrawing from a forward or high fixed point in time or space ⟨the flood waters gradually *receded*⟩. **Retreat** implies withdrawal from a point or position reached ⟨under cross-examination he *retreated* from that statement⟩. **Retrograde** implies movement contrary to a normally progressive direction ⟨the social position of women in some areas seems to be *retrograding* instead of advancing⟩. **Retract** implies drawing back from an extended position ⟨a cat *retracting* its claws⟩. **Back** is used with *up, down, out,* or *off,* to refer to any retrograde motion ⟨*backed* off when her claim was challenged⟩.

reciprocal, mutual, common mean shared or experienced by each. **Reciprocal** implies an equal return or counteraction by each of two sides toward or against or in relation to the other ⟨allies with a *reciprocal* defense agreement⟩. **Mutual** applies to feelings or effects shared by two jointly ⟨two people with a *mutual* physical attraction⟩. **Common** does not suggest reciprocity but merely a sharing with others ⟨a couple with many *common* interests⟩.

reciprocate, retaliate, requite, return mean to give back usu. in kind or in quantity. **Reciprocate** implies a mutual or equivalent exchange or a paying back of what one has received ⟨*reciprocated* their hospitality by inviting them for a visit⟩. **Retaliate** usu. implies a paying back of injury in exact kind, often vengefully ⟨the enemy *retaliated* by executing their prisoners⟩. **Requite** implies a paying back according to one's preference and often not equivalently ⟨*requited* her love with cold indifference⟩. **Return** implies a paying back of something usu. in kind but sometimes by way of contrast ⟨*returned* their kindness with ingratitude⟩.

reckless see ADVENTUROUS

reckon see CALCULATE

reclaim see RESCUE

recoil, shrink, flinch, wince, blench, quail mean to draw back in fear or distaste. **Recoil** implies a start or movement away through shock, fear, or disgust ⟨*recoils* at the sight of blood⟩. **Shrink** suggests an instinctive recoil through sensitiveness, scrupulousness, or cowardice ⟨refused to *shrink* from family responsibilities⟩. **Flinch** implies a failure to endure pain or face something dangerous or frightening with resolution ⟨faced her accusers without *flinching*⟩. **Wince** suggests a slight involuntary physical reaction (as a start or recoiling) ⟨*winced* when the new secretary called him by his first name⟩. **Blench** implies fainthearted flinching ⟨never *blenched* even as his head was lowered on the guillotine⟩. **Quail** suggests shrinking and cowering in fear ⟨*quailed* at the appearance of the ghost⟩.

recollect see REMEMBER

recollection see MEMORY

recompense see PAY

reconcile see ADAPT

rectify see CORRECT

recumbent see PRONE

redeem see RESCUE

redolence see FRAGRANCE
redolent see ODOROUS
redress see CORRECT
reduce see CONQUER, DECREASE
reflect see THINK
reform see CORRECT
refractory see UNRULY
refresh see RENEW
refuse see DECLINE
refute see DISPROVE
regard, respect, esteem, admire mean to recognize the worth
of a person or thing. **Regard** is a general term that is usu.
qualified ⟨he is not highly *regarded* in the profession⟩. **Respect** implies a considered evaluation or estimation ⟨after
many years they came to *respect* her views⟩. **Esteem** implies greater warmth of feeling accompanying a high valuation ⟨no citizen of the town was more highly *esteemed*⟩.
Admire suggests usu. enthusiastic appreciation and often
deep affection ⟨a friend that I truly *admire*⟩.
regret see SORROW
regular, normal, typical, natural mean being of the sort or
kind that is expected as usual, ordinary, or average. **Regular** stresses conformity to a rule, standard, or pattern ⟨the
regular monthly meeting of the organization⟩. **Normal** implies lack of deviation from what has been discovered or
established as the most usual or expected ⟨*normal* behavior for a two-year-old boy⟩. **Typical** implies showing all
important traits of a type, class, or group and may suggest
lack of strong individuality ⟨a *typical* small town in Amer-
ica⟩. **Natural** applies to what conforms to a thing's essential nature, function, or mode of being ⟨the *natural* love of
a mother for her child⟩.
regulation see LAW

reimburse see PAY
reject see DECLINE
rejoin see ANSWER
rejuvenate see RENEW
relate see JOIN
release see FREE
relegate see COMMIT
relent see YIELD
relevant, germane, material, pertinent, apposite, applicable, apropos mean relating to or bearing upon the matter in hand. **Relevant** implies a traceable, significant, logical connection ⟨use any *relevant* evidence to support your argument⟩. **Germane** may additionally imply a fitness for or appropriateness to the situation or occasion ⟨a topic not *germane* to our discussion⟩. **Material** implies so close a relationship that it cannot be dispensed with without serious alteration of the case ⟨the scene is *material* to the rest of the play⟩. **Pertinent** stresses a clear and decisive relevance ⟨a *pertinent* observation that cut to the heart of the matter⟩. **Apposite** suggests a felicitous relevance ⟨the anecdotes in his sermons are always *apposite*⟩. **Applicable** suggests the fitness of bringing a general rule or principle to bear upon a particular case ⟨a precedent that is not *applicable* in this case⟩. **Apropos** suggests being both relevant and opportune ⟨for your term paper use only *apropos* quotations⟩.
relieve, alleviate, lighten, assuage, mitigate, allay mean to make something less grievous. **Relieve** implies a lifting of enough of a burden to make it tolerable ⟨took drugs to *relieve* the pain⟩. **Alleviate** implies temporary or partial lessening of pain or distress ⟨new buildings that will help to *alleviate* the housing shortage⟩. **Lighten** implies reducing a burdensome or depressing weight ⟨good news that *light-*

ened his worries). **Assuage** implies softening or sweetening what is harsh or disagreeable ⟨hoped that a vacation would *assuage* the pain of the divorce⟩. **Mitigate** suggests a moderating or countering of the effect of something violent or painful ⟨ocean breezes *mitigated* the intense heat⟩. **Allay** implies an effective calming or soothing of fears or alarms ⟨the encouraging report *allayed* their fears⟩.

religious see DEVOUT

relinquish, yield, resign, surrender, abandon, waive mean to give up completely. **Relinquish** usu. does not imply strong feeling but may suggest some regret, reluctance, or weakness ⟨*relinquished* her crown with bittersweet feelings⟩. **Yield** implies concession or compliance or submission to force ⟨I *yield* to your greater expertise in this matter⟩. **Resign** emphasizes voluntary relinquishment or sacrifice without struggle ⟨the model *resigned* all her rights to the photographs⟩. **Surrender** implies a giving up after a struggle to retain or resist ⟨forced to sign a document *surrendering* all claims to the land⟩. **Abandon** stresses finality and completeness in giving up ⟨*abandon* all hope⟩. **Waive** implies conceding or forgoing with little or no compulsion ⟨*waived* the right to a trial by jury⟩.

reluctant see DISINCLINED

remarkable see NOTICEABLE

remedy see CORRECT, CURE

remember, recollect, recall, remind, reminisce mean to bring an image or idea from the past into the mind. **Remember** implies a keeping in memory that may be effortless or unwilled ⟨*remembers* that day as though it were yesterday⟩. **Recollect** implies a bringing back to mind what is lost or scattered ⟨as near as I can *recollect*⟩. **Recall** suggests an effort to bring back to mind and often to re-create in speech ⟨can't *recall* the words of the song⟩. **Remind** suggests a jogging of one's memory by an association or similarity ⟨that *reminds* me of a story⟩. **Reminisce** implies a casual often nostalgic recalling of experiences long past and gone ⟨old college friends like to *reminisce*⟩.

remembrance see MEMORY

remind see REMEMBER

reminisce see REMEMBER

reminiscence see MEMORY

remiss see NEGLIGENT

remonstrate see OBJECT

remorse see PENITENCE

remunerate see PAY

rend see TEAR

renew, restore, refresh, renovate, rejuvenate mean to make like new. **Renew** implies so extensive a remaking that what had become faded or disintegrated now seems like new ⟨efforts to *renew* a failing marriage⟩. **Restore** implies a return to an original state after depletion or loss ⟨*restored* a fine piece of furniture⟩. **Refresh** implies the supplying of something necessary to restore lost strength, animation, or power ⟨lunch *refreshed* my energy⟩. **Renovate** suggests a renewing by cleansing, repairing, or rebuilding ⟨the apartment has been entirely *renovated*⟩. **Rejuvenate** suggests the restoration of youthful vigor, powers, and appearance ⟨the change in jobs *rejuvenated* her spirits⟩.

renounce see ABDICATE, ABJURE

renovate see RENEW

renowned see FAMOUS

rent see HIRE

repair see MEND

repartee see WIT

repay see PAY

repellent see REPUGNANT

repentance see PENITENCE

replace, displace, supplant, supersede mean to put out of a usual or proper place or into the place of another. **Replace** implies a filling of a place once occupied by something lost, destroyed, or no longer usable or adequate ⟨the broken window will have to be *replaced*⟩. **Displace** implies an ousting or dislodging preceding a replacing ⟨thousands had been *displaced* by the floods⟩. **Supplant** implies either a dispossessing or usurping of another's place, possessions, or privileges or an uprooting of something and its replacement with something else ⟨discovered that he had been *supplanted* in her affections by another⟩. **Supersede** implies replacing a person or thing that has become superannuated, obsolete, or otherwise inferior ⟨the new edition *supersedes* all previous ones⟩.

replete see FULL

replica see REPRODUCTION

reply see ANSWER

reprehend see CRITICIZE

reprimand see REPROVE

reproach see REPROVE

reprobate see CRITICIZE

reproduction, duplicate, copy, facsimile, replica mean a thing made to closely resemble another. **Reproduction** implies an exact or close imitation of an existing thing ⟨*reproductions* from the museum's furniture collection⟩. **Duplicate** implies a double or counterpart exactly corresponding to another thing ⟨make a *duplicate* of the key⟩. **Copy** applies esp. to one of a number of things reproduced mechanically ⟨*copies* of the report were issued to all⟩. **Facsimile** suggests a close reproduction in the same materials that may differ in scale ⟨a *facsimile* of an illuminated medieval manuscript⟩. **Replica** implies the exact reproduction of something in all respects ⟨*replicas* of the ships used by Columbus⟩.

reprove, rebuke, reprimand, admonish, reproach, chide mean to criticize adversely. **Reprove** implies an often kindly intent to correct a fault ⟨gently *reproved* her table manners⟩. **Rebuke** suggests a sharp or stern reproof ⟨the papal letter *rebuked* dissenting church officials⟩. **Reprimand** implies a severe, formal, often public or official rebuke ⟨a general officially *reprimanded* for speaking out of turn⟩. **Admonish** suggest earnest or friendly warning and counsel ⟨*admonished* by my parents to control expenses⟩. **Reproach** and **chide** suggest displeasure or disappointment expressed in mild reproof or scolding ⟨*reproached* him for tardiness⟩ ⟨*chided* by their mother for not keeping their room clean⟩.

repudiate see DECLINE, DISCLAIM

repugnant, repellent, abhorrent, distasteful, obnoxious, invidious mean so unlikable as to arouse antagonism or aversion. **Repugnant** implies being alien to one's ideas, principles, or tastes and arousing resistance or loathing ⟨regards boxing as a *repugnant* sport⟩. **Repellent** suggests a generally forbidding or unpleasant quality that causes one to back away ⟨the public display of grief was *repellent* to her⟩. **Abhorrent** implies a repugnance causing active antagonism ⟨practices that are *abhorrent* to the American system⟩. **Distasteful** implies a contrariety to one's tastes or inclinations ⟨a family to whom displays of affection are *distasteful*⟩. **Obnoxious** suggests an objectionableness too great to tolerate ⟨the colonists found the tea tax especially *obnoxious*⟩. **Invidious** applies to what cannot be used or performed without creating ill will, odium, or envy ⟨the *invidious* task of deciding custody of the child⟩.

request see ASK

require see DEMAND

requite see RECIPROCATE

rescue, deliver, redeem, ransom, reclaim, save mean to set free from confinement or danger. **Rescue** implies freeing from imminent danger by prompt or vigorous action ⟨*rescue* the crew of a sinking ship⟩. **Deliver** implies release usu. of a person from confinement, temptation, slavery, or suffering ⟨*delivered* his people from bondage⟩. **Redeem** implies releasing from bondage or penalties by giving what is demanded or necessary ⟨*redeemed* her from her life as a bored housewife⟩. **Ransom** specif. applies to buying out of captivity ⟨subjects forced to *ransom* their king⟩. **Reclaim** suggests a bringing back to a former state or condition of someone or something abandoned or debased ⟨*reclaimed* long-abandoned farms⟩. **Save** may replace any of the foregoing terms; it may further imply a preserving or maintaining for usefulness or continued existence ⟨a social worker who *saved* youths from life as criminals⟩.

resemblance see LIKENESS

resentment see OFFENSE

reserve see KEEP

reserved see SILENT

resign see ABDICATE, RELINQUISH

resilient see ELASTIC

resist see OPPOSE

resolute see FAITHFUL

resolution see COURAGE

resolve see DECIDE

resort see RESOURCE

resource, resort, expedient, shift, makeshift, stopgap mean something one turns to in the absence of the usual means or source of supply. **Resource** and **resort** apply to anything one falls back upon ⟨haven't exhausted all of my *resources* yet⟩ ⟨favor a sales tax only as a last *resort*⟩. **Expedient** may apply to any device or contrivance used when the usual one is not at hand or not possible ⟨the flimsiest of *expedients* ends the tale⟩. **Shift** implies a tentative or temporary imperfect expedient ⟨her desperate *shifts* satisfied no one⟩. **Makeshift** implies an inferior expedient adopted because of urgent need or countenanced through indifference ⟨the space heater was supposed to be only a *makeshift*⟩. **Stopgap** applies to something used temporarily as an emergency measure ⟨the farm aid bill is no more than a *stopgap*⟩.

respect see REGARD

resplendent see SPLENDID

respond see ANSWER

responsible, answerable, accountable, amenable, liable mean subject to being held to account. **Responsible** implies holding a specific office, duty, or trust ⟨the bureau *responsible* for revenue collection⟩. **Answerable** suggests a relation between one having a moral or legal obligation and a court or other authority charged with oversight of its observance ⟨a fact-finding committee *answerable* only to the President⟩. **Accountable** suggests imminence of retribution for unfulfilled trust or violated obligation ⟨in a democracy the politicians are *accountable* to the voters⟩. **Amenable** and **liable** stress the fact of subjection to review, censure, or control by a designated authority under certain conditions ⟨laws are *amenable* to judicial review⟩ ⟨will not be *liable* for his ex-wife's debts⟩.

restful see COMFORTABLE

restive see CONTRARY

restore see RENEW

restrain, check, curb, bridle mean to hold back from or control in doing something. **Restrain** suggests holding back by force or persuasion from acting or from going to extremes ⟨*restrained* themselves from trading insults⟩. **Check** implies restraining or impeding a progress, activity, or impetus ⟨deep mud *checked* our progress⟩. **Curb** suggests an abrupt or drastic checking ⟨learn to *curb* your appetite⟩. **Bridle** implies keeping under control by subduing or holding in ⟨they could no longer *bridle* their passion⟩.

restrict see LIMIT

result see EFFECT

retain see KEEP

retaliate see RECIPROCATE

retard see DELAY

reticent see SILENT

retort see ANSWER

retract see ABJURE, RECEDE

retreat see RECEDE

retrench see SHORTEN

retrograde see RECEDE

return see RECIPROCATE

reveal, discover, disclose, divulge, tell, betray mean to make known what has been or should be concealed. **Reveal** may apply to supernatural or inspired revelation of truths beyond the range of ordinary human vision or reason ⟨the belief that divine will is *revealed* in the Bible⟩. **Discover** implies an uncovering of matters kept secret and not previously known ⟨a step-by-step comparison that *discovered* a clear case of plagiarism⟩. **Disclose** may also imply a discovering but more often an imparting of information previously kept secret ⟨candidates must *disclose* their financial assets⟩. **Divulge** implies a disclosure involving some impropriety or breach of confidence ⟨refused to *divulge* confidential information⟩. **Tell** implies an imparting of necessary or useful information ⟨never *told* her that he was married⟩. **Betray** implies a divulging that represents a breach of faith or an involuntary or unconscious disclosure ⟨a blush that *betrayed* her embarrassment⟩.

revere, reverence, venerate, worship, adore mean to honor and admire profoundly and respectfully. **Revere** stresses deference and tenderness of feeling ⟨a retiring professor *revered* by generations of students⟩. **Reverence** presupposes an intrinsic merit and inviolability in the one honored and a corresponding depth of feeling in the one honoring ⟨the general *reverenced* the army's code of honor⟩. **Venerate** implies a holding as holy or sacrosanct because of character, association, or age ⟨national heroes who are still *venerated*⟩. **Worship** implies homage usu. expressed in words or ceremony ⟨*worships* the memory of her husband⟩. **Adore** implies love and stresses the notion of an individual and personal attachment ⟨a doctor who is practically *adored* by her patients⟩.

reverence *n* see HONOR

reverence *vb* see REVERE

reverse, transpose, invert mean to change to the opposite position. **Reverse** is the most general term and may imply change in order, side, direction, meaning ⟨*reversed* his position on the arms agreement⟩. **Transpose** implies a change in order or relative position of units often through exchange of position ⟨anagrams are formed by *transposing* the letters of a word or phrase⟩. **Invert** applies chiefly to turning upside down or inside out ⟨a typo consisting of a whole line of *inverted* type⟩.

revile see SCOLD

revise see CORRECT

revolt see REBELLION

revolution see REBELLION

ribald see COARSE

rich, wealthy, affluent, opulent mean having goods, property, and money in abundance. **Rich** implies having more than enough to gratify normal needs or desires ⟨girls looking for *rich* husbands⟩. **Wealthy** stresses the possession of property and intrinsically valuable things ⟨retired from politics a *wealthy* man⟩. **Affluent** suggests prosperity and an increasing wealth ⟨an *affluent* society⟩. **Opulent** suggests lavish expenditure and display of great wealth ⟨*opulent* mansions⟩.

riddle see MYSTERY

ridicule, deride, mock, taunt, twit mean to make an object of laughter of. **Ridicule** implies a deliberate often malicious belittling ⟨consistently *ridiculed* everything she said⟩. **Deride** suggests contemptuous and often bitter ridicule ⟨*derided* their efforts to start their own business⟩. **Mock** implies scorn often ironically expressed as by mimicry or sham deference ⟨youngsters began to *mock* the helpless wino⟩. **Taunt** suggests jeeringly provoking insult or challenge ⟨terrorists *taunted* the hostages⟩. **Twit** usu. suggests mild or good-humored teasing ⟨students *twitted* their teacher about his tardiness⟩.

ridiculous see LAUGHABLE

rife see PREVAILING

right see CORRECT

righteous see MORAL

rigid, rigorous, strict, stringent mean extremely severe or stern. **Rigid** implies uncompromising inflexibility ⟨the school's admission standards are *rigid*⟩. **Rigorous** implies the imposition of hardship and difficulty ⟨the *rigorous* training of recruits⟩. **Strict** emphasizes undeviating conformity to rules, standards, or requirements ⟨her doctor put her on a *strict* diet⟩. **Stringent** suggests restrictions or limitations that curb or coerce ⟨the judge's ruling is a *stringent* interpretation of the law⟩. See in addition STIFF.

rigorous see RIGID

rile see IRRITATE

rim see BORDER

rip see TEAR

rise see SPRING

risky see DANGEROUS

rive see TEAR

roam see WANDER

robust see HEALTHY

rock see SHAKE

root see ORIGIN

rot see DECAY

rough, harsh, uneven, rugged, scabrous mean not smooth or even. **Rough** implies points, bristles, ridges, or projections on the surface ⟨a *rough* wooden board⟩. **Harsh** implies a surface or texture distinctly unpleasant to the touch ⟨the *harsh* fabric chafed his skin⟩. **Uneven** implies a lack of uniformity in height, breadth, or quality ⟨an old house with *uneven* floors⟩. **Rugged** implies irregularity or roughness of land surface and connotes difficulty of travel ⟨follow the *rugged* road up the mountain⟩. **Scabrous** implies scaliness or prickliness of surface ⟨an allergic condition that results in *scabrous* hands⟩. See in addition RUDE.

rove see WANDER

rude, rough, crude, raw mean lacking in social refinement. **Rude** implies ignorance of or indifference to good form; it may suggest intentional discourtesy ⟨consistently *rude* behavior toward her in-laws⟩. **Rough** is likely to stress lack of polish and gentleness ⟨the *rough* manners of a man used to living in the outback⟩. **Crude** may apply to thought or behavior limited to the gross, the obvious, or the primitive and ignorant of civilized amenities ⟨the *crude* antics of college students on spring break⟩. **Raw** suggests being untested, inexperienced, or unfinished ⟨charged with turning *raw* youths into young men⟩.

rugged see ROUGH

rule *vb* see DECIDE, GOVERN

rule *n* see LAW

ruminate see PONDER

rural, rustic, pastoral, bucolic mean relating to or characteristic of the country. **Rural** suggests open country and farming ⟨a diminishing portion of the island remains *rural*⟩. **Rustic** suggests more clearly a contrast with city life and connotes rudeness and lack of polish ⟨a hunting lodge filled with *rustic* furniture and decoration⟩. **Pastoral** implies an idealized simplicity and peacefulness and apartness from the world ⟨the *pastoral* setting of an exclusive health resort⟩. **Bucolic** may refer to either the desirable or undesirable aspects of country life ⟨fed-up city dwellers imagining a *bucolic* bliss⟩.

ruse see TRICK

rustic see RURAL

ruth see PITY

S

sack see RAVAGE

sadness, depression, melancholy, melancholia, dejection, gloom mean the state of mind of one who is unhappy. **Sadness** is a general term that carries no suggestion of the cause, extent, or exact nature of low spirits ⟨a feeling of *sadness* marked the farewell dinner⟩. **Depression** suggests a condition in which one feels let down, disheartened, or enervated ⟨under a doctor's care for severe *depression*⟩. **Melancholy** suggests a mood of sad and serious but not wholly unpleasant pensiveness ⟨old love letters that gave her cause for *melancholy*⟩. **Melancholia** applies to a settled deep depression verging on insanity ⟨fell into a state of *melancholia* after her husband's death⟩. **Dejection** implies a usu. passing mood of being downcast or dispirited from a natural or logical cause ⟨a struggling actor used to periods of *dejection*⟩. **Gloom** applies to the atmosphere or the effect on others created by one afflicted with any of these moods or conditions ⟨a universal *gloom* engulfed the devastated town⟩.

safeguard see DEFEND

sagacious see SHREWD

sage see WISE

salient see NOTICEABLE

salubrious see HEALTHFUL

salutary see HEALTHFUL

same, selfsame, very, identical, equivalent, equal mean not different or not differing from one another. **Same** may imply and **selfsame** always implies that the things under consideration are one thing and not two or more things

⟨we both took the *same* route⟩ ⟨it was the *selfsame* ring I had lost years ago⟩. **Very,** like *selfsame,* may imply identity, or, like *same,* may imply likeness in kind ⟨you're the *very* person I've been looking for⟩. **Identical** may imply self-sameness or suggest absolute agreement in all details ⟨their test answers were *identical*⟩. **Equivalent** implies amounting to the same thing in worth or significance ⟨two houses *equivalent* in market value⟩. **Equal** implies being identical in value, magnitude, or some specified quality ⟨divided it into *equal* shares⟩.

sample see INSTANCE
sanctimonious see DEVOUT
sanction see APPROVE
sane see WISE
sangfroid see EQUANIMITY
sanguinary see BLOODY
sanguine see BLOODY
sap see WEAKEN
sapient see WISE
sarcasm see WIT
sarcastic, satiric, ironic, sardonic mean marked by bitterness and a power or will to cut or sting. **Sarcastic** implies an intentional inflicting of pain by deriding, taunting, or ridiculing ⟨a critic famous mainly for his *sarcastic* remarks⟩. **Satiric** implies that the intent of the ridiculing is censure and reprobation ⟨a *satiric* look at contemporary sexual mores⟩. **Ironic** implies an attempt to be amusing or provocative by saying usu. the opposite of what is meant ⟨made the *ironic* observation that the government could always be trusted⟩. **Sardonic** implies scorn, mockery, or derision that is manifested by either verbal or facial expression ⟨surveyed the scene with a *sardonic* smile⟩.
sardonic see SARCASTIC

sate see SATIATE

satiate, sate, surfeit, cloy, pall, glut, gorge mean to fill to repletion. **Satiate** and **sate** may sometimes imply only complete satisfaction but more often suggest repletion that has destroyed interest or desire ⟨movies that *satiated* their interest in sex⟩ ⟨audiences were *sated* with dizzying visual effects⟩. **Surfeit** implies a nauseating repletion ⟨*surfeited* themselves with junk food⟩. **Cloy** stresses the disgust or boredom resulting from such surfeiting ⟨sentimental pictures that *cloy* after a while⟩. **Pall** emphasizes the loss of ability to stimulate interest or appetite ⟨even a tropical paradise begins to *pall* after ten trips⟩. **Glut** implies excess in feeding or supplying ⟨bookstores *glutted* with diet books⟩. **Gorge** suggests glutting to the point of bursting or choking ⟨*gorged* themselves with chocolate⟩.

satire see WIT

satiric see SARCASTIC

satisfy see PAY

saturate see SOAK

saturnine see SULLEN

savage see FIERCE

save see RESCUE

savoir faire see TACT

savory see PALATABLE

scabrous see ROUGH

scan see SCRUTINIZE

scandal see OFFENSE

scant see MEAGER

scanty see MEAGER

scarce see INFREQUENT

scathing see CAUSTIC

scatter, disperse, dissipate, dispel mean to cause to separate or break up. **Scatter** implies a force that drives parts or units irregularly in many directions ⟨the bowling ball *scattered* the pins⟩. **Disperse** implies a wider separation and a complete breaking up of a mass or group ⟨police *dispersed* the crowd⟩. **Dissipate** stresses complete disintegration or dissolution and final disappearance ⟨the fog was *dissipated* by the morning sun⟩. **Dispel** stresses a driving away or getting rid of as if by scattering ⟨an authoritative statement that *dispelled* all doubt⟩.

scent see FRAGRANCE, SMELL

scheme see PLAN

scholarship see KNOWLEDGE

school see TEACH

scoff, jeer, gibe, fleer, sneer, flout mean to show one's contempt in derision or mockery. **Scoff** stresses insolence, disrespect, or incredulity as motivating the derision ⟨*scoffed* at the religious faith of others⟩. **Jeer** suggests a coarser more undiscriminating derision ⟨the crowd *jeered* the visiting team⟩. **Gibe** implies taunting either good-naturedly or in sarcastic derision ⟨*gibed* at him for repeatedly missing the ball⟩. **Fleer** suggests grinning or grimacing derisively ⟨some freshmen were greeted by *fleering* seniors⟩. **Sneer** stresses insulting by contemptuous facial expression, phrasing, or tone of voice ⟨*sneered* at anything even remotely romantic⟩. **Flout** stresses contempt shown by refusal to heed ⟨*flouted* the conventions of polite society⟩.

scold, upbraid, berate, rail, revile, vituperate mean to reproach angrily and abusively. **Scold** implies rebuking in irritation or ill temper justly or unjustly ⟨relieved her frustrations by *scolding* the children⟩. **Upbraid** implies censuring on definite and usu. justifiable grounds ⟨the governor *upbraided* his aides for poor research⟩. **Berate** suggests prolonged and often abusive scolding ⟨*berated* continually by a violent, abusive father⟩. **Rail** (*at* or *against*) stresses an unrestrained berating ⟨*railed* loudly at the insolent bureaucrat⟩. **Revile** implies a scurrilous, abusive attack prompted by anger or hatred ⟨a President vehemently *reviled* in the press⟩. **Vituperate** suggests a violent reviling ⟨a preacher more given to *vituperating* than to inspiring⟩.

scope see RANGE

scorn see DESPISE

scout see DESPISE

scowl see FROWN

scrap see DISCARD

scrawny see LEAN

screen see HIDE

scruple see QUALM

scrupulous see CAREFUL, UPRIGHT

scrutinize, scan, inspect, examine mean to look at or over carefully and usu. critically. **Scrutinize** stresses close attention to minute detail ⟨closely *scrutinized* the bill from the hospital⟩. **Scan** implies a surveying from point to point often suggesting a cursory overall observation ⟨quickly *scanned* the wine list⟩. **Inspect** implies scrutinizing for errors or defects ⟨*inspected* the restaurant for health-code violations⟩. **Examine** suggests a scrutiny in order to determine the nature, condition, or quality of a thing ⟨*examined* the gems to see whether they were genuine⟩.

scurrility see ABUSE

scurvy see CONTEMPTIBLE

seclusion see SOLITUDE

secret, covert, stealthy, furtive, clandestine, surreptitious, underhanded mean done without attracting observation. **Secret** implies concealment on any grounds for any motive ⟨a *secret* meeting between lovers⟩. **Covert** streses the fact of not being open or declared ⟨*covert* operations against guerrilla forces⟩. **Stealthy** suggests taking pains to avoid being seen or heard esp. in some misdoing ⟨the *stealthy* movements of a cat burglar⟩. **Furtive** implies a sly or cautious stealthiness ⟨exchanged *furtive* smiles across the room⟩. **Clandestine** implies secrecy usu. for an evil or illicit purpose ⟨a *clandestine* drug deal in a back alley⟩. **Surreptitious** applies to action or behavior done secretly often with skillful avoidance of detection and in violation of custom, law, or authority ⟨the *surreptitious* stockpiling of weapons by survivalists⟩. **Underhanded** stresses fraud or deception ⟨a car dealership guilty of *underhanded* practices⟩.

secrete see HIDE

secretive see SILENT

section see PART

secure see ENSURE, GET

sedate see SERIOUS

seduce see LURE

sedulous see BUSY

seeming see APPARENT

segment see PART

seize see TAKE

selection see CHOICE

self-assertive see AGGRESSIVE

self-possession see CONFIDENCE

selfsame see SAME

sense, common sense, gumption, judgment, wisdom mean ability to reach intelligent conclusions. **Sense** implies a reliable ability to judge and decide with soundness, prudence, and intelligence ⟨hasn't the *sense* to come in out of the rain⟩. **Common sense** suggests an average degree of such ability without sophistication or special knowledge ⟨*common sense* tells me it's wrong⟩. **Gumption** suggests a readiness to use or apply common sense ⟨a shrewd busi-

nessman known for his *gumption*⟩. **Judgment** implies
sense tempered and refined by experience, training, and
maturity ⟨*judgment* is required of a camp counselor⟩.
Wisdom implies sense and judgment far above average
⟨the *wisdom* that comes from years of living⟩. See in addition MEANING.

sensible see AWARE, MATERIAL, PERCEPTIBLE, WISE

sensitive see LIABLE

sensual see CARNAL, SENSUOUS

sensuous, sensual, luxurious, voluptuous mean relating to or
providing pleasure through gratification of the senses. **Sensuous** implies gratification of the senses for the sake of aesthetic pleasure ⟨the *sensuous* delights of a Reubens paint-
ing⟩. **Sensual** tends to imply the gratification of the senses
or the indulgence of the physical appetites as ends in themselves ⟨a man who indulged his *sensual* appetites⟩. **Luxurious** suggests the providing of or indulgence of sensuous
pleasure inducing bodily ease and languor ⟨a vacation devoted to *luxurious* self-indulgence⟩. **Voluptuous** implies
more strongly an abandonment esp. to sensual pleasure
⟨promised a variety of *voluptuous* pleasures⟩.

sentiment see FEELING, OPINION

separate *vb* Separate, part, divide, sever, sunder, divorce
mean to become or cause to become disunited or dis-
jointed. **Separate** may imply any of several causes such as
dispersion, removal of one from others, or presence of an
intervening thing ⟨*separated* her personal life from her ca-
reer⟩. **Part** implies the separating of things or persons in
close union or association ⟨an argument that *parted* the
friends permanently⟩. **Divide** implies separating into
pieces or sections by cutting or breaking ⟨civil war *divided*
the nation⟩. **Sever** implies violence esp. in the removal of
a part or member ⟨his arm had been *severed* by a chain

saw). **Sunder** suggests violent rending or wrenching apart ⟨a province *sundered* by two languages⟩. **Divorce** implies separating two things that commonly interact and belong together ⟨would *divorce* scientific research from moral responsibility⟩.

separate *adj* see DISTINCT, SINGLE

serene see CALM

serious, grave, solemn, sedate, staid, sober, earnest mean not light or frivolous. **Serious** implies a concern for what really matters ⟨prefers gothic romances to *serious* fiction⟩. **Grave** implies both seriousness and dignity in expression or attitude ⟨read the pronouncement in a *grave* voice⟩. **Solemn** suggests an impressive gravity utterly free from levity ⟨the *solemn* occasion of a coronation⟩. **Sedate** implies a composed and decorous seriousness ⟨amidst the frenzy of activity the bride remained *sedate*⟩. **Staid** suggests a settled, accustomed sedateness and prim self-restraint ⟨her dinner parties were *staid* affairs⟩. **Sober** stresses seriousness of purpose and absence of levity or frivolity ⟨an objective and *sober* look at the situation⟩. **Earnest** suggests sincerity or often zealousness of purpose ⟨an *earnest* attempt at dramatizing the Bible⟩.

servile see SUBSERVIENT

setting see BACKGROUND

settle see DECIDE

sever see SEPARATE

several see DISTINCT

severe, stern, austere, ascetic mean given to or marked by strict discipline and firm restraint. **Severe** implies standards enforced without indulgence or laxity and may suggest harshness ⟨the *severe* dress of the Puritans⟩. **Stern** stresses inflexibility and inexorability of temper or character ⟨a *stern* judge who seemed immune to pleas for mercy⟩. **Austere** stresses absence of warmth, color, or feeling and may apply to rigorous restraint, simplicity, or self-denial ⟨the view that modern architecture is *austere*, brutal, and inhuman⟩. **Ascetic** implies abstention from pleasure and comfort or self-indulgence as spiritual discipline ⟨the *ascetic* life of the monastic orders⟩.

shackle see HAMPER

shake, agitate, rock, convulse mean to move up and down or to and fro with some violence. **Shake** often carries a further implication of a particular purpose ⟨*shake* well before using⟩. **Agitate** suggests a violent and prolonged tossing or stirring ⟨strong winds *agitated* the ship for hours⟩. **Rock** suggests a swinging or swaying motion resulting from violent impact or upheaval ⟨the entire city was *rocked* by the explosion⟩. **Convulse** suggests a violent pulling or wrenching as of a body in a paroxysm ⟨we were *convulsed* with laughter⟩.

shallow see SUPERFICIAL

sham *vb* see ASSUME

sham *n* see IMPOSTURE

shape *n* see FORM

shape *vb* see MAKE

share, participate, partake mean to have, get, or use in common with another or others. **Share** implies that one as the original holder grants to another the partial use, enjoyment, or possession of a thing though it may merely imply a mutual use or possession ⟨*shared* my tools with the others⟩. **Participate** implies a having or taking part in an undertaking, activity, or discussion ⟨students are encouraged to *participate* in outside activities⟩. **Partake** implies accepting or acquiring a share esp. of food or drink ⟨invited everyone to *partake* freely in the refreshments⟩.

sharp, keen, acute mean having or showing alert competence and clear understanding. **Sharp** implies quick perception, clever resourcefulness, or sometimes questionable trickiness ⟨*sharp* enough to know a con job when he saw one⟩. **Keen** suggests quickness, enthusiasm, and a penetrating mind ⟨a *keen* observer of the political scene⟩. **Acute** implies a power to penetrate and may suggest subtlety and sharpness of discrimination ⟨an *acute* sense of what is linguistically effective⟩.

shed see DISCARD

sheer see STEEP

shield see DEFEND

shift see RESOURCE

shimmer see FLASH

short see BRIEF

shorten, curtail, abbreviate, abridge, retrench mean to reduce in extent. **Shorten** implies reduction in length or duration ⟨*shorten* the speech to fit the allotted time⟩. **Curtail** adds an implication of cutting that in some way deprives of completeness or adequacy ⟨the ceremonies were *curtailed* because of the rain⟩. **Abbreviate** implies a making shorter usu. by omitting some part ⟨hostile questioning had the effect of *abbreviating* the interview⟩. **Abridge** implies a reduction in compass or scope with retention of essential elements and a relative completeness in the result ⟨the *abridged* version of the novel⟩. **Retrench** suggests a reduction in extent or costs of something felt to be excessive ⟨falling prices forced the company to *retrench*⟩.

shove see PUSH

show, exhibit, display, expose, parade, flaunt mean to present so as to invite notice or attention. **Show** implies no more than enabling another to see or examine ⟨*showed* her snapshots to the whole group⟩. **Exhibit** stresses putting forward prominently or openly ⟨*exhibit* paintings at a gallery⟩. **Display** emphasizes putting in a position where others may see to advantage ⟨*display* sale items⟩. **Expose** suggests bringing forth from concealment and displaying ⟨sought to *expose* the hypocrisy of the town fathers⟩. **Parade** implies an ostentatious or arrogant displaying ⟨*parading* their piety for all to see⟩. **Flaunt** suggests a shameless, boastful, often offensive parading ⟨nouveaux riches *flaunting* their wealth⟩.

show, manifest, evidence, evince, demonstrate mean to reveal outwardly or make apparent. **Show** is the general term but sometimes implies that what is revealed must be gained by inference from acts, looks, or words ⟨careful not to *show* what he feels⟩. **Manifest** implies a plainer, more immediate revelation ⟨*manifested* musical ability at an early age⟩. **Evidence** suggests serving as proof of the actuality or existence of something ⟨her deep enmity is *evidenced* by her silent glaring⟩. **Evince** implies a showing by outward marks or signs ⟨*evinced* not the slightest grief at the funeral⟩. **Demonstrate** implies showing by action or by display of feeling ⟨*demonstrated* her appreciation in her own way⟩.

showy, pretentious, ostentatious mean given to excessive outward display. **Showy** implies an imposing or striking appearance but usu. suggests cheapness or poor taste ⟨the *showy* costumes of the circus performers⟩. **Pretentious** implies an appearance of importance not justified by the thing's value or the person's standing ⟨for a family-style restaurant, the menu was far too *pretentious*⟩. **Ostentatious** stresses vainglorious display or parade ⟨very *ostentatious*, even for a debutante party⟩.

shrewd, sagacious, perspicacious, astute mean acute in perception and sound in judgment. **Shrewd** stresses practical, hardheaded cleverness and judgment ⟨a *shrewd* judge of character⟩. **Sagacious** suggests wisdom, penetration, and farsightedness ⟨a series of *sagacious* investments tripled her wealth⟩. **Perspicacious** implies unusual power to see through and understand what is puzzling or hidden ⟨a *perspicacious* counselor saw through his facade⟩. **Astute** suggests shrewdness, perspicacity, and diplomatic skill ⟨an *astute* player of party politics⟩.

shrink see CONTRACT, RECOIL

shun see ESCAPE

shy, bashful, diffident, modest, coy mean not inclined to be forward. **Shy** implies a timid reserve and a shrinking from familiarity or contact with others ⟨*shy* in front of total strangers⟩. **Bashful** implies a frightened or hesitant shyness characteristic of childhood and adolescence ⟨the *bashful* boy rarely told us how he felt about anything⟩. **Diffident** stresses a distrust of one's own ability or opinion that causes hesitation in acting or speaking ⟨felt *diffident* about raising an objection⟩. **Modest** suggests absence of undue confidence or conceit ⟨very *modest* about reciting his achievements⟩. **Coy** implies an assumed or affected shyness ⟨don't be misled by her *coy* demeanor⟩.

side see PHASE

sign, mark, token, note, symptom mean a discernible indication of what is not itself directly perceptible. **Sign** applies to any indication to be perceived by the senses or the reason ⟨interpreted her smile as a good *sign*⟩. **Mark** suggests something impressed on or inherently characteristic of a thing often in contrast to general outward appearance ⟨integrity is the *mark* of a gentleman⟩. **Token** applies to something that serves as a proof of something intangible ⟨this gift is a *token* of our esteem⟩. **Note** suggests a distinguishing mark or characteristic ⟨a *note* of despair pervades her poetry⟩. **Symptom** suggests an outward indication of an internal change or condition ⟨rampant violence is a *symptom* of that country's decline⟩.

significance see IMPORTANCE, MEANING

signification see MEANING

silent, taciturn, reticent, reserved, secretive mean showing restraint in speaking. **Silent** implies a habit of saying no more than is needed ⟨her husband was the *silent* type, not given to idle chatter⟩. **Taciturn** implies a temperamental disinclination to speech and usu. connotes unsociability ⟨the locals are *taciturn* and not receptive to outsiders⟩. **Reticent** implies a reluctance to speak out or at length, esp. about one's own affairs ⟨our guest was strangely *reticent* about his plans⟩. **Reserved** implies reticence and suggests the restraining influence of caution or formality in checking easy informal conversational exchange ⟨greetings were brief, formal, and *reserved*⟩. **Secretive**, too, implies reticence but usu. carries a suggestion of deviousness and lack of frankness or of an often ostentatious will to conceal ⟨a *secretive* public official usually stingy with news stories⟩.

silhouette see OUTLINE

silken see SLEEK

silly see SIMPLE

similar, analogous, parallel mean closely resembling each other. **Similar** implies the possibility of being mistaken for each other ⟨all the houses in the development are *similar*⟩. **Analogous** applies to things belonging in essentially different categories but nevertheless having many similarities ⟨*analogous* political systems⟩. **Parallel** suggests a marked likeness in the development of two things ⟨the *parallel* careers of two movie stars⟩.

similarity see LIKENESS

similitude see LIKENESS

simple, foolish, silly, fatuous, asinine mean actually or ap-

parently deficient in intelligence. **Simple** implies a degree
of intelligence inadequate to cope with anything complex
or involving mental effort ⟨*simple* peasants afraid of rev-
olutionary ideas⟩. **Foolish** implies the character of being or
seeming unable to use judgment, discretion, or good sense
⟨*foolish* people believed the ghost story⟩. **Silly** suggests
failure to act as a rational being esp. by ridiculous behavior
⟨the *silly* stunts of vacationing college students⟩. **Fatuous**
implies foolishness, inanity, and disregard of reality ⟨the
fatuous conspiracy theories of these extremists⟩. **Asinine**
suggests utter and contemptible failure to use normal rationality or perception ⟨a soap opera with an especially *asinine* plot⟩. See in addition EASY.

simulate see ASSUME

simultaneous see CONTEMPORARY

sin see OFFENSE

sincere, wholehearted, heartfelt, hearty, unfeigned mean
genuine in feeling. **Sincere** stresses absence of hypocrisy,
feigning, or any falsifying embellishment or exaggeration
⟨offered a *sincere* apology⟩. **Wholehearted** suggests sincerity and earnest devotion without reservation or misgiving
⟨promised our *wholehearted* support to the cause⟩. **Heartfelt** suggests depth of genuine feeling outwardly expressed
⟨a gift that expresses our *heartfelt* gratitude⟩. **Hearty** suggests honesty, warmth, and exuberance in displaying feeling ⟨received a *hearty* welcome at the door⟩. **Unfeigned**
stresses spontaneity and absence of pretense ⟨her *unfeigned* delight at receiving the award⟩.

single, sole, unique, separate, solitary, particular mean one
as distinguished from two or more or all others. **Single** implies being unaccompanied by or unsupported by any
other ⟨a *single* example will suffice⟩. **Sole** applies to the
one of its kind or character in existence ⟨my *sole* reason

for moving there). **Unique** applies to the only one of its kind or character in existence ⟨the medal is *unique,* for no duplicates were made⟩. **Separate** stresses discreteness and disconnection from every other one ⟨a country with a *separate* set of problems⟩. **Solitary** implies being both single and isolated ⟨the television was her *solitary* link to the outside world⟩. **Particular** implies numerical distinctness from other instances, examples, or members of a class ⟨a *particular* kind of wine⟩.

singular see STRANGE

sinister, baleful, malign mean seriously threatening evil or disaster. **Sinister** suggests a general or vague feeling of fear or apprehension on the part of the observer ⟨a *sinister* aura surrounded the place⟩. **Baleful** imputes perniciousness or destructiveness to something whether working openly or covertly ⟨the *baleful* influence of recreational drugs on our society⟩. **Malign** applies to what is inherently evil or harmful ⟨smoking's *malign* effects on one's health⟩.

skepticism see UNCERTAINTY

sketch see COMPENDIUM

skill see ART

skilled see PROFICIENT

skillful see PROFICIENT

skimpy see MEAGER

skinny see LEAN

skulk see LURK

slack see NEGLIGENT

slacken see DELAY

slander see MALIGN

slang see DIALECT

slavish see SUBSERVIENT

slay see KILL

sleek, slick, glossy, silken mean having a smooth bright surface or appearance. **Sleek** suggests a smoothness or brightness resulting from attentive grooming or physical conditioning ⟨a *sleek* racehorse⟩. **Slick** suggests extreme smoothness that results in a slippery surface ⟨slipped and fell on the *slick* floor⟩. **Glossy** suggests a surface that is smooth and highly polished ⟨photographs having a *glossy* finish⟩. **Silken** implies the smoothness and luster as well as the softness of silk ⟨*silken* hair⟩.

slender see THIN
slick see SLEEK
slight *vb* see NEGLECT
slight *adj* see THIN
slighting see DEROGATORY
slim see THIN
sling see THROW
slink see LURK
slip see ERROR
slothful see LAZY
slough see DISCARD
slow see DELAY

sly, cunning, crafty, tricky, foxy, artful mean attaining or seeking to attain one's ends by devious means. **Sly** implies furtiveness, lack of candor, and skill in concealing one's aims and methods ⟨a *sly* corporate-takeover scheme⟩. **Cunning** suggests the inventive use of sometimes limited intelligence in overreaching or circumventing ⟨relentlessly *cunning* in her pursuit of the governorship⟩. **Crafty** implies cleverness and subtlety of method ⟨a *crafty* trial lawyer⟩. **Tricky** is more likely to suggest shiftiness and unreliability than skill in deception and maneuvering ⟨a *tricky* interviewer who usually got what she wanted from her subject⟩. **Foxy** implies a shrewd and wary craftiness usu. involving devious dealing ⟨a *foxy* thief got away with her jewels). **Artful** implies alluring indirectness in dealing and often connotes sophistication or coquetry or cleverness ⟨an *artful* matchmaker⟩.

small, little, diminutive, minute, tiny, miniature mean noticeably below average in size. **Small** and **little** are often interchangeable, but *small* applies more to relative size determined by capacity, value, number; *little* is more absolute in implication often carrying the idea of petiteness, pettiness, insignificance, or immaturity ⟨the theater was relatively *small*⟩ ⟨your pathetic *little* smile⟩. **Diminutive** implies abnormal smallness ⟨the *diminutive* gymnast outshone her larger competitors⟩. **Minute** implies extreme smallness ⟨a beverage with only a *minute* amount of caffeine⟩. **Tiny** is an informal equivalent to *minute* ⟨*tiny* cracks have formed in the painting⟩. **Miniature** applies to an exactly proportioned reproduction on a very small scale ⟨a doll house complete with *miniature* furnishings⟩.

smell, scent, odor, aroma mean the quality that makes a thing perceptible to the olfactory sense. **Smell** implies solely the sensation without suggestion of quality or character ⟨an odd *smell* permeated the room⟩. **Scent** applies to the characteristic smell given off by a substance, an animal, or a plant ⟨dogs trained to detect the *scent* of narcotics⟩. **Odor** may imply a stronger or more readily distinguished scent or it may be equivalent to *smell* ⟨a type of cheese with a very pronounced *odor*⟩. **Aroma** suggests a somewhat penetrating usu. pleasant odor ⟨the *aroma* of freshly ground coffee⟩.

smooth see EASY, LEVEL, SUAVE

snare see CATCH

snatch see TAKE

sneak see LURK

sneer see SCOFF

snug see COMFORTABLE

soak, saturate, drench, steep, impregnate mean to permeate or be permeated with a liquid. **Soak** implies usu. prolonged immersion as for softening or cleansing ⟨*soak* the clothes in bleach and water to remove the stains⟩. **Saturate** implies a resulting effect of complete absorption until no more liquid can be held ⟨gym clothes *saturated* with sweat⟩. **Drench** implies a thorough wetting by something that pours down or is poured ⟨the cloudburst *drenched* us to the skin⟩. **Steep** suggests either the extraction of an essence (as of tea leaves) by the liquid or the imparting of a quality (as a color) to the thing immersed ⟨*steep* the tea leaves for exactly five minutes⟩. **Impregnate** implies a thorough interpenetration of one thing by another ⟨a cake strongly *impregnated* with brandy⟩.

sober see SERIOUS

sociable see GRACIOUS

society see ARISTOCRACY

solace see COMFORT

sole see SINGLE

solemn see SERIOUS

solicit see ASK, INVITE

solicitude see CARE

solid see FIRM

solidarity see UNITY

solitary see ALONE, SINGLE

solitude, isolation, seclusion mean the state of one who is alone. **Solitude** may imply a condition of being apart from all human beings or of being cut off by wish or compulsion from one's usual associates ⟨the *solitude* enjoyed by the long-distance trucker⟩. **Isolation** stresses detachment from others often involuntarily ⟨the oppressive *isolation* of the village during winter⟩. **Seclusion** suggests a shutting away or keeping apart from others often connoting deliberate withdrawal from the world or retirement to a quiet life ⟨lived in bucolic *seclusion* surrounded by his art collection⟩.

somatic see BODILY

sophisticated, worldly-wise, blasé mean experienced in the ways of the world. **Sophisticated** often implies refinement, urbanity, cleverness, and cultivation ⟨guests at her salon were usu. rich and *sophisticated*⟩. **Worldly-wise** suggests a close and practical knowledge of the affairs and manners of society and an inclination toward materialism ⟨a *worldly-wise* woman with a philosophy of personal independence⟩. **Blasé** implies a lack of responsiveness to common joys as a result of a real or affected surfeit of experience and cultivation ⟨*blasé* travelers who claimed to have been everywhere⟩.

sordid see MEAN

sorrow, grief, anguish, woe, regret mean distress of mind. **Sorrow** implies a sense of loss or a sense of guilt and remorse ⟨a nation united in *sorrow* upon the death of the President⟩. **Grief** implies poignant sorrow for an immediate cause ⟨gave his father much *grief*⟩. **Anguish** suggests torturing grief or dread ⟨the *anguish* felt by the hostages⟩. **Woe** is deep or inconsolable grief or misery ⟨cries of *woe* echoed throughout the bombed city⟩. **Regret** implies pain caused by deep disappointment, fruitless longing, or unavailing remorse ⟨never felt a moment of *regret* following the divorce⟩.

sorry see CONTEMPTIBLE

sort see TYPE

sound see HEALTHY, VALID

source see ORIGIN

sovereign see DOMINANT, FREE

spacious, commodious, capacious, ample mean larger in extent or capacity than the average. **Spacious** implies great length and breadth ⟨a mansion with a *spacious* front lawn⟩. **Commodious** stresses roominess and comfortableness ⟨a *commodious* and airy penthouse apartment⟩. **Capacious** stresses the ability to hold, contain, or retain more than the average ⟨a *capacious* suitcase⟩. **Ample** implies having a greater size, expanse, or amount than that deemed adequate ⟨we have *ample* means to buy the house⟩.

spare see LEAN, MEAGER

sparing, frugal, thrifty, economical mean careful in the use of one's money or resources. **Sparing** stresses abstention and restraint ⟨mother was *sparing* in buying luxuries for herself⟩. **Frugal** implies absence of luxury and simplicity of life-style ⟨carried on in the *frugal* tradition of the Yankees⟩. **Thrifty** stresses good management and industry ⟨the store prospered under his *thrifty* management⟩. **Economical** stresses prudent management, lack of wastefulness, and use of things to their best advantage ⟨trucking remains an *economical* means of transport⟩.

sparkle see FLASH

sparse see MEAGER

spasmodic see FITFUL

spat see QUARREL

special, especial, specific, particular, individual mean of or relating to one thing or class. **Special** stresses having a quality, character, identity, or use of its own ⟨airline passengers who require *special* meals⟩. **Especial** may add implications of preeminence or preference ⟨a matter of *especial* importance⟩. **Specific** implies a quality or character distinguishing a kind or a species ⟨children with *specific* nutritional needs⟩. **Particular** stresses the distinctness of something as an individual ⟨an Alpine scene of *particular* beauty⟩. **Individual** implies unequivocal reference to one of a class or group ⟨valued each *individual* opinion⟩.

specific see EXPLICIT, SPECIAL

specimen see INSTANCE

speculate see THINK

speed see HASTE

speedy see FAST

spirit see COURAGE

spite see MALICE

spleen see MALICE

splendid, resplendent, gorgeous, glorious, sublime, superb mean extraordinarily or transcendently impressive. **Splendid** implies outshining the usual or customary ⟨the royal wedding was a *splendid* occasion⟩. **Resplendent** suggests a glowing or blazing splendor ⟨the church was *resplendent* in its Easter decorations⟩. **Gorgeous** implies a rich splendor esp. in display of color ⟨a *gorgeous* red dress⟩. **Glorious** suggests radiance that heightens beauty or distinction ⟨a *glorious* sunset over the ocean⟩. **Sublime** implies an exaltation or elevation almost beyond human comprehension ⟨the *sublime* grandeur of the thunderous falls⟩. **Superb** suggests a magnificence or excellence reaching the highest conceivable degree ⟨a three-star restaurant offering *superb* cuisine⟩.

splenetic see IRASCIBLE

split see TEAR

spoil *n* Spoil, pillage, plunder, booty, prize, loot mean something taken from another by force or craft. **Spoil,** more commonly **spoils,** applies to what belongs by right or custom to the victor in war or political contest ⟨a governor who relished doling out the *spoils* of office⟩. **Pillage** stresses more open violence or lawlessness ⟨filled his cap-

ital city with the *pillage* of Europe⟩. **Plunder** applies to
what is taken not only in war but in robbery, banditry,
grafting, or swindling ⟨a fortune that was the *plunder* of
years of political corruption⟩. **Booty** implies plunder to be
shared among confederates ⟨the thieves planned to divide
their *booty* later⟩. **Prize** applies to spoils captured on the
high seas or territorial waters of the enemy ⟨a pirate ship
ruthlessly seizing *prizes*⟩. **Loot** applies esp. to what is taken
from victims of a catastrophe ⟨prowlers searched the
storm-damaged cottages for *loot*⟩.

spoil *vb* see DECAY, INDULGE

sponge see PARASITE

spontaneous, impulsive, instinctive, automatic, mechanical
mean acting or activated without deliberation. **Spontaneous** implies lack of prompting and connotes naturalness
⟨a *spontaneous* burst of applause⟩. **Impulsive** implies acting under stress of emotion or spirit of the moment ⟨*impulsive* acts of violence⟩. **Instinctive** stresses spontaneous
action involving neither judgment nor will ⟨blinking is an
instinctive reaction⟩. **Automatic** implies action engaging
neither the mind nor the emotions and connotes a predictable response ⟨his denial was *automatic*⟩. **Mechanical**
stresses the lifeless, often perfunctory character of the response ⟨over the years her style of teaching became
mechanical⟩.

sporadic see INFREQUENT

sport see FUN

sprightly see LIVELY

**spring, arise, rise, originate, derive, flow, issue, emanate,
proceed, stem** mean to come up or out of something into
existence. **Spring** implies rapid or sudden emerging ⟨a brilliant idea that had *sprung* out of nowhere⟩. **Arise** and **rise**
may both convey the fact of coming into existence or no-

tice but *rise* often stresses gradual growth or ascent ⟨a dispute *arose* over the property⟩ ⟨as time passed legends about the house *rose*⟩. **Originate** implies a definite source or starting point ⟨the theory did not *originate* with Darwin⟩. **Derive** implies a prior existence in another form ⟨their system of justice *derives* from British colonial law⟩. **Flow** adds to *spring* a suggestion of abundance or ease of inception ⟨the belief that all good *flows* from God⟩. **Issue** suggests emerging from confinement through an outlet ⟨shouts of joy *issued* from the team's locker room⟩. **Emanate** applies to the coming of something immaterial (as a principle or thought) from a source ⟨serenity *emanated* from her⟩. **Proceed** stresses place of origin, derivation, parentage, or logical cause ⟨bitterness that *proceeded* from an unhappy marriage⟩. **Stem** implies originating by dividing or branching off from something as an outgrowth or subordinate development ⟨a whole new industry *stemmed* from the discovery⟩.

springy see ELASTIC

spry see AGILE

spur see MOTIVE

spurn see DECLINE

squabble see QUARREL

squalid see DIRTY

squeamish see NICE

stable see LASTING

staid see SERIOUS

stalwart see STRONG

stand see BEAR

standard, criterion, gauge, yardstick, touchstone mean a means of determining what a thing should be. **Standard** applies to any definite rule, principle, or measure established by authority ⟨the book is a classic by any *standard*⟩.

Criterion may apply to anything used as a test of quality whether formulated as a rule or principle or not ⟨in art there are no hard-and-fast *criteria*⟩. **Gauge** applies to a means of testing a particular dimension (as thickness, depth, diameter) or figuratively a particular quality or aspect ⟨congressional mail is not always an accurate *gauge* of public opinion⟩. **Yardstick** is an informal substitute for *criterion* that suggests quantity more often than quality ⟨the movie was a flop by most *yardsticks*⟩. **Touchstone** suggests a simple test of the authenticity or value of something intangible ⟨fine service is one *touchstone* of a first-class restaurant⟩.

stare see GAZE

start see BEGIN

stately see GRAND

statute see LAW

staunch see FAITHFUL

stay see DEFER

steadfast see FAITHFUL

steady, even, equable mean not varying throughout a course or extent. **Steady** implies lack of fluctuation or interruption of movement ⟨ran the race at a *steady* pace⟩. **Even** suggests a lack of variation in quality or character ⟨read the statement in an *even* voice⟩. **Equable** implies lack of extremes or of sudden sharp changes ⟨during exercise keep your pulse as *equable* as possible⟩.

steal, pilfer, filch, purloin mean to take from another without right or without detection. **Steal** may apply to any surreptitious taking of something and differs from the other terms by commonly applying to intangibles as well as material things ⟨*steal* jewels⟩ ⟨*stole* a look at her⟩. **Pilfer** implies stealing repeatedly in small amounts ⟨dismissed for *pilfering* from the company⟩. **Filch** adds a suggestion of snatching quickly and surreptitiously ⟨*filched* an apple when the man looked away⟩. **Purloin** stresses removing or carrying off for one's own use or purposes ⟨had *purloined* a typewriter and other office equipment⟩.

stealthy see SECRET

steep *adj* **Steep, abrupt, precipitous, sheer** mean having an incline approaching the perpendicular. **Steep** implies such sharpness of pitch that ascent or descent is very difficult ⟨a *steep* staircase leading to the attic⟩. **Abrupt** implies a sharper pitch and a sudden break in the level ⟨a beach with an *abrupt* drop-off⟩. **Precipitous** applies to an incline approaching the vertical ⟨the airplane went into a *precipitous* nosedive⟩. **Sheer** suggests an unbroken perpendicular expanse ⟨climbers able to ascend *sheer* cliffs⟩.

steep *vb* see SOAK

steer see GUIDE

stem see SPRING

stentorian see LOUD

stereotyped see TRITE

stern see SEVERE

stick, adhere, cohere, cling, cleave mean to become closely attached. **Stick** implies attachment by affixing or by being glued together ⟨the gummed label will *stick* just by pressing⟩. **Adhere** is often interchangeable with *stick* but sometimes implies a growing together ⟨muscle fibers will *adhere* following surgery⟩. **Cohere** suggests a sticking together of parts so that they form a unified mass ⟨eggs will make the mixture *cohere*⟩. **Cling** implies attachment by hanging on with arms or tendrils ⟨always *cling* to a capsized boat⟩. **Cleave** stresses strength of attachment ⟨barnacles *cleaving* to the hull of a boat⟩.

stiff, rigid, inflexible mean difficult to bend. **Stiff** may apply to any degree of this condition ⟨muscles will become *stiff* if they are not stretched⟩. **Rigid** applies to something so stiff that it cannot be bent without breaking ⟨a *rigid* surfboard⟩. **Inflexible** stresses lack of suppleness or pliability ⟨for adequate support, rock-climbers wear shoes with *inflexible* soles⟩.

stimulate see PROVOKE

stingy, close, niggardly, parsimonious, penurious, miserly mean being unwilling or showing unwillingness to share with others. **Stingy** implies a marked lack of generosity ⟨a *stingy* child, not given to sharing⟩. **Close** suggests keeping a tight grip on one's money and possessions ⟨folks who are very *close* when charity calls⟩. **Niggardly** implies giving or spending the very smallest amount possible ⟨gave his wife a *niggardly* household allowance⟩. **Parsimonious** suggests a frugality so extreme as to lead to stinginess ⟨a *parsimonious* life-style with no room for luxuries⟩. **Penurious** implies niggardliness that gives an appearance of actual poverty ⟨the *penurious* old woman left behind a fortune⟩. **Miserly** suggests a sordid avariciousness and a morbid pleasure in hoarding ⟨a *miserly* man indifferent to the cries of the needy⟩.

stinking see MALODOROUS

stint see TASK

stoic see IMPASSIVE

stolid see IMPASSIVE

stoop, condescend, deign mean to descend from one's level to do something. **Stoop** may imply a descent in dignity or from a relatively high moral plane to a much lower one ⟨how can you *stoop* to such childish name-calling⟩. **Condescend** implies a stooping by one of high rank or position to socialize with social inferiors ⟨the boss's wife *condescending* to mingle with the employees⟩. **Deign** suggests a reluctant condescension of one in a haughty mood ⟨scarcely *deigned* to speak with her poor relations⟩.

stop, cease, quit, discontinue, desist mean to suspend or cause to suspend activity. **Stop** applies to action or progress or to what is operating or progressing and may imply suddenness or definiteness ⟨*stopped* at the red light⟩. **Cease** applies to states, conditions, or existence and may add a suggestion of gradualness and a degree of finality ⟨by nightfall the fighting had *ceased*⟩. **Quit** may stress either finality or abruptness in stopping or ceasing ⟨the engine faltered, sputtered, then *quit* altogether⟩. **Discontinue** applies to the stopping of an accustomed activity or practice ⟨we have *discontinued* the manufacture of that item⟩. **Desist** implies forbearance or restraint as a motive for stopping or ceasing ⟨*desisted* from further efforts to persuade them⟩.

stopgap see RESOURCE
storm see ATTACK
stout see STRONG
straits see JUNCTURE
strange, singular, unique, peculiar, eccentric, erratic, odd, queer, quaint, outlandish mean departing from what is ordinary, usual, or to be expected. **Strange** stresses unfamiliarity and may apply to the foreign, the unnatural, the unaccountable ⟨the *strange* sights of a trip to the Orient⟩. **Singular** suggests individuality or puzzling strangeness ⟨a *singular* feeling of impending disaster⟩. **Unique** implies singularity and the fact of being without a known parallel ⟨a career that is *unique* in the annals of science⟩. **Peculiar** implies a marked distinctiveness ⟨problems *peculiar* to inner-city areas⟩. **Eccentric** suggests a wide divergence from the usual or normal esp. in behavior ⟨the *eccentric* eating habits of young children⟩. **Erratic** stresses a capri-

cious and unpredictable wandering or deviating ⟨disturbed by his friend's *erratic* behavior⟩. **Odd** applies to a departure from the regular or expected ⟨an *odd* sense of humor⟩. **Queer** suggests a dubious sometimes sinister oddness ⟨puzzled by the *queer* happenings since her arrival⟩. **Quaint** suggests an old-fashioned but pleasant oddness ⟨a *quaint* and remote village in the mountains⟩. **Outlandish** applies to what is uncouth, bizarre, or barbaric ⟨islanders having *outlandish* customs and superstitions⟩.

stratagem see TRICK

strength see POWER

strenuous see VIGOROUS

strict see RIGID

strident see LOUD, VOCIFEROUS

strife see DISCORD

strike see AFFECT

striking see NOTICEABLE

stringent see RIGID

strive see ATTEMPT

strong, stout, sturdy, stalwart, tough, tenacious mean showing power to resist or to endure. **Strong** may imply power derived from muscular vigor, large size, structural soundness, intellectual or spiritual resources ⟨*strong* arms⟩ ⟨a *strong* desire to succeed⟩. **Stout** suggests an ability to endure stress, pain, or hard use without giving way ⟨wear *stout* boots when hiking⟩. **Sturdy** implies strength derived from vigorous growth, determination of spirit, solidity of construction ⟨a *sturdy* table⟩ ⟨people of *sturdy* independence⟩. **Stalwart** suggests an unshakable dependability and connotes great physical strength ⟨*stalwart* supporters of the environmental movement⟩. **Tough** implies great firmness and resiliency ⟨a *tough* political opponent⟩. **Te-**

nacious suggests strength in seizing, retaining, clinging to, or holding together ⟨*tenacious* of their right to privacy⟩.

stubborn see OBSTINATE

study see CONSIDER

stupendous see MONSTROUS

stupid, dull, dense, crass, dumb mean lacking in power to absorb ideas or impressions. **Stupid** implies a slow-witted or dazed state of mind that may be either congenital or temporary ⟨you're too *stupid* to know what's good for you⟩. **Dull** suggests a slow or sluggish mind such as results from disease, depression, or shock ⟨monotonous work that left his mind *dull*⟩. **Dense** implies a thickheaded imperviousness to ideas ⟨was too *dense* to take a hint⟩. **Crass** suggests a grossness of mind precluding discrimination or delicacy ⟨a *crass,* materialistic people⟩. **Dumb** applies to an exasperating obtuseness or lack of comprehension ⟨too *dumb* to figure out what's going on⟩.

stupor see LETHARGY

sturdy see STRONG

style see FASHION

suave, urbane, diplomatic, bland, smooth, politic mean pleasantly tactful and well-mannered. **Suave** suggests a specific ability to deal with others easily and without friction ⟨a luxury restaurant with an army of *suave* waiters⟩. **Urbane** implies high cultivation and poise coming from wide social experience ⟨the *urbane* host of a televised anthology series⟩. **Diplomatic** stresses an ability to deal with ticklish situations tactfully ⟨be *diplomatic* in asking them to leave⟩. **Bland** emphasizes mildness of manner and absence of irritating qualities ⟨a *bland* manner suitable for early morning radio⟩. **Smooth** suggests often a deliberately assumed suavity ⟨the *smooth* sales pitch of a car dealer⟩. **Politic** implies shrewd as well as tactful and suave handling of people ⟨an ambassador's wife must be *politic* and discreet⟩.

subdue see CONQUER

subject *n* see CITIZEN

subject *adj* see LIABLE

sublime see SPLENDID

submit see YIELD

subscribe see ASSENT

subservient, servile, slavish, obsequious mean showing or characterized by extreme compliance or abject obedience. **Subservient** implies the cringing manner of one very conscious of a subordinate position ⟨domestic help was expected to be properly *subservient*⟩. **Servile** suggests the mean or fawning behavior of a slave ⟨a political boss and his entourage of *servile* hangers-on⟩. **Slavish** suggests abject or debased servility ⟨the *slavish* status of migrant farm workers⟩. **Obsequious** implies fawning or sycophantic compliance and exaggerated deference of manner ⟨waiters who are *obsequious* in the presence of celebrities⟩.

subside see ABATE

substantiate see CONFIRM

subterfuge see DECEPTION

succeed see FOLLOW

succinct see CONCISE

succumb see YIELD

sudden see PRECIPITATE

suffer see BEAR

suffering see DISTRESS

sufficient, enough, adequate, competent mean being what is necessary or desirable. **Sufficient** suggests a close meeting of a need ⟨had supplies *sufficient* to last a month⟩. **Enough** is less exact in suggestion than *sufficient* ⟨do you have *enough* food?⟩. **Adequate** may imply barely meeting a requirement ⟨the room was *adequate,* no more⟩. **Competent** suggests measuring up to all requirements without question or being adequately adapted to an end ⟨a *competent* income for their life-style⟩.

suffuse see INFUSE

suggest, imply, hint, intimate, insinuate mean to convey an idea indirectly. **Suggest** may stress putting into the mind by association of ideas, awakening of a desire, or initiating a train of thought ⟨an actress who can *suggest* a whole character with one gesture⟩. **Imply** is close to *suggest* but may indicate a more definite or logical relation of the unexpressed idea to the expressed ⟨pronouncements that *imply* he has lost touch with reality⟩. **Hint** implies the use of slight or remote suggestion with a minimum of overt statement ⟨*hinted* that she might have a job lined up⟩. **Intimate** stresses delicacy of suggestion without connoting any lack of candor ⟨*intimated* that he was ready to pop the question⟩. **Insinuate** applies to the conveying of a usu. unpleasant idea in a sly underhanded manner ⟨*insinuated* that the neighbors were not what they appeared to be⟩.

suitable see FIT

sulky see SULLEN

sullen, glum, morose, surly, sulky, crabbed, saturnine, gloomy mean showing a forbidding or disagreeable mood. **Sullen** implies a silent ill humor and a refusal to be sociable ⟨remained *sullen* throughout the party⟩. **Glum** suggests a silent dispiritedness ⟨the whole team was *glum* following the defeat⟩. **Morose** adds to *glum* an element of bitterness or misanthropy ⟨became *morose* after the death of his wife⟩. **Surly** implies gruffness and sullenness of speech or manner ⟨a *surly* teenage boy⟩. **Sulky** suggests childish resentment expressed in peevish sullenness ⟨a period of *sulky* behavior followed every argument⟩. **Crabbed** applies to a forbidding morose harshness of manner ⟨his *crabbed* exterior was only a pose⟩. **Saturnine** describes a heavy forbidding aspect or suggests a bitter disposition ⟨a *saturnine* cynic always finding fault⟩. **Gloomy** implies a depression in mood making for seeming sullenness or glumness ⟨bad news that put everyone in a *gloomy* mood⟩.

summary see CONCISE

summative see CUMULATIVE

summit, peak, pinnacle, climax, apex, acme, culmination mean the highest point attained or attainable. **Summit** implies the topmost level attainable ⟨a singer at the *summit* of his career⟩. **Peak** suggests the highest among other high points ⟨an artist working at the *peak* of his powers⟩. **Pinnacle** suggests a dizzying and often insecure height ⟨the *pinnacle* of success in the entertainment world⟩. **Climax** implies the highest point in an ascending series ⟨the moon landing marked the *climax* of the program⟩. **Apex** implies the point where all ascending lines converge ⟨Dutch culture reached its *apex* in the 17th century⟩. **Acme** implies a level of quality representing the perfection of a thing ⟨a statue that was once deemed the *acme* of beauty⟩. **Culmination** suggests the outcome of a growth or development representing an attained objective ⟨the bill marked the *culmination* of the civil rights movement⟩.

summon, call, cite, convoke, convene, muster mean to demand the presence of. **Summon** implies the exercise of authority ⟨*summoned* by the court to appear as a witness⟩. **Call** may be used less formally for *summon* ⟨the President *called* Congress for a special session⟩. **Cite** implies a summoning to court usu. to answer a charge ⟨*cited* to answer the charge of drunken driving⟩. **Convoke** implies a summons to assemble for deliberative or legislative purposes ⟨*convoked* an assembly of the world's leading scientists⟩.

Convene is somewhat less formal than *convoke* ⟨*convened* the students in the school auditorium⟩. **Muster** suggests a calling up of a number of things that form a group in order that they may be exhibited, displayed, or utilized as a whole ⟨*muster* the troops for an inspection⟩.

sumptuous see LUXURIOUS

sunder see SEPARATE

superb see SPLENDID

supercilious see PROUD

supererogatory, gratuitous, uncalled-for, wanton mean done without need or compulsion or warrant. **Supererogatory** implies a giving above what is required by rule and may suggest adding something not needed or not wanted ⟨an abrupt man who regarded the usual pleasantries as *supererogatory*⟩. **Gratuitous** usu. applies to something offensive or unpleasant given or done without provocation ⟨my civil question received a *gratuitous* insult⟩. **Uncalled-for** implies impertinence or logical absurdity ⟨resented her *uncalled-for* advice⟩. **Wanton** implies not only a lack of provocation but a malicious or sportive motive ⟨the *wanton* destruction of property by vandals⟩.

superficial, shallow, cursory mean lacking in depth or solidity. **Superficial** implies a concern only with surface aspects ⟨a *superficial* examination of the wound⟩. **Shallow** is more generally derogatory in implying lack of depth in knowledge, reasoning, emotions, or character ⟨a *shallow* interpretation of the character Hamlet⟩. **Cursory** suggests a lack of thoroughness or a neglect of details ⟨even a *cursory* reading of the work will reveal that⟩.

supersede see REPLACE

supervene see FOLLOW

supine see INACTIVE, PRONE

supplant see REPLACE

supple see ELASTIC

supplicate see BEG

support, uphold, advocate, back, champion mean to favor
actively one that meets opposition. **Support** is least explicit
about the nature of the assistance given ⟨people who *support* the development of the area⟩. **Uphold** implies extended support given to something attacked ⟨*upheld* the
legitimacy of the military action⟩. **Advocate** stresses urging
or pleading ⟨*advocated* a return to basics in public school
education⟩. **Back** suggests supporting by lending assistance to one failing or falling ⟨allies refused to *back* the call
for sanctions⟩. **Champion** suggests publicly defending one
unjustly attacked or too weak to advocate his own cause
⟨*championed* the rights of pregnant women⟩.

suppress see CRUSH

sure, certain, positive, cocksure mean having no doubt or
uncertainty. **Sure** usu. stresses the subjective or intuitive
feeling of assurance ⟨felt *sure* that he had forgotten some-
thing⟩. **Certain** may apply to a basing of a conclusion or
conviction on definite grounds or indubitable evidence
⟨scientists are now *certain* what caused the explosion⟩.
Positive intensifies sureness or certainty and may imply
opinionated conviction or forceful expression of it ⟨she is
positive that he is the killer⟩. **Cocksure** implies presumptuous or careless positiveness ⟨you're always so *cocksure*
about everything⟩.

surfeit see SATIATE

surly see SULLEN

surmise see CONJECTURE

surpass see EXCEED

surprise, astonish, astound, amaze, flabbergast mean to impress forcibly through unexpectedness. **Surprise** stresses
causing an effect through being unexpected at a particular

time or place rather than by being essentially unusual or novel ⟨*surprised* to find his mother in a bar⟩. **Astonish** implies surprising so greatly as to seem incredible ⟨the young player *astonished* the chess masters⟩. **Astound** stresses the shock of astonishment ⟨news of the atomic bomb *astounded* everyone⟩. **Amaze** suggests an effect of bewilderment ⟨*amazed* by the immense size of the place⟩. **Flabbergast** may suggest thorough astonishment and bewilderment or dismay ⟨*flabbergasted* by his daughter's precocious comments⟩.

surrender see RELINQUISH

surreptitious see SECRET

survey see COMPENDIUM

susceptible see LIABLE

suspend see DEFER, EXCLUDE

suspicion see UNCERTAINTY

sway *vb* see AFFECT, SWING

sway *n* see POWER

sweep see RANGE

swell see EXPAND

swerve, veer, deviate, depart, digress, diverge mean to turn aside from a straight course. **Swerve** may suggest a physical, mental, or moral turning away from a given course, often with abruptness ⟨suddenly *swerved* to avoid hitting an animal⟩. **Veer** implies a major change in direction ⟨at that point the road *veers* to the right⟩. **Deviate** implies a turning from a customary or prescribed course ⟨the witness never *deviated* from her story⟩. **Depart** suggests a deviation from a traditional or conventional course or type ⟨a book that *departs* from the usual memoirs of a film star⟩. **Digress** applies to a departing from the subject of one's discourse ⟨frequently *digressed* during his lecture⟩. **Diverge** may equal *depart* but usu. suggests a branching of a main path into two or more leading in different directions ⟨after medical school their paths *diverged*⟩.

swift see FAST

swindle see CHEAT

swing *vb* Swing, wave, flourish, brandish, thrash mean to wield or cause to move to and fro or up and down. **Swing** implies regular or uniform movement ⟨*swing* the rope back and forth⟩. **Wave** usu. implies smooth or continuous motion ⟨a flag *waving* in the breeze⟩. **Flourish** suggests vigorous, ostentatious, or graceful movement ⟨*flourishing* her racket, she challenged me to a match⟩. **Brandish** implies threatening or menacing motion ⟨*brandishing* his fist, he vowed vengeance⟩. **Thrash** suggests vigorous, abrupt, violent movement ⟨a child *thrashing* his arms about in a tantrum⟩.

swing *vb* Swing, sway, oscillate, vibrate, fluctuate, waver, undulate mean to move from one direction to its opposite. **Swing** implies a movement of something attached at one end or one side ⟨the door suddenly *swung* open⟩. **Sway** implies a slow swinging or teetering movement ⟨the drunk *swayed* a little and then fell⟩. **Oscillate** stresses a usu. rapid alternation of direction ⟨a fan that *oscillates* will cool more effectively⟩. **Vibrate** suggests the rapid oscillation of an elastic body under stress or impact ⟨the *vibrating* strings of a piano⟩. **Fluctuate** suggests constant irregular changes of level, intensity, or value ⟨monetary exchange rates *fluctuate* constantly⟩. **Waver** stresses irregular motion suggestive of reeling or tottering ⟨his whole body *wavered* as he crossed the finish line⟩. **Undulate** suggests a gentle wavelike motion ⟨an *undulating* sea of grass⟩.

sycophant see PARASITE

syllabus see COMPENDIUM

sympathetic see CONSONANT

sympathy see ATTRACTION, PITY
symptom see SIGN
synchronous see CONTEMPORARY
synopsis see ABRIDGMENT
synthetic see ARTIFICIAL
system see METHOD
systematize see ORDER

T

taciturn see SILENT
tact, address, poise, savoir faire mean skill and grace in dealing with others. **Tact** implies delicate and considerate perception of what is appropriate ⟨use *tact* when inquiring
about the divorce⟩. **Address** stresses dexterity and grace in
dealing with new and trying situations and may imply success in attaining one's ends ⟨brought off her first dinner
party with remarkable *address*⟩. **Poise** may imply both tact
and address but stresses self-possession and ease in meeting difficult situations ⟨the *poise* of one who has been of-
ficiating all his life⟩. **Savoir faire** is likely to stress worldly
experience and a sure awareness of what is proper or expedient ⟨has little of the *savoir faire* expected of a Wash-
ington hostess⟩.
taint see CONTAMINATE
take, seize, grasp, clutch, snatch, grab mean to get hold of
by or as if by catching up with the hand. **Take** is a general
term applicable to any manner of getting something into
one's possession or control ⟨*take* some salad from the
bowl⟩ ⟨*took* control of the company⟩. **Seize** implies a sudden and forcible movement in getting hold of something
tangible or an apprehending of something fleeting or elu-

sive when intangible ⟨*seized* the crook as he tried to escape⟩. **Grasp** stresses a laying hold so as to have firmly in possession ⟨firmly *grasp* the handle and pull⟩. **Clutch** suggests avidity or anxiety in seizing or grasping and may imply less success in holding ⟨frantically *clutching* the bush at the edge of the cliff⟩. **Snatch** suggests more suddenness or quickness but less force than *seize* ⟨*snatched* a doughnut before running out the door⟩. **Grab** implies more roughness or rudeness than ⟨roughly *grabbed* her by the arm⟩.

talent see GIFT

talkative, loquacious, garrulous, voluble mean given to talk or talking. **Talkative** may imply a readiness to engage in talk or a disposition to enjoy conversation ⟨not the *talkative* type who would enjoy a party⟩. **Loquacious** suggests the power of expressing oneself articulately, fluently, or glibly ⟨the corporation needs a spokesperson who is *loquacious* and telegenic⟩. **Garrulous** implies prosy, rambling, or tedious loquacity ⟨forced to endure a *garrulous* companion the whole trip⟩. **Voluble** suggests a free, easy, and unending loquacity ⟨the Italians are a *voluble* people⟩.

tall see HIGH

tangible see PERCEPTIBLE

task, duty, job, chore, stint, assignment mean a piece of work to be done. **Task** implies work imposed by a person in authority or an employer or by circumstance ⟨performed a variety of *tasks* for the company⟩. **Duty** implies an obligation to perform or responsibility for performance ⟨the *duties* of a lifeguard⟩. **Job** applies to a piece of work voluntarily performed; it may sometimes suggest difficulty or importance ⟨took on the *job* of turning the company around⟩. **Chore** implies a minor routine activity necessary for maintaining a household or farm ⟨every child had a list of *chores* to do⟩. **Stint** implies a carefully allotted or measured quantity of assigned work or service ⟨during his *stint* as governor⟩. **Assignment** implies a definite limited task assigned by one in authority ⟨your *assignment* did not include interfering with others⟩.

tasty see PALATABLE

taunt see RIDICULE

tawdry see GAUDY

teach, instruct, educate, train, discipline, school mean to cause to acquire knowledge or skill. **Teach** applies to any manner of imparting information or skill so that others may learn ⟨*teach* French⟩ ⟨*taught* them how to ski⟩. **Instruct** suggests methodical or formal teaching ⟨*instruct* the recruits in calisthenics at boot camp⟩. **Educate** implies attempting to bring out latent capabilities ⟨*educate* students so that they are prepared for the future⟩. **Train** stresses instruction and drill with a specific end in view ⟨*trained* foreign pilots to operate the new aircraft⟩. **Discipline** implies subordinating to a master for the sake of controlling ⟨*disciplined* herself to exercise daily⟩. **School** implies training or disciplining esp. in what is hard to master or to bear ⟨*schooled* myself not to flinch at the sight of blood⟩.

tear, rip, rend, split, cleave, rive mean to separate forcibly. **Tear** implies a pulling apart by force and leaving jagged edges ⟨*tear* up lettuce for a salad⟩. **Rip** implies a pulling apart in one rapid uninterrupted motion often along a seam or joint ⟨*ripped* the jacket along the side seams⟩. **Rend** implies very violent or ruthless severing or sundering ⟨an angry mob *rent* his clothes⟩. **Split** implies a cutting or breaking apart in a continuous, straight, and usu. lengthwise direction or in the direction of grain or layers ⟨*split* logs for firewood⟩. **Cleave** implies very forceful splitting or cutting with a blow ⟨a bolt of lightning *cleaved* the giant oak⟩. **Rive** suggests action rougher and more violent than *split* or *cleave* ⟨a friendship *riven* by jealousy⟩.

tease see WORRY

tell see REVEAL

telling see VALID

temerity, audacity, hardihood, effrontery, nerve, cheek, gall, chutzpah mean conspicuous or flagrant boldness. **Temerity** suggests boldness arising from rashness and contempt of danger ⟨had the *temerity* to ask for a favor after that insult⟩. **Audacity** implies a disregard of restraints commonly imposed by convention or prudence ⟨an entrepreneur with *audacity* and vision⟩. **Hardihood** suggests firmness in daring and defiance ⟨no serious scientist has the *hardihood* to claim that⟩. **Effrontery** implies shameless, insolent disregard of propriety or courtesy ⟨had the *effrontery* to tell me how to do my job⟩. **Nerve, cheek, gall,** and **chutzpah** are informal equivalents for *effrontery* ⟨the *nerve* of that guy⟩ ⟨has the *cheek* to bill herself as a singer⟩ ⟨had the *gall* to demand some evidence⟩ ⟨her *chutzpah* got her into the exclusive party⟩.

temper see DISPOSITION

temperament see DISPOSITION

tempt see LURE

tenacious see STRONG

tenacity see COURAGE

tendency, trend, drift, tenor, current mean movement in a particular direction. **Tendency** implies an inclination sometimes amounting to an impelling force ⟨the *tendency* to expand the limits of what is art⟩. **Trend** applies to the general direction maintained by a winding or irregular course ⟨the long-term *trend* of the stock market is upward⟩. **Drift** may apply to a tendency determined by external forces ⟨the *drift* of the population away from large cities⟩ or it may apply to an underlying or obscure trend of meaning or discourse ⟨a racist *drift* runs through all of his works⟩. **Tenor** stresses a clearly perceptible direction and a continuous, undeviating course ⟨a suburb seeking to maintain its *tenor* of tranquility⟩. **Current** implies a clearly defined but not necessarily unalterable course ⟨an encounter that altered forever the *current* of my life⟩.

tenor see TENDENCY

tenuous see THIN

tergiversation see AMBIGUITY

terminal see LAST

terminate see CLOSE

termination see END

terminus see END

terror see FEAR

terse see CONCISE

testy see IRASCIBLE

theatrical see DRAMATIC

theory see HYPOTHESIS

thick see CLOSE

thin, slender, slim, slight, tenuous mean not thick, broad, abundant, or dense. **Thin** implies comparatively little extension between surfaces or in diameter, or it may imply lack of substance, richness, or abundance ⟨*thin* wire⟩ ⟨soup that was *thin* and tasteless⟩. **Slender** implies leanness or spareness often with grace and good proportion ⟨the *slender* legs of a Sheraton chair⟩. **Slim** applies to slenderness that suggests fragility or scantiness ⟨a *slim* volume of poetry⟩ ⟨a *slim* chance of success⟩. **Slight** implies smallness as well as thinness ⟨the *slight* build of a professional jockey⟩. **Tenuous** implies extreme thinness, sheerness, or lack of substance and firmness ⟨the sword hung by a *tenuous* thread⟩.

think *vb* **Think, conceive, imagine, fancy, realize, envisage, envision** mean to form an idea of. **Think** implies the entrance of an idea into one's mind with or without deliberate consideration or reflection ⟨I just *thought* of a good story⟩. **Conceive** suggests the forming and bringing forth and usu. developing of an idea, plan, or design ⟨*conceive* of a plan to rescue the hostages⟩. **Imagine** stresses a visualization ⟨*imagine* a permanently operating space station⟩. **Fancy** suggests an imagining often unrestrained by reality but spurred by desires ⟨*fancied* himself a super athlete⟩. **Realize** stresses a grasping of the significance of what is conceived or imagined ⟨*realized* the enormity of the task ahead⟩. **Envisage** and **envision** imply a conceiving or imagining that is esp. clear or detailed ⟨*envisaged* a totally computerized operation⟩ ⟨*envisioned* a world free from hunger and want⟩.

think *vb* **Think, cogitate, reflect, reason, speculate, deliberate** mean to use one's powers of conception, judgment, or inference. **Think** is general and may apply to any mental activity, but used alone often suggests attainment of clear ideas or conclusions ⟨a course that really teaches you to *think*⟩. **Cogitate** implies deep or intent thinking ⟨quietly sitting and *cogitating* on the mysteries of nature⟩. **Reflect** suggests unhurried consideration of something recalled to the mind ⟨*reflected* on fifty years of married life⟩. **Reason** stresses consecutive logical thinking ⟨*reasoned* that the murderer and victim knew each other⟩. **Speculate** implies reasoning about things theoretical or problematic ⟨historians have *speculated* about the fate of the Lost Colony⟩. **Deliberate** suggests slow or careful reasoning before forming an opinion or reaching a conclusion or decision ⟨the jury *deliberated* for five hours⟩.

thirst see LONG

thought see IDEA
thrash see SWING
threadbare see TRITE
thrifty see SPARING
throng see CROWD
throw, cast, toss, fling, hurl, pitch, sling, mean to cause to
  move swiftly through space by a propulsive movement or
  a propelling force. **Throw** is general and interchangeable
  with the other terms but may specif. imply a distinctive
  motion with bent arm ⟨*throws* the ball with great accu-
  racy⟩. **Cast** usu. implies lightness in the thing thrown and
  sometimes a scattering ⟨*cast* bread crumbs to the birds⟩.
  Toss suggests a light or careless or aimless throwing and
  may imply an upward motion ⟨*tossed* her racket on the
  bed⟩. **Fling** stresses a violent throwing ⟨*flung* the ring back
  in his face⟩. **Hurl** implies power as in throwing a massive
  weight ⟨*hurled* the intruder out the window⟩. **Pitch** suggests throwing carefully at a target ⟨*pitch* horseshoes⟩.
  Sling suggests propelling with a sweeping or swinging motion, usu. with force and suddenness ⟨*slung* the bag over
  his shoulder⟩.
thrust see PUSH
thwart see FRUSTRATE
tiff see QUARREL
tight see DRUNK
tiny see SMALL
tipsy see DRUNK
tire, weary, fatigue, exhaust, jade, fag mean to make or become unable or unwilling to continue. **Tire** implies a
  draining of one's strength or patience ⟨the long ride *tired*
  us out⟩. **Weary** stresses tiring until one is unable to endure
  more of the same thing ⟨*wearied* of the constant arguing⟩.
  Fatigue suggests causing great lassitude through excessive

strain or undue effort ⟨*fatigued* by the long, hard climb⟩.
Exhaust implies complete draining of strength by hard exertion ⟨shoveling snow *exhausted* him⟩. **Jade** suggests the
loss of all freshness and eagerness ⟨*jaded* with the endless
round of society parties⟩. **Fag** implies a drooping with fatigue ⟨arrived home, all *fagged* out by a day's shopping⟩.

tireless see INDEFATIGABLE

toady *vb* see FAWN

toady *n* see PARASITE

toil see WORK

token see SIGN

tolerant see FORBEARING

tolerate see BEAR

tool see IMPLEMENT

toothsome see PALATABLE

torment see AFFLICT

torpor see LETHARGY

torture see AFFLICT

toss see THROW

total see WHOLE

touch see AFFECT

touching see MOVING

touchstone see STANDARD

touchy see IRASCIBLE

tough see STRONG

toy see TRIFLE

trace, vestige, track mean a perceptible sign made by something that has passed. **Trace** may suggest any line, mark,
or discernible effect ⟨an animal species believed to have
vanished without a *trace*⟩. **Vestige** applies to a tangible reminder such as a fragment or remnant of what is past and
gone ⟨boulders that are *vestiges* of the last ice age⟩. **Track**

implies a continuous line that can be followed ⟨the fossilized tracks of dinosaurs⟩.

track see TRACE

tractable see OBEDIENT

trade see BUSINESS

traduce see MALIGN

traffic see BUSINESS

trail see CHASE

train see TEACH

traipse see WANDER

traitorous see FAITHLESS

trammel see HAMPER

tranquil see CALM

transcend see EXCEED

transfigure see TRANSFORM

transform, metamorphose, transmute, convert, transmogrify, transfigure mean to change a thing into a different thing. **Transform** implies a major change in form, nature, or function ⟨*transformed* a small company into a corporate giant⟩. **Metamorphose** suggests an abrupt or startling change induced by or as if by magic or a supernatural power ⟨*metamorphosed* awkward girls into graceful ballerinas⟩. **Transmute** implies transforming into a higher element or thing ⟨*transmuted* a shopworn tale into a psychological masterpiece⟩. **Convert** implies a change fitting something for a new or different use or function ⟨*converted* the boys' room into a guest bedroom⟩. **Transmogrify** suggests a grotesque or preposterous metamorphosis ⟨the prince was *transmogrified* into a frog⟩. **Transfigure** implies a change that exalts or glorifies ⟨ecstasy *transfigured* her face⟩.

transient, transitory, ephemeral, momentary, fugitive, fleeting, evanescent mean lasting or staying only a short time.

Transient applies to what is actually short in its duration or stay ⟨a hotel catering primarily to *transient* guests⟩. **Transitory** applies to what is by its nature or essence bound to change, pass, or come to an end ⟨fame in the movies is *transitory*⟩. **Ephemeral** implies striking brevity of life or duration ⟨many slang words are *ephemeral*⟩. **Momentary** suggests coming and going quickly and therefore being merely a brief interruption of a more enduring state ⟨my feelings of guilt were only *momentary*⟩. **Fugitive** and **fleeting** imply passing so quickly as to make apprehending difficult ⟨in winter the days are short and sunshine is *fugitive*⟩ ⟨a life with only *fleeting* moments of joy⟩. **Evanescent** suggests a quick vanishing and an airy or fragile quality ⟨the story has an *evanescent* touch of whimsy that is lost on stage⟩.

transitory see TRANSIENT

translucent see CLEAR

transmogrify see TRANSFORM

transmute see TRANSFORM

transparent see CLEAR

transport *vb* see BANISH, CARRY

transport *n* see ECSTASY

transpose see REVERSE

trap see CATCH

travail see WORK

travesty see CARICATURE

treacherous see FAITHLESS

treasure see APPRECIATE

tremendous see MONSTROUS

trenchant see INCISIVE

trend see TENDENCY

trepidation see FEAR

trespass *vb* Trespass, encroach, entrench, infringe, invade mean to make inroads upon the property, territory, or rights of another. **Trespass** implies an unwarranted, unlawful, or offensive intrusion ⟨warned people about *trespassing* on their land⟩. **Encroach** suggests gradual or stealthy entrance upon another's territory or usurpation of his rights or possessions ⟨on guard against laws that *encroach* upon our civil rights⟩. **Entrench** suggests establishing and maintaining oneself in a position of advantage or profit at the expense of others ⟨opposed to regulations that *entrench* upon free enterprise⟩. **Infringe** implies an encroachment clearly violating a right or prerogative ⟨a product that *infringes* upon another's patent⟩. **Invade** implies a hostile and injurious entry into the territory or sphere of another ⟨practices that *invade* our right to privacy⟩.

trespass *n* see BREACH

tribute see ENCOMIUM

trick *n* Trick, ruse, stratagem, maneuver, artifice, wile, feint mean an indirect means to gain an end. **Trick** may imply deception, roguishness, illusion, and either an evil or harmless end ⟨used every *trick* in the book to nail a husband⟩. **Ruse** stresses an attempt to mislead by a false impression ⟨secured a papal audience through a clever *ruse*⟩. **Stratagem** implies a ruse used to entrap, outwit, circumvent, or surprise an opponent or enemy ⟨a series of *stratagems* that convinced both sides he was their agent⟩. **Maneuver** suggests adroit and skillful avoidance of difficulty ⟨a bold *maneuver* that won him the nomination⟩. **Artifice** implies ingenious contrivance or invention ⟨his fawning smile was just an *artifice*⟩. **Wile** suggests an attempt to entrap or deceive with false allurements ⟨used all of his *wiles* to win his uncle's favor⟩. **Feint** implies a diversion or distraction of attention away from one's real intent ⟨ballcarriers use *feints* to draw defensemen out of position⟩.

trick *vb* see DUPE

trickery see DECEPTION

tricky see SLY

trifle, toy, dally, flirt, coquet mean to deal with or act toward without serious purpose. **Trifle** may imply playfulness, unconcern, indulgent contempt ⟨*trifled* with her boyfriend's feelings⟩. **Toy** implies acting without full attention or serious exertion of one's powers ⟨*toying* with the idea of taking a cruise⟩. **Dally** suggests indulging in thoughts or plans merely as an amusement ⟨likes to *dally* with the idea of writing a book someday⟩. **Flirt** implies an interest or attention that soon passes to another object ⟨*flirted* with one college major after another⟩. **Coquet** implies attracting interest or admiration without serious intention ⟨brazenly *coquetted* with the husbands of her friends⟩.

trite, hackneyed, stereotyped, threadbare mean lacking the freshness that evokes attention or interest. **Trite** applies to a once effective phrase or idea spoiled from long familiarity ⟨"you win some, you lose some" is a *trite* expression⟩. **Hackneyed** stresses being worn out by overuse so as to become dull and meaningless ⟨all of the metaphors and images in the poem are *hackneyed*⟩. **Stereotyped** implies falling invariably into the same pattern or form ⟨views of American Indians that are *stereotyped* and out-of-date⟩. **Threadbare** applies to what has been used until its possibilities of interest have been totally exhausted ⟨a mystery novel with a *threadbare* plot⟩.

trouble see EFFORT

truckle see FAWN

truth, veracity, verity, verisimilitude mean the quality of keeping close to fact or reality. **Truth** may apply to an ideal abstraction conforming to a universal or generalized reality or it may represent a quality of statements, acts, or feelings of adhering to reality and avoiding error or falsehood ⟨swore to the *truth* of the statement he had made⟩. **Veracity** implies rigid and unfailing observance of truth ⟨a politician not known for his *veracity*⟩. **Verity** refers to things of lasting, ultimate, or transcendent value ⟨a teacher still believing in the old *verities* of school pride and loyalty⟩. **Verisimilitude** implies the quality of an artistic or literary representation that causes one to accept it as true to life or to human experience ⟨a novel about contemporary marriage that was praised for its *verisimilitude*⟩.

try see AFFLICT, ATTEMPT

tug see PULL

tumult see COMMOTION

turmoil see COMMOTION

turn see CURVE

twist see CURVE

twit see RIDICULE

type, kind, sort, nature, description, character mean a number of individuals thought of as a group because of a common quality or qualities. **Type** may suggest strong and clearly marked similarity throughout the items included so that each is typical of the group ⟨one of three basic body *types*⟩. **Kind** may suggest natural grouping ⟨a zoo with animals of every *kind*⟩. **Sort** often suggests some disparagement ⟨the *sort* of newspaper dealing in sensational stories⟩. **Nature** may imply inherent, essential resemblance rather than obvious or superficial likenesses ⟨two problems of a similar *nature*⟩. **Description** implies a group marked by agreement in all details belonging to a type as described or defined ⟨not all individuals of that *description* are truly psychotic⟩. **Character** implies a group marked by distinctive likenesses peculiar to the type ⟨a society with little of the *character* of an advanced culture⟩.

typical see REGULAR

tyrannical see ABSOLUTE

tyro see AMATEUR

U

ubiquitous see OMNIPRESENT

ultimate see LAST

umbrage see OFFENSE

unbecoming see INDECOROUS

unbiased see FAIR

uncalled-for see SUPEREROGATORY

uncanny see WEIRD

uncertainty, doubt, dubiety, skepticism, suspicion, mistrust mean lack of sureness about someone or something. **Uncertainty** may range from a falling short of certainty to an almost complete lack of definite knowledge esp. about an outcome or result ⟨general *uncertainty* about the program's future⟩. **Doubt** suggests both uncertainty and inability to make a decision ⟨plagued by *doubts* about his upcoming marriage⟩. **Dubiety** stresses a wavering between conclusions ⟨in times of crisis a leader must be free of all *dubiety*⟩. **Skepticism** implies unwillingness to believe without conclusive evidence ⟨an economic forecast that was met with *skepticism*⟩. **Suspicion** stresses lack of faith in the truth, reality, fairness, or reliability of something or someone ⟨viewed the new neighbors with *suspicion*⟩. **Mistrust** implies a genuine doubt based upon suspicion ⟨had a great *mistrust* of all doctors⟩.

uncommon see INFREQUENT

unconcerned see INDIFFERENT

unctuous see FULSOME

underhanded see SECRET

undermine see WEAKEN

understand, comprehend, appreciate mean to have a clear or complete idea of. **Understand** may differ from **comprehend** in implying a result whereas *comprehend* stresses the mental process of arriving at a result ⟨*understood* the instructions without *comprehending* their purpose⟩. **Appreciate** implies a just estimation of a thing's value ⟨failed to *appreciate* the risks involved⟩.

undulate see SWING

unearth see DISCOVER

unerring see INFALLIBLE

uneven see ROUGH

unfeigned see SINCERE

unflagging see INDEFATIGABLE

ungovernable see UNRULY

union see UNITY

unique see SINGLE, STRANGE

unite see JOIN

unity, solidarity, integrity, union mean the quality of a whole made up of closely associated parts. **Unity** implies oneness esp. of what is varied and diverse in its elements or parts ⟨a multiplicity of styles effectively combined into a *unity* of architectural design⟩. **Solidarity** implies a unity in a group or class that enables it to manifest its strength and exert its influence as one ⟨an ethnic minority with a strong sense of *solidarity*⟩. **Integrity** implies unity that indicates interdependence of the parts and completeness and perfection of the whole ⟨a farcical scene that destroys the play's *integrity*⟩. **Union** implies a thorough integration and harmonious cooperation of the parts ⟨the *union* of 13 diverse colonies into one nation⟩.

universal, general, generic mean of or relating to all or the whole. **Universal** implies reference to every one without exception in the class, category, or genus considered; **general** implies reference to all or nearly all ⟨the theory has met *general* but not *universal* acceptance⟩. **Generic** implies reference to every member of a genus ⟨*generic* likenesses among all dogs⟩.

unlearned see IGNORANT

unlettered see IGNORANT

unman see UNNERVE

unmindful see FORGETFUL

unnatural see IRREGULAR

unnerve, enervate, unman, emasculate mean to deprive of strength or vigor and the capacity for effective action. **Unnerve** implies marked often temporary loss of courage, self-control, or power to act ⟨*unnerved* by the near midair collision⟩. **Enervate** suggests a gradual physical or moral weakening (as through luxury or indolence) until one is too feeble to make an effort ⟨totally *enervated* after a week's vacation⟩. **Unman** implies a loss of manly vigor, fortitude, or spirit ⟨the sight of blood usually *unmanned* him⟩. **Emasculate** stresses a depriving of characteristic force by removing something essential ⟨an amendment that *emasculates* existing gun-control laws⟩.

unpremeditated see EXTEMPORANEOUS

unruffled see COOL

unruly, ungovernable, intractable, refractory, recalcitrant, willful, headstrong mean not submissive to government or control. **Unruly** implies lack of discipline or incapacity for discipline and often connotes waywardness or turbulence of behavior ⟨*unruly* children⟩. **Ungovernable** implies either an escape from control or guidance or a state of being unsubdued and incapable of controlling oneself or being controlled by others ⟨*ungovernable* rage⟩. **Intractable** suggests stubborn resistance to guidance or control ⟨the farmers were *intractable* in their opposition to the hazardous-waste dump⟩. **Refractory** stresses resistance to attempts to manage or to mold ⟨special schools for *refractory* children⟩. **Recalcitrant** suggests determined resistance to or defiance of authority ⟨acts of sabotage by a *recalcitrant* populace⟩. **Willful** implies an obstinate determination to have one's own way ⟨a *willful* disregard for the rights of others⟩. **Headstrong** suggests self-will impatient of restraint, advice, or suggestion ⟨a *headstrong* young cavalry officer⟩.

unseemly see INDECOROUS
unsophisticated see NATURAL
unstable see INCONSTANT
untangle see EXTRICATE
untiring see INDEFATIGABLE
untruthful see DISHONEST
untutored see IGNORANT
unwearied see INDEFATIGABLE
upbraid see SCOLD
upheaval see COMMOTION
uphold see SUPPORT
upright, honest, just, conscientious, scrupulous, honorable mean having or showing a strict regard for what is morally right. **Upright** implies a strict adherence to moral principles ⟨ministers of the church must be *upright* and unimpeachable⟩. **Honest** stresses adherence to such virtues as truthfulness, candor, fairness ⟨doctors must be *honest* with the terminally ill⟩. **Just** stresses conscious choice and regular practice of what is right or equitable ⟨a reputation for

being entirely *just* in business dealings⟩. **Conscientious** and **scrupulous** imply an active moral sense governing all one's actions and painstaking efforts to follow one's conscience ⟨*conscientious* in doing all of her chores⟩ ⟨*scrupulous* in carrying out the terms of the will⟩. **Honorable** suggests a firm holding to codes of right behavior and the guidance of a high sense of honor and duty ⟨the *honorable* thing would be to resign my position⟩.

uprising see REBELLION

uproot see EXTERMINATE

upset see DISCOMPOSE

urbane see SUAVE

usage see HABIT

use, employ, utilize mean to put into service esp. to attain an end. **Use** implies availing oneself of something as a means or instrument to an end ⟨willing to *use* any means to achieve her ends⟩. **Employ** suggests the use of a person or thing that is available but idle, inactive, or disengaged ⟨your time might have been better *employed* by reading⟩. **Utilize** may suggest the discovery of a new, profitable, or practical use for something ⟨meat processors *utilize* every part of the animal⟩.

usual, customary, habitual, wonted, accustomed mean familiar through frequent or regular repetition. **Usual** stresses the absence of strangeness or unexpectedness ⟨my *usual* order for lunch⟩. **Customary** applies to what accords with the practices, conventions, or usages of an individual or community ⟨a *customary* waiting period before remarrying⟩. **habitual** suggests a practice settled or established by much repetition ⟨an *habitual* exercise regime that served her well⟩. **Wonted** stresses habituation but usu. applies to what is favored, sought, or purposefully cultivated ⟨his *wonted* pleasures had lost their appeal⟩. **Accustomed**

is less emphatic than *wonted* or *habitual* in suggesting fixed habit or invariable custom ⟨accepted the compliment with her *accustomed* modesty⟩.

usurp see APPROPRIATE
utensil see IMPLEMENT
utilize see USE
utter see EXPRESS

V

vacant see EMPTY
vacillate see HESITATE
vacuous see EMPTY
vagary see CAPRICE
vague see OBSCURE
vain, nugatory, otiose, idle, empty, hollow mean being without worth or significance. **Vain** implies either absolute or relative absence of value ⟨it is *vain* to think that we can alter destiny⟩. **Nugatory** suggests triviality or insignificance ⟨a monarch with *nugatory* powers⟩. **Otiose** suggests that something serves no purpose and is either an encumbrance or a superfluity ⟨not a single scene in the film is *otiose*⟩. **Idle** suggests being incapable of worthwhile use or effect ⟨it is *idle* to speculate on what might have been⟩. **Empty** and **hollow** suggest a deceiving lack of real substance or soundness or genuineness ⟨an *empty* attempt at reconciliation⟩ ⟨a *hollow* victory that benefited no one⟩. See in addition FUTILE.
valid, sound, cogent, convincing, telling mean having such force as to compel serious attention and usu. acceptance. **Valid** implies being supported by objective truth or generally accepted authority ⟨absences will be excused for

valid reasons). **Sound** implies a basis of flawless reasoning or of solid grounds ⟨a *sound* proposal for combatting terrorism⟩. **Cogent** may stress either weight of sound argument and evidence or lucidity of presentation ⟨the prosecutor's *cogent* summation won over the jury⟩. **Convincing** suggests a power to overcome doubt, opposition, or reluctance to accept ⟨a documentary that makes a *convincing* case for court reform⟩. **Telling** stresses an immediate and crucial effect striking at the heart of a matter ⟨a *telling* example of the bureaucratic mentality⟩.

validate see CONFIRM
valor see HEROISM
valuable see COSTLY
value see APPRECIATE, ESTIMATE
vanquish see CONQUER
vapid see INSIPID
variance see DISCORD
various see DIFFERENT
vary see CHANGE
vast see ENORMOUS
vaunt see BOAST
veer see SWERVE
venerable see OLD
venerate see REVERE
vent see EXPRESS
venturesome see ADVENTUROUS
veracity see TRUTH
verbose see WORDY
verge see BORDER
verify see CONFIRM
verisimilitude see TRUTH
veritable see AUTHENTIC
verity see TRUTH

vernacular see DIALECT

vertical, perpendicular, plumb mean being at right angles to a base line. **Vertical** suggests a line or direction rising straight upward toward a zenith ⟨the side of the cliff is almost *vertical*⟩. **Perpendicular** may stress the straightness of a line making a right angle with any other line, not necessarily a horizontal one ⟨the parallel bars are *perpendicular* to the support posts⟩. **Plumb** stresses an exact verticality determined (as with a plumb line) by earth's gravity ⟨make sure that the wall is *plumb*⟩.

very see SAME

vestige see TRACE

vex see ANNOY

vibrate see SWING

vice see FAULT, OFFENSE

vicious, villainous, iniquitous, nefarious, corrupt, degenerate mean highly reprehensible or offensive in character, nature, or conduct. **Vicious** may directly oppose *virtuous* in implying moral depravity, or may connote malignancy, cruelty, or destructive violence ⟨a *vicious* gangster wanted for murder⟩. **Villainous** applies to any evil, depraved, or vile conduct or characteristic ⟨*villainous* behavior that must be punished⟩. **Iniquitous** implies absence of all signs of justice or fairness ⟨an *iniquitous* tyrant, ruling by fear and intimidation⟩. **Nefarious** suggests flagrant breaching of time-honored laws and traditions of conduct ⟨pornography, prostitution, and organized crime's other *nefarious* activities⟩. **Corrupt** stresses a loss of moral integrity or probity causing betrayal of principle or sworn obligations ⟨city hall was filled with *corrupt* politicians⟩. **Degenerate** suggests having sunk to an esp. vicious or enervated condition ⟨a *degenerate* regime propped up by foreign support⟩.

view see OPINION
vigilant see WATCHFUL
vigorous, energetic, strenuous, lusty, nervous mean having
  great vitality and force. **Vigorous** further implies showing
  no signs of depletion or diminishing of freshness or robustness ⟨still *vigorous* and sharp in her seventieth year⟩.
  Energetic suggests a capacity for intense activity ⟨an *energetic* wife, mother, and career woman⟩. **Strenuous** suggests a preference for coping with the arduous or the challenging ⟨moved to Alaska in search of the *strenuous* life⟩.
  Lusty implies exuberant energy and capacity for enjoyment ⟨a huge meal to satisfy the men's *lusty* appetites⟩.
  Nervous suggests esp. the forcibleness and sustained effectiveness resulting from mental vigor ⟨a *nervous* energy in-
  forms his sculptures⟩.
vile see BASE
vilify see MALIGN
villainous see VICIOUS
vindicate see EXCULPATE, MAINTAIN
violation see BREACH
virtuous see MORAL
visage see FACE
visionary see IMAGINARY
vital see ESSENTIAL, LIVING
vitiate see DEBASE
vituperate see SCOLD
vituperation see ABUSE
vivacious see LIVELY
vivid see GRAPHIC
vivify see QUICKEN
**vociferous, clamorous, blatant, strident, boisterous, obstrep-
  erous** mean so loud or insistent as to compel attention. **Vociferous** implies a vehement deafening shouting or calling

out ⟨*vociferous* cries of protest and outrage⟩. **Clamorous** may imply insistency as well as vociferousness in demanding or protesting ⟨*clamorous* demands for prison reforms⟩. **Blatant** implies an offensive bellowing or insensitive loudness ⟨a *blatant* and abusive drunkard⟩. **Strident** suggests harsh and discordant noise ⟨heard the *strident* cry of the crow⟩. **Boisterous** suggests a noisiness and turbulence due to high spirits ⟨a *boisterous* crowd of partygoers⟩. **Obstreperous** suggests unruly and aggressive noisiness and resistance to restraint ⟨the *obstreperous* demonstrators were removed from the hall⟩.

vogue see FASHION

voice see EXPRESS

void see EMPTY

volatility see LIGHTNESS

voluble see TALKATIVE

volume see BULK

voluntary, intentional, deliberate, willing mean done or brought about of one's own will. **Voluntary** implies freedom and spontaneity of choice or action without external compulsion ⟨*voluntary* enlistment in the armed services⟩. **Intentional** stresses an awareness of an end to be achieved ⟨the *intentional* concealment of vital information⟩. **Deliberate** implies full consciousness of the nature of one's act and its consequences ⟨the *deliberate* sabotaging of a nuclear power plant⟩. **Willing** implies a readiness and eagerness to accede to or anticipate the wishes of another ⟨a *willing* accomplice in a bank robbery⟩.

voluptuous see SENSUOUS

voracious, gluttonous, ravenous, rapacious mean excessively greedy. **Voracious** applies esp. to habitual gorging with food or drink ⟨teenagers are often *voracious* eaters⟩. **Gluttonous** applies to one who delights in eating or acquiring things esp. beyond the point of necessity or satiety ⟨an admiral who was *gluttonous* for glory⟩. **Ravenous** implies excessive hunger and suggests violent or grasping methods of dealing with food or with whatever satisfies an appetite ⟨football practice usu. gives them *ravenous* appetites⟩. **Rapacious** often suggests excessive and utterly selfish acquisitiveness or avarice ⟨*rapacious* land developers indifferent to the ruination of the environment⟩.

vouch see CERTIFY

vouchsafe see GRANT

vulgar see COARSE, COMMON

W

waive see RELINQUISH

wander, roam, ramble, rove, traipse, meander mean to move about more or less aimlessly. **Wander** implies an absence of or an indifference to a fixed course ⟨found her *wandering* about the square⟩. **Roam** suggests wandering about freely and often far afield ⟨liked to *roam* through the woods⟩. **Ramble** stresses carelessness and indifference to one's course or objective ⟨the speaker *rambled* on without ever coming to the point⟩. **Rove** suggests vigorous and sometimes purposeful roaming ⟨armed brigands *roved* over the countryside⟩. **Traipse** implies an erratic if purposeful course ⟨*traipsed* all over town looking for the right dress⟩. **Meander** implies a winding or intricate course suggestive of aimless or listless wandering ⟨the river *meanders* for miles through rich farmland⟩.

wane see ABATE

want *vb* see DESIRE

want *n* see POVERTY

wanton see SUPEREROGATORY

ward off see PREVENT

warp see DEFORM

wary see CAUTIOUS

waste see RAVAGE

watchful, vigilant, wide-awake, alert mean being on the lookout esp. for danger or opportunity. **Watchful** is the least explicit term ⟨played under the *watchful* eyes of their mothers⟩. **Vigilant** suggests intense, unremitting, wary watchfulness ⟨*vigilant* taxpayers forestalled all attempts to raise taxes⟩. **Wide-awake** applies to watchfulness for opportunities and developments more often than dangers ⟨*wide-awake* observers will recall other summit meetings⟩. **Alert** stresses readiness or promptness in meeting danger or in seizing opportunity ⟨*alert* traders anticipated the stock market's slide⟩.

wave see SWING

waver see HESITATE, SWING

way see METHOD

wayward see CONTRARY

weak, feeble, frail, fragile, infirm, decrepit mean not strong enough to endure strain, pressure, or strenuous effort. **Weak** applies to deficiency or inferiority in strength or power of any sort ⟨a *weak* government likely to topple soon⟩. **Feeble** suggests extreme weakness inviting pity or contempt ⟨a *feeble* attempt to resist the enemy attack⟩. **Frail** implies delicacy and slightness of constitution or structure ⟨a once-robust man now *frail* with disease⟩. **Fragile** suggest frailty and brittleness unable to resist rough usage ⟨a *fragile* beauty that the camera cannot convey⟩. **Infirm** suggests instability, unsoundness, and insecurity due to old age or crippling illness ⟨an *infirm* old woman confined to her home⟩. **Decrepit** implies being worn-out or broken-down from long use or old age ⟨the *decrepit* butler had been with the family for years⟩.

weaken, enfeeble, debilitate, undermine, sap, cripple, disable mean to lose or cause to lose strength or vigor. **Weaken** may imply loss of physical strength, health, soundness, or stability or of quality, intensity, or effective power ⟨a disease that *weakens* the body's defenses against infection⟩. **Enfeeble** implies an obvious and pitiable condition of weakness and helplessness ⟨so *enfeebled* by arthritis that he requires constant care⟩. **Debilitate** suggests a less marked or more temporary impairment of strength or vitality ⟨the operation has a temporary *debilitating* effect⟩. **Undermine** and **sap** suggest a weakening by something working surreptitiously and insidiously ⟨a poor diet *undermines* your health⟩ ⟨drugs had *sapped* his ability to think⟩. **Cripple** implies causing a serious loss of functioning power through damaging or removing an essential part or element ⟨inflation had *crippled* the economy⟩. **Disable** suggests a usu. sudden crippling or enfeebling ⟨*disabled* soldiers received an immediate discharge⟩.

wealthy see RICH

wean see ESTRANGE

weary see TIRE

weigh see CONSIDER

weight see IMPORTANCE, INFLUENCE

weighty see HEAVY

weird, eerie, uncanny mean mysteriously strange or fantastic. **Weird** may imply an unearthly or supernatural strangeness or it may stress queerness or oddness ⟨*weird* creatures from another world⟩. **Eerie** suggests an uneasy or fearful consciousness that mysterious and malign powers are at work ⟨an *eerie* calm preceded the bombing raid⟩.

Uncanny implies disquieting strangeness or mysteriousness ⟨bore an *uncanny* resemblance to his dead wife⟩.

well see HEALTHY

wet, damp, dank, moist, humid mean covered or more or less soaked with liquid. **Wet** usu. implies saturation but may suggest a covering of a surface with water or something (as paint) not yet dry ⟨slipped on the *wet* pavement⟩. **Damp** implies a slight or moderate absorption and often connotes an unpleasant degree of moisture ⟨clothes will mildew if stored in a *damp* place⟩. **Dank** implies a more distinctly disagreeable or unwholesome dampness ⟨a prisoner in a cold, *dank* cell⟩. **Moist** applies to what is slightly damp or not felt as dry ⟨treat the injury with *moist* heat⟩. **Humid** applies to the presence of much water vapor in the air ⟨the hot, *humid* conditions brought on heatstroke⟩.

wheedle see COAX

whim see CAPRICE

whole, entire, total, all mean including everything or everyone without exception. **Whole** implies that nothing has been omitted, ignored, abated, or taken away ⟨read the *whole* book⟩. **Entire** may suggest a state of completeness or perfection to which nothing can be added ⟨the *entire* population was wiped out⟩. **Total** implies that everything has been counted, weighed, measured, or considered ⟨the *total* number of people present⟩. **All** may equal *whole, entire,* or *total* ⟨*all* their money went to pay the rent⟩. See in addition PERFECT.

wholehearted see SINCERE

wholesome see HEALTHFUL, HEALTHY

wicked see BAD

wide see BROAD

wide-awake see WATCHFUL

wield see HANDLE

wile see TRICK
willful see UNRULY
willing see VOLUNTARY
win see GET
wince see RECOIL
wisdom see SENSE
wise, sage, sapient, judicious, prudent, sensible, sane mean
having or showing sound judgment. **Wise** suggests great
understanding of people and of situations and unusual discernment and judgment in dealing with them ⟨*wise*
enough to know what really mattered in life⟩. **Sage** suggests wide experience, great learning, and wisdom ⟨sought
the *sage* advice of her father in times of crisis⟩. **Sapient**
suggests great sagacity and discernment ⟨the *sapient* obser-
vations of a veteran foreign correspondent⟩. **Judicious**
stresses a capacity for reaching wise decisions or just conclusions ⟨*judicious* parents using kindness and discipline
in equal measure⟩. **Prudent** suggests exercise of the restraint of sound practical wisdom and discretion ⟨a *prudent* decision to wait out the storm⟩. **Sensible** applies to
action guided and restrained by good sense and rationality
⟨a *sensible* woman who was not fooled by flattery⟩. **Sane**
stresses mental soundness, rationality, and levelheaded-
ness ⟨remained *sane* even as the war raged around him⟩.
wisecrack see JEST
wish see DESIRE
wit, humor, irony, sarcasm, satire, repartee mean a mode of
expression intended to arouse amusement. **Wit** suggests
the power to evoke laughter by remarks showing verbal fe-
licity or ingenuity and swift perception esp. of the incon-
gruous ⟨appreciate the *wit* of Wilde and Shaw⟩. **Humor**
implies an ability to perceive the ludicrous, the comical,
and the absurd in human life and to express these usu.

without bitterness ⟨a person with a finely honed sense of *humor*⟩. **Irony** applies to a manner of expression in which the intended meaning is the opposite of what is seemingly expressed ⟨with wry *irony,* he said to the priest, "Thank God I'm an atheist!"⟩. **Sarcasm** applies to expression frequently in the form of irony that is intended to cut or wound ⟨a cynic much given to heartless *sarcasm*⟩. **Satire** applies to writing that exposes or ridicules conduct, doctrines, or institutions either by direct criticism or more often through irony, parody, or caricature ⟨the play is a *satire* on contemporary living arrangements⟩. **Repartee** implies the power of answering quickly, pointedly, or wittily ⟨a partygoer well known for razor-sharp *repartee*⟩.

withhold see KEEP

withstand see OPPOSE

witness see CERTIFY

witticism see JEST

witty, humorous, facetious, jocular, jocose mean provoking or intended to provoke laughter. **Witty** suggests cleverness and quickness of mind and often a caustic tongue ⟨a film critic remembered for his *witty* reviews⟩. **Humorous** applies broadly to anything that evokes usu. genial laughter and may contrast with *witty* in suggesting whimsicality or eccentricity ⟨laced her lectures with *humorous* anecdotes⟩. **Facetious** stresses a desire to produce laughter and may be derogatory in implying dubious or ill-timed attempts at wit or humor ⟨*facetious* comments that were unappreciated at the funeral⟩. **Jocular** implies a usu. habitual fondness for jesting and joking ⟨a *jocular* fellow whose humor often brightened spirits⟩. **Jocose** is somewhat less derogatory than *facetious* in suggesting habitual waggishness or playfulness ⟨the dim-witted took his *jocose* proposals seriously⟩.

woe see SORROW

woebegone see DOWNCAST

wont see HABIT

wonted see USUAL

wordy, verbose, prolix, diffuse mean using more words than necessary to express thought. **Wordy** may also imply loquaciousness or garrulity ⟨a *wordy* speech that said nothing⟩. **Verbose** suggests a resulting dullness, obscurity, or lack of incisiveness or precision ⟨*verbose* position papers that no one reads⟩. **Prolix** suggests unreasonable and tedious dwelling on details ⟨habitually transformed brief anecdotes into *prolix* sagas⟩. **Diffuse** stresses lack of compactness and pointedness of style ⟨*diffuse* memoirs that are so many shaggy-dog stories⟩.

work *n* Work, labor, travail, toil, drudgery, grind mean activity involving effort or exertion. **Work** may imply activity of body, of mind, of a machine, or of a natural force ⟨too tired to do any *work*⟩. **Labor** applies to physical or intellectual work involving great and often strenuous exertion ⟨believes that farmers are poorly paid for their *labor*⟩. **Travail** is bookish for labor involving pain or suffering ⟨years of *travail* were lost when the building burned⟩. **Toil** implies prolonged and fatiguing labor ⟨his lot would be years of back-breaking *toil*⟩. **Drudgery** suggests dull and irksome labor ⟨a job with a good deal of *drudgery*⟩. **Grind** implies labor exhausting to mind or body ⟨the *grind* of performing the play eight times a week⟩.

work *n* Work, employment, occupation, calling, pursuit, métier, business mean a specific sustained activity engaged in esp. in earning one's living. **Work** may apply to any purposeful activity whether remunerative or not ⟨her *work* as a hospital volunteer⟩. **Employment** implies work for which one has been engaged and is being paid by an employer ⟨*employment* will be terminated in cases of chronic tardiness⟩. **Occupation** implies work in which one engages regularly esp. as a result of training ⟨his *occupation* as a trained auto mechanic⟩. **Calling** applies to an occupation viewed as a vocation or profession ⟨I feel the ministry is my true *calling*⟩. **Pursuit** suggests a trade, profession, or avocation followed with zeal or steady interest ⟨her family considered medicine the only proper *pursuit*⟩. **Métier** implies a calling or pursuit for which one believes oneself to be esp. fitted ⟨from childhood I considered acting my *métier*⟩. **Business** suggests activity in commerce or the management of money and affairs ⟨the *business* of managing a hotel⟩.

worldly see EARTHLY

worldly-wise see SOPHISTICATED

worry *vb* Worry, annoy, harass, harry, plague, pester, tease mean to disturb or irritate by persistent acts. **Worry** implies an incessant goading or attacking that drives one to desperation ⟨pursued a policy of *worrying* the enemy⟩. **Annoy** implies disturbing one's composure or peace of mind by intrusion, interference, or petty attacks ⟨you're doing that just to *annoy* me⟩. **Harass** implies petty persecutions or burdensome demands that exhaust one's nervous or mental power ⟨*harassed* on all sides by creditors⟩. **Harry** may imply heavy oppression or maltreatment ⟨*harried* mothers trying to cope with small children⟩. **Plague** implies a painful and persistent affliction ⟨*plagued* all her life by poverty⟩. **Pester** stresses the repetition of petty attacks ⟨the bureau was constantly *pestered* with trivial complaints⟩. **Tease** suggests an attempt to break down one's resistance or rouse to wrath ⟨malicious children *teased* the dog⟩.

worry *n* see CARE
worship see REVERE
wrangle see QUARREL
wrath see ANGER
wrong *vb* **Wrong, oppress, persecute, aggrieve** mean to injure unjustly or outrageously. **Wrong** implies inflicting injury either unmerited or out of proportion to what one deserves ⟨a penal system that had *wronged* him⟩. **Oppress** suggests inhumane imposing of burdens one cannot endure or exacting more than one can perform ⟨a people *oppressed* by a warmongering tyrant⟩. **Persecute** implies a relentless and unremitting subjection to annoyance or suffering ⟨a boy with a clubfoot *persecuted* by his playmates⟩. **Aggrieve** implies suffering caused by an infringement or denial of rights ⟨a legal aid society representing *aggrieved* minority groups⟩.
wrong *n* see INJUSTICE

Y

yardstick see STANDARD
yearn see LONG
yield, submit, capitulate, succumb, relent, defer mean to give way to someone or something that one can no longer resist. **Yield** may apply to any sort or degree of giving way before force, argument, persuasion, or entreaty ⟨*yields* too easily in any argument⟩. **Submit** suggests full surrendering after resistance or conflict to the will or control of another ⟨voluntarily *submitted* to an inspection of the premises⟩. **Capitulate** stresses the fact of ending all resistance and may imply either a coming to terms (as with an adversary) or hopelessness in the face of an irresistible opposing force

⟨the college president *capitulated* to the protesters' demands⟩. **Succumb** implies weakness and helplessness to the one that gives way or an overwhelming power to the opposing force ⟨a stage actor *succumbing* to the lure of Hollywood⟩. **Relent** implies a yielding through pity or mercy by one who holds the upper hand ⟨finally *relented* and let the children stay up late⟩. **Defer** implies a voluntary yielding or submitting out of respect or reverence for or deference and affection toward another ⟨I *defer* to your superior expertise in these matters⟩. See in addition RELINQUISH.

Z

zeal see PASSION